JUNG & STEINER

THE BIRTH OF A NEW PSYCHOLOGY

GERHARD WEHR

WITH

THE RIDDLES OF THE SOUL :

DEPTH PSYCHOLOGY AND ANTHROPOSOPHY

BY HANS ERHARD LAUER

Translated by Magdalene Jaeckel

FOREWORD BY ROBERT SARDELLO

ANTHROPOSOPHIC
PRESS

Translated with permission from the German *C.G. Jung und Rudolf Steiner: Konfrontation und Synopse*, copyright © 1990 by Gerhard Wehr, and from Hans Erhard Lauer, *Die Rätsel der Seele: Tiefenpsychologie und Anthroposophie*, copyright © 1960, 1975 by Hans Erhard Lauer.

Translation copyright © 2002 by Magdalene Jaeckel

Excerpts from C.G. Jung: *Collected Works*, volumes 4 (1961), 6 (1974), 7 (1966), 8 (1969), 9.1 (1990), 9.2 (1968), 10 (1975), 11 (1969), 12 (1968), 13 (1968), 14 (1970), and 17 (1954); *Two essays in Analytical Psychology* (1966); and *Answer to Job* (1969), copyright © by Princeton University Press. Reprinted by permission of Princeton University Press.

Published by Anthroposophic Press
P.O. Box 799, Great Barrington, MA 01230
www.anthropress.org

Publication of the work was made possible in part by a grant from the Waldorf Curriculum Fund.

Library of Congress Cataloging-in-Publication Data

Wehr, Gerhard.
[C.G. Jung und Rudolf Steiner. English]
Jung and Steiner : the birth of a new psychology / by Gerhard Wehr ;
with an appendix by Hans Erhard Lauer ; translated by Magdalene Jaeckel.
p. cm.
Includes bibliographical references.
ISBN 0-88010-496-1
1. Jung, C. G. (Carl Gustav), 1875-1961. 2. Steiner, Rudolf,
1861-1925. 3. Psychoanalysis. 4. Anthroposophy. I. Lauer, Hans
Erhard. II. Title.
BF173.J85 W4413 2002
299'.935—dc21
2001002163

10 9 8 7 6 5 4 3 2 1

CONTENTS

Foreword by Robert Sardello   7

JUNG AND STEINER

by Gerhard Wehr

PREFACE   33

1. Introducing the Problem   35

2. A Biographical Comparison   48

3. Jung's *Psychology of the Unconscious* and Steiner's Lectures on Psychoanalysis 77

4. Spiritual Backgrounds   85

5. Two Images of the Human Being   90

6. Steiner's "Second Self" and the Unconscious   105

7. Natural Science as a Starting Point   119

8. Forms of Consciousness   136

9. Soul and Spirit   160

10. Initiation and Individuation   183

11. Contrasts and Similarities in East and West   209

12. Allegations of Gnosticism   231

APPENDICES   240

1. Mental Health through Spiritual Discipline   240

2. Evil as Shadow and Double   241

3. Androgyny   247

4. Soul and Spirit Research as *Praeambulum Fidei*   249

5. *Unus Mundus* and the Cosmic Christ   252

Final Remarks   258

๙

APPENDIX

THE RIDDLES OF THE SOUL: DEPTH PSYCHOLOGY AND ANTHROPOSOPHY

by Hans Erhard Lauer

PREFACE   262

1. The Riddles of the Human Soul in the Light
of Depth Psychology   263

2. The Riddles of the Human Soul in the Light
of Anthroposophy   280

3. Depth Psychology and Anthroposophy   302

NOTES   320

Foreword

by Robert Sardello

For the past fifteen years I have worked to institute a new orientation in psychology. This effort has centered on bringing the soul psychology of C.G. Jung into a relation with the spiritual science of Rudolf Steiner. This creative synthesis would, I believe, give birth to a new psychology—one that is fully cognizant of the spiritual and soul worlds and how human consciousness forms in association with them.

Imagine, then, my excitement in learning of this book by Gerhard Wehr, the author of an important biography of Jung, and an Anthroposophist. Reading and rereading his book, I felt assured that these years had not been wasted, for here at last was a linking work, one that would be appreciated by Anthroposophists and depth psychologists alike. Even more, the concerns addressed in this remarkable book were living questions that applied to everyone, not just to the practitioners of each of these movements: How can we live and be open and receptive to the spiritual realms? How can we know what is going on in the depths of our soul? How can we approach others and our work and the world soulfully and with spiritual intent?

Psychology is vastly misunderstood in our time. It is regarded either as a therapeutic endeavor or as a rather meaningless scientific discipline that tries, mostly unsuccessfully, to model itself after the physical sciences. Thanks to Jung, the field has been ennobled, and the word "psychology" has been somewhat restored as the discipline of the soul. A true discipline is far more than an academic area of interest. One takes up a discipline, enters it—one becomes it. It then becomes a way of knowing oneself and knowing the world. Thanks to Steiner, the possibility exists of taking this discipline of the soul and placing it within the context of understanding the place and work of the human being in the whole cosmos. The kind of psychology that could come from working through the whole of Jung and Steiner in an inner, experiential way is a practical psychology. It is not confined to the therapy office but is rather the work of living a conscious soul life.

If one goes even a little way into the labor of self-knowledge, it soon becomes necessary to reimagine one's place within whole world and indeed the whole of existence. Most of us do not have the capacities to do this on our own. Thus many of us find ourselves in a liminal place. No longer dominated by mass consciousness, we are left on our own, without ground or the capacity to steer a course for ourselves. Then we find we no longer belong to the guiding myth of the time—the technological myth, the myth of materialism. Where do we go? We need a new myth, a large imagination within which understanding of who we are makes sense. In medieval times, Dante offered a whole soul cosmology of this kind. He couched it in Christian tradition, language, and practice, because that satisfied his need for a means to convey large picture within which we can find our place. Such a cosmology interprets us; it tells us who we are, what we are doing, where we came from, where we are going.

Both Jung and Steiner have given us a cosmology within which we can see ourselves soulfully. That is why both are worth lifetimes of study. We should not make our task easy by considering these two individuals as only providing systems that agree in certain ways and diverge in others. Nor should we try to simply determine which one to follow. Both decried followers, but hoped to see independent workers inspired by their efforts.

Jung and Steiner does not merely offer a comparison of two creative individuals, each of whom has brought something decidedly new to the world. That approach might be interesting, but it would create nothing more than another academic study. This book goes much further, and its reach has to do with the method employed, which Wehr calls the "synoptic" method. Rather than setting the externals of two systems side by side and looking at each for similarities and differences, Wehr sets the core meaning of each beside the other. Out of the tension something new comes into being. Jung himself knew that this method

Love need the Eternal and Boundless contained within in The Temporal + Bound belongs to the very nature of the psyche. He employed it many times. It requires developing the capacity to hold two irreconcilable positions together without seeking resolution. Something new will then emerge. Steiner advocated something similar when he advised developing the capacity to hold twelve different views on the same issue. Moreover Steiner's lectures are full of contradictions, demanding that one enter into his work with an awakened imagination in which these contradictions become pregnant with new meanings.

Jung and Steiner, for all its merits, does not push this method as far as it could. In this introduction, I want to push it even further to begin to show the outlines of a new psychology, a spiritual psychology that emerges from holding the tension of the opposites of depth psychology and Anthroposophy without seeking resolution.

The opposites involved here are extreme. They consist of bringing the greatest possible development of waking consciousness into relation with the deepest level of unconsciousness. The tension is exacerbated by the fact that these two ways of viewing the human being are separated by no more than a thin veneer. When we go into that seemingly thin separation, we find two sides of the same thing. That is to say, there is a central element that unknowingly joins depth psychology and Anthroposophy. This union is the image of the Grail as the central myth of each of these cultural creations.

In *An Outline of Esoteric Science*, Steiner spoke explicitly of Anthroposophy as a Grail science. He meant that if Anthroposophy is a science of the cosmos working into the earthly and the earthly working into the cosmos, then the human being is at the very center of this relation. Jung for his part was a Westerner through and through, and his central myth was the Grail. He had a very clear dream of the Grail, which is described in chapter eleven of Wehr's book. He had this dream when he was on a long journey in India and when everything in this environment seemed to verify all he had to say about culture, symbolism, and myth.

The new psychology that begins to emerge from the flying sparks of a path founded in the reality of soul and a path founded in the reality of spirit will be one that is symbolized by the Grail cup. Among its many other aspects, this symbol gives us a picture of the spiritual soul.

The vessel itself symbolizes the soul, open and receptive, receiving whatever it needs from the spiritual worlds. This image perfectly represents the spiritual psychology of which I speak. It also represents the current of psychology that comes about by holding in tension a love for the soul and a love for the spirit. I define that psychology as follows:

> Spiritual psychology is an active practice that develops embodied, conscious, soul life to make that life open and receptive to the spiritual realms. This is done as an act of love toward ourselves, others, and the world.

Steiner followed the spirit side of the Grail myth; Jung, the soul side. The great appeal of both is the quest. We cannot undervalue the tremendous motivating power of an image of questing. Thus in both Jung and Steiner, we find a continual criticism of the way things are in the world, an urging to throw off the immediate past and to seek to establish both a soul and a spirit perspective for the future of humanity. But unless their endeavors are seen as quests, each of these two very strong conceptions of the human future is bound to gather dogmatic disciples.

The content of the Grail cup must be taken into account as well. It is blood, which is an image of the very essence of desire. Desire is essential. So if the desire of soul or the desire of spirit is not addressed, then it gets at you from behind. It is mistaken for what we think the founders wanted, which will be confused with our own unexamined desires. But the blood of the Grail is also the blood of Christ. Thus it represents purified desire, which can be wholly oriented toward the divine rather than becoming confused with personal desires.

Both Jung and Steiner went through personal transformations that ensured as much as possible that the desires they followed were free of personal taints. There is no doubt that both individuals were also tremendously ambitious, wanting to see their views adopted in the world. But their followers tend to foolishly ignore the factor of desire in themselves, and the necessity of working with this before all else. They think they are being good Anthroposophists or good Jungians if they adopt the master's content, oblivious of how their own desires figure in. In Anthroposophy, the follower's desire tends to be falsely purified. Anthroposophists often act as if they had no bodies and were already pure spirits,

Consciousness of Desire

bringing the world exactly what it needed. In depth psychology, there is often a reveling in the experience of following soul down into the depths, completely unaware of anything like a need for purifying desire. There is a temptation to allow the content of those depths to take hold in the foolish belief that because it is soul, it has to be good.

Working with desire requires holding irresolvable tensions without seeking resolution. Our main cultural model for working with the desire of the blood, placing that desire within the Grail cup, may be neither Steiner nor Jung but Dante. The whole of the *Purgatorio* is explicitly concerned with holding opposites together without resolving them. Remorse is held in tension with joy, pride with humility, contemplation with action, responsibility toward the timeless with responsibility toward timely need. This play of opposites finally opens the soul to the spiritual realms. So perhaps we have a greater psychology in Dante than can be found in either Jung or Steiner. Or perhaps we can follow the lead of Dante, whom Steiner quite seriously called "the greatest man." This would mean holding Steiner and Jung in a tension of opposites, noticing that the inherent reason for such tension is that, as Dante shows, this is the one and only way that love enters, a love that is greater than any of our desires. We do not *do* love, in spite of our glorification of the possibility of loving. Our desire is too confused for us to love otherwise than out of our own self-oriented desires. The purifying power of love enters through the opening, the soul space created by holding impossible contradictions.

Love enters the discussion here because it is the central dimension of the spiritual psychology that emerges from holding Jung and Steiner in tension. Love is not mere feeling, but the very essence of the action of the spiritual soul. It is what the spiritual soul *does*. Love is not desire already purified; it is desire in process of being purified.

Jung had little to do with the world beyond his circle and his soul interests. Steiner had a great deal to do with the world. He created new systems of education, medicine, and agriculture and new forms of painting, dance, architecture, drama. He inspired a religious movement known as the Christian Community, thought through a new social order, and engaged in many other cultural endeavors. Jung is characterized by an innerness without which dedication to soul life is impossible. His whole autobiography is written as an inner biography, an entirely new form of biography, a memoir of the soul. Steiner's biography, on the other hand, is completely external, so objective that it is downright dull. It belongs to the genre of esoteric spiritual biographies where it is not uncommon for the writer to speak of his own life in the third person. So here is one tension to hold: soul as inwardness, spirit as being out in the world. Soul as where we have been, the depth of memory, and memory as imagination. Spirit as where we are going, the not-yet, the yet to-be-established in the world.

When read closely, Wehr's chapter comparing the biographies of Jung and Steiner reveals something amazing about the inner origins of spiritual science and depth psychology. Both Steiner and Jung had a particular and profound relationship with the dead. When he was only four years old, Steiner was visited by a woman who had died—an experience that made a lasting impression. He later gave numerous lectures on the importance of remaining in connection with those who have died, even providing methods for doing so. Jung also had experiences with the dead. Wehr points to Jung's experience (also at age four) of seeing a funeral over which his father presided and the strange impression it made on Jung. His depth psychology began with association experiments he carried out with his cousin, who had contact with the dead as well.

The mysteries of death impress themselves on both of these figures, but in different ways. In Steiner's vision, the dead woman asks for help. The experience originates a scientific interest in him: what are the methods for remaining in connection with the dead? Jung leaves the impression of having a simultaneous fear and attraction to the realm of the dead. For him, there is more of a sense of a struggle against the mysteries of death, characteristic of one who is fully aware of the tragedy of death, the leaving of life.

The death experiences of these two individuals, when held in inner tension, open the way of spiritual psychology. It is the way of a double consciousness that characterizes both Steiner and Jung. They both lived an ongoing relation with the dead, a relation of actual presence, but one that must be understood as an act of the active imagination.

not of ordinary consciousness. And they both lived an ongoing connection with the world (albeit Steiner seemed to do this more effectively). In both we observe two forms of consciousness side by side: for Jung, personality 1 and personality 2; for Steiner, ordinary consciousness and clairvoyant consciousness. This dual consciousness is the consciousness of the future. It belongs to the Grail myth, and is what we are all being asked to develop. We are asked to be consciously open, in soul, to the spiritual realms and to work effectively in the world.

If we look at these two individuals as initiates, forerunners for the rest of humanity, this is what they introduce as a human possibility. We can work for the world and work for the soul and spirit at the same time. That is the kind of consciousness spiritual psychology encourages. Jung and Steiner were born into this consciousness and lived with it in different ways. The next step is to develop this consciousness in full awareness. This is now possible because of the initiation experiences of these two individuals. We can say that double consciousness was initiated in both of these individuals by the dead. The real founders of spiritual psychology are those who have died and have a continuing interest and love for the world; they are tremendously interested in what happens here. They concern themselves with whether we can meet the challenge of living as soul and spirit beings housed in earthly garments.

The way of double consciousness is well known in the mystery traditions. We see it, for example, in the *Bacchae* of Euripides. When Pentheus, who is one-sidedly rational, is overtaken by Dionysus, the god of embodied imagination, he looks up into the sky and suddenly sees two suns. The two suns signify a consciousness of earth alongside a consciousness of death. While this doesn't do much good for Pentheus (who ends up torn to pieces by Maenads), it does renew the community. We need Jung's psychology in order to remain imaginal. We need Steiner's spiritual science in order to apply this imagination to the forming of the world. These two together make possible a conscious, imaginal sun alongside the sun of our usual earthly consciousness.

In the past the experience of two suns signified extreme danger. Like Pentheus, one might go off the deep end. The right capacities must be formed. We cannot jump into this kind of consciousness. We need to undergo the throes of transformation, and the way to go about radical change of capacities is found in the written work of Jung and Steiner. Their writing is completely unlike other writing. You can't go through it and come out the same. However, they need to be read together or in tandem, and read with the whole of one's being, not just through the intellect.

Spiritual psychology is a result of working this tandem approach. It founded in the consciousness of death, and signifies the importance—and even the method—of working toward something without doing so for our own benefit. We know, of course, that even when we seem to be generously working for the benefit of others, our own self-interests are involved; usually they are at the forefront. The spiritual-psychological perspective, a mode of consciousness rather than a theory, operates within a continual undoing of itself—dying as a way of living. This is the only way to allow soul to be genuinely open to the spiritual worlds and serving those worlds truthfully.

Closely related to the presence of the dead as a central factor of human consciousness is the problem of the term "the unconscious." For Steiner, there are many kinds of consciousness—waking, dreaming, sleep, trance, to name but a few. There is no *unconscious*: that is only the way waking consciousness speaks of other forms of consciousness. Furthermore these different consciousnesses are not states but beings. Psychological symptoms that appear seemingly out of nowhere, for example, are sometimes due to the living presence of the dead who have not been remembered. That is to say, one of the worlds of consciousness is the spirits of the dead. This is a much more forceful way of speaking than Jung's references to a psychic structure that has a certain content much of which remains under the surface. The right and proper field of psychology includes not only the dead, but all sorts of other beings who are not *in* the unconscious, but *are* different *worlds* of consciousness—spirits, angels, gods.

If we try to speak of these different worlds of beings without developing the capacity of the spiritual soul, we run the risk either of completely literalizing them (when approaching them in terms of Anthroposophy) or of regarding them as mere images (when working from a depth-psychological perspective). The spiritual soul, the goal of spiritual psychology, does not make a sharp division between what is literal and what is imaginal. Are these beings real? Yes. Are they physical, affecting us in terms of the laws of cause and effect? No. When the beings of a certain world of consciousness affect us, we *are* that consciousness. It is not a matter of something external impinging on us like rocks hitting the flesh; nor is it a matter of their imaginal presence acting as content of the soul. Soul is not a container of contents but the inherent capacity for perceiving spiritual realities. We are soul and spiritual beings, not beings with a soul and with a spirit. We are also embodied, but even so soul and spirit do not hover around phantomlike within our physical being. Rather than being caught by the laws of cause and effect, as Jung still was to a greater or lesser extent, we have to grow accustomed to working within the laws of sympathetic and antipathetic currents. The presence of such currents creates a resonance within us. We are like harps, sounding when the beings of the soul and spiritual worlds sound. And this resounding is possible only because we are of the substance of those beings.

There is a differentiation in understanding the structure and functioning of the body in Anthroposophy that makes it clear how something completely immaterial, such as the dead, or other spirit-beings affect us in such a way that physical symptoms would arise. The living body consists of matter, but also of subtle, etheric forces, which provide a link with the immaterial. There is nothing theoretical about the etheric body. It is recognized by all spiritual and esoteric traditions; moreover it can be quite easily experienced through the life-forming processes of the physical body. When Steiner criticizes psychoanalysis, saying that it lacks the proper tools to address the kind of reality that it is trying to investigate, he is, among other things, referring to the absence of an understanding of the etheric body.

The concept of the etheric body makes for completely different understandings of psychological symptoms in Jung and in Steiner. Jung always traces a symptom back to an archetypal image, looks for the gods or spirits or dead in the disease, and speaks always of such figures as images in the soul. Steiner looks at the same symptoms and also traces the symptom back to the gods, the spirits, or the dead, but he takes these spirits as directly acting on the human being. Without Jung's perspective, these acts by spiritual beings would be taken literally, as if they were just like earthly beings, except perhaps a little more shadowy. Without Steiner's perspective, on the other hand, the truth of the actual presence of spiritual beings is sidestepped.

Another expression of the irresolvable tensions of opposites between Steiner and Jung concerns soul and spirit. Everywhere I have taught for the past fifteen years, someone inevitably asks me to define soul and spirit and tell how they differ. Such a question goes nowhere because it shifts something known and felt to the level of the ordinary intellect, where it cannot be answered. The question assumes that there is some way out of the confusion other than finding deeper ways into the question's substance.

This book takes us further and deeper into the tension between soul and spirit. Here also the two are sometimes interchanged. This confusion persists, for example, in the essays by Hans Erhard Lauer in the second part of this book. But holding the tension begins to bring some clarity. For example, we find that both soul and spirit reveal themselves as inner experiences, even though the "inner" of soul is different from the "inner" of spirit. Jung speaks of how, at an early age, he was initiated into the earth mysteries. Steiner speaks of being taken into the cosmic mysteries. Both speak of archetypal realities. However, Jung is always concerned with the archetypal patterns and figures that reveal themselves as contents of soul life. Steiner is always concerned with the archetypal beings that shape the human being and the earth.

Another difference: for Jung, psyche is image, and image is understood as a particular content, whether dream content or mythic content. Jung, of course, is more sophisticated concerning image than this, and we have the distinct feeling in his work that image, more than picture content, is that through which content appears. In Steiner, image is activity, the pure activity of forming or coming into form of the actual presence of spiritual beings. Image is the first way in which we can be present to the activity of spiritual beings. Image, in Steiner, is a decidedly spiritual notion, while in Jung it is the very heart of soul.

We can focus on the fruitfulness of keeping these two orientations in relation rather than on the divisiveness that arises by separating soul and spirit too sharply. Taken alone, the soul perspective leads to a forgetfulness of the human being in the context of the world. Jung seals soul off from the world and unwittingly promotes self-absorption. Taken alone, Steiner's perspective leads to a literalizing, unimaginative, sometimes manic working to bring practical endeavors of a spiritual nature into the world, expecting that artistic endeavors, rather than conscious soul work, will answer the soul's needs. When we hold both the spirit and the soul perspectives together, we have spiritual psychology. This new psychology, which has its precursors in Jung and Steiner, places the spiritual soul at the heart of its endeavors. Holding the tension between soul and spirit is the attempt to provide the practical way of working in the world that is the forming of a spiritual culture. Our task concerns developing the capacities of allowing the spiritual realms to work through us into the world, and keeping this conscious. How this work happens remains open to inspiration; it is not a work of applying what Steiner said to the world.

The two perspectives of soul and spirit show up in another way—Jung's notion of the goal of inner development as the awakening to the Self and Steiner's call for the development of the "I." Are these two goals the same? Wehr puts them together, but I think it might be better to avoid collapsing them and keep the inherent tension between the two. The Self can be imagined as soul at the border of spirit. The "I" can be imagined as spirit at the border of the soul. The "I" is the Self from spirit's point of view. The Self is the "I" from the soul's point of view. The Self is the collective soul raised to the level of individuality. The "I" is individuality in connection with the whole. Holding this tension between Self and "I" can help Anthroposophists, who are forever confusing Steiner's understanding of the "I" with their own egotism because they often lack a sense of soul. (Steiner also uses the word "ego" in multiple ways. Sometimes he is speaking of the "I" when using the term "ego." Sometimes he is speaking of ego in the ordinary sense.) Similarly, this tension can help those in the Jungian stream because the notion of the "I," while somewhat linguistically awkward, has a solidity about it that prevents the misconception that adhering to soul life leads to mysticism.

The knot holding together "I," "Self," "self," and "ego" still persists. Neither "I" and "Self" nor should "self" and "ego," it seems, should be collapsed. Nor should we try to untie the knot with definitions. The value of seeing these notions collide in Jung and Steiner is precisely so that they collide in us. We have to find the way into the problem, which is a living problem for each of us. For example, in light of the spiritual individuality that is described as "I," a specific relation to ego has to be worked through. Ego is not quite the same in Jung and Steiner. For Steiner, ego would be the reflection of the spirit individuality within us, a kind of a shadow of our true spirit being. It takes conscious inner development to come to the "I"; it takes a long process of the purification of desire, developing a presence to creative thinking, a conscious awakening to imagination, inspiration, and intuition. For Jung, ego is a part of the whole of soul life that takes itself to be the whole. Consciously entering the whole process of individuation, something that is never complete, is required for coming to the point of a presence of the Self. It is of vast importance, both personally and culturally, to know when we are in ego and when in Self. It is vital to have a clear sense of the kind of experience characterizing the "I" and the kind characterizing the Self.

The relation between the "inner worlds" and the "outer world" is another tension to be worked through. Steiner belongs more to the Aristotelian line, Jung to the Platonic. Thus in setting the work of Jung and Steiner side by side, as Wehr has done, we have to hold this tension and try to see into it as clearly as we can. For Steiner there are three domains to research with respect to the human being: the realm of the senses; how sense experience lives on in soul life; and how the human being knows. This approach seems decidedly different from Jung's. Jung is far more interested in preexisting patterns, traced back to the acts of archetypal beings who still live on as contents in the soul. The contrast between the Aristotelian and Platonic points of view could not be greater, except that Steiner's approach to working through his three domains of research is wholly and entirely *internal*. It is not subjective, but inner. He may, for example, start by describing the senses and their functions from an external point of view. But he never stops with the external. He goes on to explore sensing from an inner point of view, skillfully taking us further and further into an inner view of the human being and of the whole of the cosmos from within. He is no simple Aristotelian. As he moves us gradually inward, it is done with impeccable logic. Mysticism is not an option.

The inner way of working that characterizes Anthroposophy is completely free of dualism. Approaching the human being's physical innerness does not mean "inside" versus "outside." The "outside," too, can be approached in an inner way. For example, among the most important researches of Steiner into the inner physical being are his studies of human physiology. He avoids dualism by seeing that the whole human being participates in three worlds—the physical, soul, and spirit worlds. Each of these worlds can be explored with equal precision, but only through the development of the capacity of nondualistic perception and thought, the "I." Dualism is founded on the mistake that there is only one world. Thus it separates mind from body, locating the body as part of the physical world. It also separates soul and spirit from body and from world, and then searches for peculiar connections, such as parallelism or reductionism.

Jung is also completely faithful to the inner world. Strictly speaking, he is not Platonic but Kantian (the archetypal psychologist James Hillman emphasizes Jung's Platonic side, minimizing his Kantian side). His emphasis on soul is somewhat misleading because he does not and cannot reach the cosmological level of soul with his psychology. He is always concerned with the contents of the soul and steers completely away from saying anything about whether the contents reflect the actions of "real" spiritual beings. This is important because, with the help of Steiner, it is possible to reset Jung into more of a Platonic imagination. It is simply a matter of taking the archetypal figures as real, as existing in themselves. But it takes Steiner to make that move because it is not sufficient to simply state that this is so. Capacities of consciousness have to be developed that reveal the nature of spiritual beings. Steiner developed such capacities and wrote extensively concerning how others can develop them as well.

Kant stated that the object, the transcendent, the thing-in-itself is absolutely inaccessible, so that you have to confine yourself to the empirical world, to the finite, to appearances. Jung adopted as his own unshakable foundation for psychology the restriction of Kant's phenomenal world and the closing of the door to the noumenon. This is why Jung posited the existence of the archetypes but would never say anything of their reality beyond what could be said "psychologically." Thus, for Jung, the question of truth is closed, or at best we have a special notion of truth, easily susceptible to being completely misused— "the truth within."

Once we have exposed Jung's decision to remain completely empirical, confining his work to inner soul images, it may seem that the comparison between Jung and Steiner must cease. Steiner says a lot about the reality of spiritual beings; they are, in his view, completely autonomous, and we are required to develop the soul as the organ for the perception of these realities. The tension, though, needs to be maintained because of the phenomenological acumen Jung brings to the inner life.

Steiner does have a clear notion of the transcendent and goes after it with incredible descriptive capacities along with an accuracy of observation equal to that of any scientist. In addition, he develops the capacities for making observations of the invisible spiritual realms. He goes about this in such a way, however, that he reports what he has seen, not as interior conversations with the spirits, but as ideas—the closest we can come with our consciousness to the realities he experienced. We have no direct reports of Steiner's immediate experiences of the spiritual worlds. We have the ideas he gives as descriptive of those realms. However, because the spiritual realms remain closed for most people, there is an extremely strong tendency to take Steiner's ideas at face value, even though he himself says over and over again to test them. But to test them requires the capacity to enter into the interior of those ideas. Rather than merely examining them with our ordinary consciousness, we must experience them within; we must enter into the soul of the ideas. This is where Jung comes in as absolutely necessary. He shows how to find the way into and inhabit the interior of things. Without Jung, I propose, Anthroposophy becomes the dogmatic application of the ideas of a remarkable individual without inner understanding. The application of these ideas, without the capacity to discover their soul nature, becomes the imposition of those ideas onto others. In the long run, such imposition can fare no better than, say, the imposition of the technological worldview on us because it will supposedly make life better.

A number of years ago I spoke to a large gathering of Anthroposophists, introducing a basic view of spiritual psychology as being founded in Jung and Steiner. The address was met with little enthusiasm; in fact, I could hear a number of stomachs turning over. One person forcefully stood up and said something to the effect that because of Steiner we have absolutely no need for psychology. Many of those gathered agreed with this naïve view. Nevertheless the fact that Steiner explored soul does not acquit us of the need to be present to soul realities from within rather than accepting Steiner's findings. Steiner shows us much concerning the ways of soul, but then there is the problem of living them. This can only be done by finding the way into the interior of soul, which is Jung's forte.

A significant question arises at this point. If Jung's reliance on Kant confines him to immediate appearances, why go to Steiner for the way through to the reality of spiritual beings rather than someone like Hegel, as the very astute Jungian Wolfgang Geigerich has done? (See his book *The Logical Life of the Soul.*) The answer is that while Hegel perhaps provides a better philosophical basis for Jung than Kant, his approach would be devastating to soul. Image-consciousness would be lost to abstract thinking. Only Steiner provides the needed basis capable of comprising both soul and spirit, and as such is a basis within psychology itself. The very fact that Wehr can put the work of these two individuals side by side and make a meaningful comparison of them is due to their shared basis of soul and spirit.

The problem of seeing soul in terms of the picture content of myths, memories, and stories is unfortunately perpetuated somewhat by Wehr, who often uses content-oriented language in his text. Speaking of the soul as having contents gives the impression of some kind of container filled with images. Yet soul, at least in part, concerns the act of picturing, not the picture contents. Myths too are not picture contents, but worlds of picturings; that is, if you take myths as still living. If myth are now completed and dead, then indeed all we have left are the corpses, the picture contents.

Learning to imagine in terms of *picturing* rather than *pictures* is one of the most important things I have learned from Steiner. In his most profound work on the soul, *A Psychology of Body, Soul, and Spirit,* he describes how soul functions. Among the most significant aspects is the soul's apprehension of a time current from the future. This is the picturing act I am talking about. It does not concern a content, because the future coming toward us has no content. The moment it does have a content, it is necessarily from the past; this is a reflection occurring in the etheric body, where there is something like pictures from the past, both personal and archetypal. But this time current from the future is something real and actual. The future here concerns the possibilities of our being. While the notion sounds remote, it is not. We experience this time current with every movement we make. I get up and go to the door. Within the deep will, what is to come is already happening before it happens. I could not get to the door if it were only a mental idea. Getting to the door is already in my movement as I approach the door. This little example is but a shortened version of how our whole life approaches us from out of the future.

Each act that we do is internally connected with the whole of our life and expresses itself as belonging to the whole. But much of that whole has not yet happened. This is the time current from the future, and in *A Psychology of Body, Soul, and Spirit,* Steiner calls this current the *astral body* of the soul. It is picturing in the process of coming-to-be. The life of the soul is being formed out of the whole of the cosmos: "astral" comes from a root meaning "star." This world is whole, but it is open, unfinished. The pictures as content—memories, but also archetypal images—are from the past, from what has already happened. Steiner speaks of this current as the *etheric body* of the soul. The pictures of the etheric body are completed, done. They are not necessarily dead and gone; they still live on but are closed to new meanings. I thus make a distinction between the soul's immersion in fate—how we are shaped by the past—and the soul's immersion in destiny—how we are shaped from the future. Jung's psychology belongs more to the former, Anthroposophy more to the latter. Spiritual psychology works with both at once, but tries to be conscious of the difference.

For example, when in our lives we encounter a real deviation from our usual experience, is this fate or is it destiny? The words are often used interchangeably, but they are definitely distinct experiences; if you know how to be present to each, the difference is very clear. Here depth psychology has a lot to learn from Anthroposophy. It is as if half of psychology has been neglected because of the discipline's bias toward explanations in terms of the past. It is a matter of looking at images, even archetypal and mythic images, in terms of what they intimate about what is coming rather than looking backward to their past.

Methods of individual inner development reveal another area where it is fruitful to hold both Jung and Steiner together without seeking resolution. Jung speaks of analysis as the only initiatory path available in the modern Western world. He either was unfamiliar with Steiner or scornfully chose not to acknowledge that Steiner's work is above all a path of individual inner development. The methods of Jung and Steiner seem at first unrelated. For Jung, the method is analysis of others (though one must have gone through analysis oneself). Then, within analysis, it is constant inner work with dreams, trying to get close to the images, feeling their living presence, amplifying the images through myths, and, most of all, engaging in the transference, where the real transformation occurs. For a few, there is the work of active imagination, which is the work of those initiated into the process of individuation.

Steiner's method is meditation, which focuses on developing the capacity of remaining in full control of consciousness, not allowing anything to enter consciousness that is not put there deliberately by the meditator. And what is supposed to be put there is a thought or an image of something unrelated to the sense world. One might, for example, meditate on the Rose Cross, which does not exist in the sensory world. After holding this in consciousness for a while, letting nothing else enter, the content focused on is erased, creating an empty consciousness. Then one waits, as the consciousness does not remain empty. An image, a thought, an insight enters, a response from the spiritual worlds.

Steiner recommends a host of other exercises, such as the backward review of the day; exercises for controlling thought, feeling, and will; and special meditative practices for developing the capacity to experience karma. Steiner's recommendations for each area he worked in—such as medicine, agriculture, and education—also include particular meditative exercises.

A primary difference between these two methods is that Jung's meditative work takes place primarily in the presence of another person, the therapist, while Steiner's takes place in private. In Anthroposophy, group meditative work has been discouraged and even disparaged.

In looking at the methods of Jung and Steiner, what is most important is to look at the capacities that are being developed, not the way the meditations are structured. Steiner is actually very clear about this. For example, in such practices as the Rose Cross meditation described above, it is the force of building up the thought and the force it takes to erase it that is central. Here it is as if the soul is a muscle that is being exercised to build up its strength. This makes it possible for the practitioner to be in soul in a conscious way.

For Jung, if we look at his methods closely, what is most essential is the relation between the individual and the therapist. This is where the strength to go on with analysis, dream work, and active imagination is centered. Much, of course, comes from working the material, but the soul transformation has to do with the transference. And transference is a name for the capacity to feel the autonomous presence of love without acting it out, without reducing it to something personal.

There is actually an element of something like transference in the methods of Steiner. This element is Steiner's insistence that all meditations be done with a strong sense of reverence. Here a relationship of love is established with an as-yet-unknown other. It is, I think, going in the wrong direction to say that Steiner's mediations are solitary while Jung's are communal, though that is what strikes one most at first. If we hold both of these methods together, we come to the method of spiritual psychology. Spiritual psychology values group meditative work, recognizing, mainly from Jung, that the element of feeling is as important as the element of thought in meditative work. At the same time, following Steiner's lead, spiritual psychology refuses to literalize therapy but sees individual meditative work as inherently therapeutic. It is perfectly possible to do individual meditative work in a group context. Here the exercises are like those proposed by Steiner, so that building up inner strength of soul is what is most important. The results of the exercises are discussed in the group, which develops the feeling dimension of the soul, and also serves as a way of doing soul research together. The method of spiritual psychology is a new form of therapeutic work that takes therapy away from concentration on the personal, which easily becomes ego-centered, and yet strengthens the soul and spirit forces that are, in any case, central to any therapeutic healing.

The valuable lectures by Hans Erhard Lauer, printed here as an appendix, look at the relation between Jung and Steiner from a slightly different point of view. I want to mine this material, too, for what it contributes to spiritual psychology with depth psychology and Anthroposophy as a base.

The first essay gives a good picture of how an Anthroposophist who is sympathetic to depth psychology interprets the vision, meaning, and methods of the latter. At first the essay may seem to resemble what one might find in a textbook about depth psychology. Notice, however, the inner clarity of the thinking and how Lauer slowly builds his theme.

Lauer first finds within the stream of depth psychology the play between individuality and collective forces. The polarity of that play is represented by Freud at the collective end—with his emphasis on the collective force known as sex—and by Adler on the end of individuality. Jung lands right in between. For Jung, illness manifests when these polarities conflict. His depth psychology explores the collective forces of the soul and the archetypes, as well as how autonomous symbolic forms seep into consciousness, producing illness when there is no capacity to receive these forms consciously. Lauer sees Jung as helping to prevent a total split between collective inner forces and individuality.

Steiner also wishes to heal this split, but from an entirely different angle than Jung. His work consists of developing the capacities of individuality to the point that the ego becomes the conscious "I," the spirit individuality that can make spiritual sense of what comes from the depths while doing practical spiritual work in the world. This is a very large order indeed. When these capacities are not developed spiritually, the split widens. For the many Anthroposophists who work to develop the practical cultural forms Steiner initiated—education, medicine, agriculture, painting, science, drama, movement, and so on—there is the inherent possibility of developing severe disturbances that go unnoticed. The content of the various areas of Steiner's work is taken up, but often not the meditative work. Even those who do practice the meditative work do not reckon with the size and degree of the split in the culture between the individual and the collective, or perhaps they somehow feel exempt from this split. In actual fact, the split has proceeded so far that it is highly dangerous, I think, to do spiritual practices without accompanying soul work.

There is a notion in Anthroposophy that the content of what Steiner created can be beneficial in the world on its own. But taken alone, without conscious connection to soul life, and without inner connection to the *activity* of conscious life, not just its contents, Anthroposophy is just another content, operating out of the same sleepy consciousness as the world at large. Furthermore, evoking spiritual authority that has no actual basis in oneself is deadly when accompanied by upsurging forces that leak into consciousness. This stance of authority can lead to abuse, cruelty, dogmatism, false superiority, and a self-isolation of anthroposophical communities from the rest of the world.

According to Lauer, depth psychology works out of the same kind of consciousness as modern science: it makes theories and hypotheses concerning the human soul that are then investigated through therapy. Lauer here misses Jung's phenomenological basis as well as the central significance of the transference. On the other hand, according to Lauer, those who take up Anthroposophy can, through meditative work, come to experience the soul inwardly, independently of the body. This meditative work potentially leads to a fully conscious "I." It is the fully conscious "I" that is supposed to be able to meet whatever rises from the collective forces of the soul.

Much of ego life is not conscious. This is the real discovery of Anthroposophy, but one that goes unnoticed, even in Anthroposophy. There is always an inner collusion going on between the unconscious aspects of the ego and the collective realms of the soul. Our ordinary ego is filled with pride, self-aggrandizement, anger, envy, and much besides. Most of all, the ego is the structure of fear. Freud's wonderful list of some fifty ego defense mechanisms are very descriptive of the unconscious aspects of ego life. Ego defends itself, but in wholly unconscious ways, such as denial, projection, introjection, and so on. For the very few people who do follow through with the meditative regimen recommended by Steiner, there is the possibility of doing conscious spiritual work of a practical nature in the world, with the capacity of meeting whatever comes from the depths. However, anthroposophical training goes on without any guidance in inner soul work, with no recognition of the importance of depth psychology, and almost no guidance in the meditative work recommended by Steiner. In these matters the student is left to fend alone. The ego is thus left isolated from the usual forms of ego gratification and development. It is cut off from help in finding a healthy connection with the collective forces of the soul; it is also cut off from guidance in coming to the "I."

The anthroposophical path, taken alone, requires one, through meditative exercises, to experience the soul as independent of the body. It requires one to be able to enter into the activity, rather than the content, of thinking. This development opens imaginative consciousness. This path then requires one to go through exercises that make it possible to enter into the activity, rather than the content, of feeling life, where inspiration is experienced as the activity of actual spiritual beings. Then one goes through exercises that make it possible to enter into the activity, rather than the content, of the will, where intuition is experienced as direct participation with spiritual beings. All this, it is expected, can happen in a culture in which the most severe split has occurred in soul life, a split in which individualism reigns and there is no connection to the collective forces of the soul.

Spiritual psychology, a creative synthesis of depth psychology and Anthroposophy, sees inner soul work as a necessary preliminary to any kind of spiritual work. "Preliminary" here is meant as something akin to doing warmup exercises, as, for example, done by a musician. You can be a very advanced musician, but you cannot do away with finger exercises. In our time, it is utter foolishness to try to take on meditative exercises without coming into healthy connection with one's soul life and doing a lot of work to keep that connection. How to keep open and keep these connections, and how to do so specifically within the kind of work one does in the world, is the work of spiritual psychology. Spiritual psychology as a practice, a doing, needs to be a part of every Waldorf training program, every anthroposophical medical training program, and all other anthroposophical endeavors.

In contemplating Lauer's essays, it might occur to the reader that the body must be gotten away from in order to work within the spiritual soul. Lauer strongly implies this. Lauer does not mention (nor does Wehr) that there is a whole dimension of Steiner's work that concerns developing the capacities to enter into imagination of the organs of the body and, through these, to enter into the soul and spirit worlds underlying them. Anthroposophy mostly touts body-free meditation, but this is not the direction that is necessarily required. It would be extremely fruitful to develop a synoptic comparison of Jung and Steiner by going to Steiner's meditative exercises and the results of those exercises reported in his book *Occult Physiology*.

I do not want to avoid contemplating the most difficult issue of all in this synoptic comparison of Jung and Steiner and the forming of spiritual psychology. This is the placement of Christ at the center of Anthroposophy and the importance of Christ in Jung.

Unfortunately, in Anthroposophy this focus is almost always sentimentalized, although Steiner does not sentimentalize it. He underwent a profound spiritual experience that showed him something of the true mysteries of Christ, reorienting the direction of Anthroposophy. But when the meditative side of Steiner's work is not practiced, the central freedom of the human being slides into a veiled religion, justified by Steiner's esoteric Christian viewpoint. Anthroposophy is practiced as a

Christian religion (although this is vehemently denied). Many Anthroposophists want to have it both ways. They want to experience themselves as completely free "I-beings," but they also want to believe that Christ is working in them—without working through all the baggage of Christian belief that each and everyone lives, whether Christian or not.

Neither Jung nor Steiner asks for Christian belief. But both realize the utter foolishness of speaking of a psychology of the dead, the gods, and the spiritual worlds without coming up against the status of Christ. Jung clearly emphasizes the religious character of the psyche, but wants to hold that soul is influenced by many archetypal myths besides the Christian myth. He does, however, see the Christian myth as the future of the psyche, that is, individuation as realization of the Self and Christ as the archetype of the Self.

If one does not just accept Jung's view, but meditates on it deeply as well as on Jung's writings concerning Christ, then what he says makes good sense and provides a way through the barrier encountered by Anthroposophists. This barrier is simply that there is no other way to apprehend Christ from the consciousness of the ordinary ego than through what we are given from outside, by others. In Anthroposophy, the risk is that of forming a relationship to the religious notions of Christ, thinking that it is an immediate experience of developed spiritual consciousness. The development of the true capacity of the "I" would be needed, and if that takes place, we might well have Christian spiritual psychology. Steiner's writings have disseminated concepts of Christ that are more powerful and astute than religions that either completely humanize Christ or completely deify him. But to simply accept what Steiner has to say would be falling into religion. (Actually, there is nothing wrong with falling into religion. Far worse is doing so without knowing that has happened.)

The concern here is whether there is or can be such a thing as a Christian spiritual psychology that is something other than imposing a certain belief structure onto a discipline. Here Steiner is more helpful than Jung, but the whole of Steiner has to be worked through. This means coming to see that the very structure and meaning of consciousness, of the natural world, of culture and civilization, of the earth, of the human being in body, soul, and spirit, is permeated with the forces that are Christ. Thus it is impossible *not* to have a Christian spiritual psychology. It is only possible to deny the fact that spiritual psychology is completely the same as Christian psychology. Speaking in this way, at the end of this introduction, is not intended to be a pronouncement. It is deliberately provocative, a call for the working through the details of Christian spiritual psychology without falling into institutional religion, actual or veiled.

JUNG
AND
STEINER

GERHARD WEHR

PREFACE

The rationale for a book like this cannot be given in a short—or even a long—preface. A work like this, which must be regarded as an experiment, has to be seen as part of a whole.

First of all, sincere thanks to those who have made this book possible. I owe it to the initiative of Dr. Wilhelm Bitter, the eminent founder and director of the Internationale Gesellschaft Arzt und Seelsorger (International Society of Doctors and Pastors), Stuttgart, that this attempt was possible at all. My short 1969 essay on C.G. Jung provided a stimulus, even though that was not my original intention. Thanks to the effective help of the Wilhelm Bitter Fund, the project—which was originally conceived by only a small circle of colleagues—could be realized.

I owe special thanks to Dr. Käthe Weizsäcker-Hoss of Tübingen, who, together with a number of colleagues, went to the considerable trouble of critically reading the whole manuscript. Her advice and faithful encouragement were very valuable to me, as was that of Manuela Jaeger, an experienced psychotherapist who led me to the first steps on the path of self-knowledge. Prof. Bitter thoroughly evaluated the project from his depth-psychological and psychotherapeutic perspective. Dr. Hans Erhard Lauer did the same from the anthroposophical point of view. The critical remarks of these two scholars were of great value to me, as was, fortunately, their overall approval.

Since I see no reason to deny the doubts and reservations that are bound to arise in the course of writing a work like this, I want to remember all those whose encouragement I received: Dr. Irmgard Buck; Dr. Marie-Louise von Franz; Jung's biographer, Aniela Jaffé; and the psychotherapist Marie Laiblin. I thank my German publisher, especially Dr. Hubert Arbogast and Dr. Hanne Lenz, for their

33

appreciation and careful attention during publication. Finally, this work could never have been brought to a good end if it was not for the understanding and patience of my dear wife, Else, and of my children, Gabriele and Matthias.

GERHARD WEHR

Schwarzenberg bei Nürnberg
June 6, 1971, the tenth anniversary of C.G. Jung's death

1

INTRODUCING THE PROBLEM

GREAT PEOPLE OF HISTORY, especially those who are felt to be outsiders and nonconformists, usually pose some riddles for their contemporaries as well as their descendants. First, they demand that one come to understand the special contribution they have made to our quest for knowledge. A circle of pupils as well as a group of opponents forms. All too often, it is detrimental to the further development of the founder's original intentions when there is a group of uncritical admirers who swear by every word the "master" has uttered—detrimental because others draw the wrong conclusions about the original achievement of the personality whose cause these people claim to represent. Because of their demeanor, their dogmatism, and their spiritual stubbornness, prejudices arise, especially if the content of the founder's original message is considered strange or disturbing by the general public. For example, it may seem strange when a new, holistic viewpoint is offered that embraces the whole cosmos and demands a high measure of open-mindedness and the ability to follow new concepts. These demands can usually be met by only a relatively small group of people. Yet there are many who feel the need to counteract the increasing specialization into different scientific disciplines, whether through popularizations, or through various comparative efforts.

The enigma of great figures in the history of the mind, if they are contemporaries, is that they are often able to thoroughly and correctly diagnose the times they live in, but fail to appreciate the significance of someone they may see as a competitor. It is not unusual for outstanding personalities to live as if they had nothing in common, even though they might have complemented each other, could perhaps even have corrected and inspired each other in the pursuit of a common goal.[1]

It must be part of the psychology, of the inner law of a spiritual pioneer—or rather, of the founder of a new way of thinking—that he pursues their path with the greatest concentration and inner consistency in order to reach his life's goal. This consistency and inner urgency demand that, risking one-sidedness, he may be "blind and intolerant" of others' efforts. The pioneer simply does not have the time and strength to pay proper attention to the apparent competitor; occasionally, his attitude is one of disregard or even condemnation. It is only too easy then for pupils and overeager disciples, remembering their master's "anathema," to consider the work of the assumed competitor inconsequential.

After the pioneering phase during which a new spiritual movement has to accomplish its breakthrough, there follows a scholastic phase and a period of orthodoxy. One is sufficiently occupied with editing, commenting on, and quoting the work in question—not to mention the army of intellectually challenged parrots. Yet it would be an important task for the pupils to do the work that the master left unfinished, like trying to create lateral connections as well as building mental bridges to other, related endeavors.

Here lies a real problem, however. Aside from the wealth of material that needs to be addressed in each case, the significance of a great work shows itself in the fact that it really is incomparable. The thoughts of its creator, his or her beginning and aims, do not readily correspond to the thoughts of another person. This already follows from the biological and social conditions into which destiny has cast the individual, shaping his or her life. Differing approaches to knowledge, often preconditioned, shape the background of an individual's worldview, and these differ in each person. In every conceptualization there is a certain innate way of looking at things that differs fundamentally from the thought forms of another author, even if the text itself seems, at first glance, to suggest a similar meaning. On the other hand, it also happens that related ideas are hidden behind different terminologies. Whoever confuses statements of different origin that seem to be in agreement with ideas that are truly in accord, overlooking the true character of certain thought-connections and the deep disparity that separates the two mental creations, will often be in danger of comparing apples and oranges.

The analytic psychology of C.G. Jung and Rudolf Steiner's Anthroposophy constitute two disparate entities in regard to their points of departure as well as their aim, and in regard to the fundament of their knowledge and their initial understanding. Rudolf Steiner has to be recognized as the founder of the anthroposophical spiritual science that seeks to convey an understanding of the physical-soul-spiritual wholeness of the human being. Anthroposophy, as will be shown in a later chapter—and in the biographical context—is primarily a path of research that should enable a person to act according to this view of the human being and recognition of its reality. The immediate fruits of Anthroposophy are manifest in a variety of endeavors and specialties: the Waldorf school movement, biodynamic agriculture, the production of high-quality remedies (for instance, by the Weleda Company), the work of anthroposophical physicians and curative educators. These anthroposophical activities are widely known throughout the world, as are anthroposophical contributions in natural science and the arts. An impulse for religious renewal has created the Christian Community.[2]

Jung has also directed his cognitive efforts toward a new understanding of the human being. As a psychiatrist he appreciated early on the groundbreaking achievements of Sigmund Freud. One cannot, however, call him merely a pupil of Freud, as after several years of cooperation, he distanced himself from the "master." Proof of this is his earlier work, which was done before he met Freud. But most of all he proved himself by his great discoveries in the field of depth psychology, his studies of the collective unconscious and of the world of archetypal images. With these he went far beyond Freud and his classical psychoanalysis.[3] His insights into the reality of the psyche have borne fruit in many ways and have considerably deepened our understanding of reality, as we see in the dialogue between the different scientific disciplines that is now underway.[4] No doubt the foremost focus of work for Jung the analytical psychologist was his medical practice. But anyone who studies Jung's work thoroughly notices that his psychotherapy does not only address the mental patient. Beyond this it has an important cognitive function to fulfill. It encourages self-discovery and accompanies the process of maturation.

Steiner and Jung never had any immediate exchange of ideas during their lifetime, although they were contemporaries for half a century (from 1875, Jung's birth year, to 1925, Steiner's death year), and lived in close proximity to each other. The Anthroposophist and the depth psychologist each speak a language that is by nature foreign to the representative of the other discipline; but aside from the technical differences in their fields, there are definitely other factors that reinforced their distance. Steiner mentioned psychoanalysis and analytic psychology in some of his lectures. He also occasionally spoke of Jung as a scientist, but never did so in the thorough and detailed manner that would have been desirable. This occurred at a time when Jung's psychology was just beginning to distinguish itself from Freud's older psychoanalysis and to come into its own. Jung on his part mentions Anthroposophy several times and refers to Steiner without showing any interest in him. One gets the impression that the circumspect depth psychologist Jung ignored the essence and significance of Anthroposophy. One can conclude this because Anthroposophy is mentioned on occasion in one breath, without any differentiation, with the Anglo-Indian Theosophy of H.P. Blavatsky or with Christian Science. This is surprising and unfortunate, especially since Jung outlived Steiner for three and a half decades, and could have had occasion to observe the activities of the Anthroposophical Society from nearby.

A factual dialogue between Anthroposophy and Jungian psychology has so far never been conducted. From the side of Anthroposophy there are only a few works that could contribute to such a dialogue. For the most part we have apologetic, critical remarks in which the author refers to Steiner's rejection of psychoanalysis and considers a serious study of the material to be superfluous. Representatives of the Jungian school have also shown little interest thus far in occupying themselves with the results of Steiner's work or any of his suggestions. For instance, a representative anthroposophical work like Friedrich Husemann's *Image of Man as Foundation for the Healing Arts*,[5] which discusses the relationship between body and psyche and devotes space to the psychotherapeutic view of the anthroposophical neurologist, mentions Freud only once, and only refers twice—very briefly—to Jung. In the same work the author laments the fact that Steiner is not mentioned in several psychological works, and then refers the reader to Steiner's *Theosophy* (1904) and *Riddles of the Soul* (1917). It is obvious that such encouragement to read Steiner's books is not sufficient in view of the fact that such books necessitate a thorough study of Anthroposophy. This situation of mutual disregard is untenable.

From within Anthroposophy, there is a lack not only of pertinent preparatory work, but even of suitable material for such inquiry. Only a few experts have access to the vast body of Steiner's work, because most of it consists of lecture notes. There is one register listing subjects and names mentioned in the first fifty lecture cycles.[6] The laudable complete edition of all of Steiner's books and lectures, which is still in the making, does contain short annotations with cross-references and brief biographical notes. But there is no index that would facilitate compilation of Steiner's widely scattered remarks on a particular subject. The content and stylistic presentation of the lectures add to the difficulties. As a final obstacle, the publisher must preface each of the nearly 350 volumes of lectures with a statement that they were printed from written notes unedited by the lecturer, and to understand them, a certain familiarity with Anthroposophy is necessary. In any event, real caution is needed if one wants to evaluate the lectures as time, location, the particular audience and, last but not least, the reliability of the handwritten notes must all be taken into consideration.

Many people have considerable trouble with Steiner's communications regarding the results of his spiritual research. His mode of expression, especially in the lectures, has also been heavily criticized. All this leaves an unprepared reader perplexed. A solid education in natural science, philosophy or even psychology is not necessarily sufficient to understand basic anthroposophical literature. One needs special hermeneutic help. Readers who are unfamiliar with the character of imaginative writings and their special language may ask how they should interpret communications of occult facts that seem to be clothed in language that is either mythological, symbolic, or allegorical.

These facts do not seem to be accessible to normal, rational thinking. Of course, it is also often unclear what a particular reader means by mythological, symbolic, or allegorical. (It is well-known that many self-appointed anthroposophical experts maintain a faithful master-pupil relationship and swear by every word the "master" has said. These people should not constitute a serious obstacle to honest investigation, but they do exist.)

There is another fundamental problem to which Jung and Steiner both referred frequently—a characteristic fear that seizes people when they are faced with the supersensible. "We are used to thought patterns founded on sense observation and experimentation, and we fear falling prey to nebulous, fantastic ideas when they are not anchored in what we can learn from our sense impressions, our way of measuring and weighing things." Steiner points out that people shy away from the complete rethinking that is required if one wants to attain accurate spiritual-scientific knowledge. "Out of unconscious fear they accuse Anthroposophy of being fantastic, when in reality Anthroposophy wants to proceed in the realm of the spirit just as cautiously as natural science does in the physical world."[7]

Jung acknowledges the fear that appears in the face of the unconscious when he says: "Fear and resistance are the signposts that stand beside the *via regia* to the unconscious, and it is obvious that what they primarily signify is a preconceived opinion of the thing that they are pointing at."[8]

Aside from the fear that one could be overwhelmed or inundated by the powerful forces of the unconscious, which is not entirely unfounded, there is our tendency to avoid "conversions, enlightenment, upsets, and new experiences." Modern people either have such confused ideas about the "mystical" or such a rationalistic fear of it that they misinterpret the true character of their experience and either reject its numinosity or repress it. It is then considered to be an inexplicable, irrational, or even pathological phenomenon. It is obviously a fear that one does not like to admit, and it leads to denial or suppression of one's inner experiences when one becomes aware of things that appear in the soul-mirror. This is, by the way, a well-known phenomenon, and is referred to in religious documents as fear of the gods, fear when encountering angels, and so on. For modern people, estranged as we are from the supersensible world, this fear acquires a special significance. Steiner writes: "Before cognizing it, the spiritual world is something quite foreign to the soul. It has no attributes that the soul can experience in the sensory world." Therefore there are no safeguards, there is no possibility of confirming one's impressions as a scientist does in the sense world. "Thus the soul may find itself facing the spiritual world and see there only a complete 'nothing.' In this case, the soul feels as though it were looking into an endless, empty, deserted abyss. This feeling of facing the abyss—a kind of dread—actually exists in the depths of the soul. At first, the soul is unconscious of these depths. The soul feels only that this experience of dread is related to fear; and that it lives in this fear without knowing it."[9] In this connection Steiner speaks of "materialism as a psychological phenomenon of fear" and sees in this an "important chapter in psychology."

In the following we will have to come back to the observation that both Steiner and Jung give us very little definite information when they describe soul life as a process in flux. This has led to accusations of vagueness and conceptual haziness. In this respect, when one compares Jung and Freud, the latter has done somewhat better: Freud's accounts have an immediacy that speaks without difficulty to the rational mind. We will see that Steiner as well as Jung had to create a method of research that was dictated by their object, namely the psychic-spiritual dimensions. The list of difficulties and obstacles in comparing Steiner and Jung would be long enough as it is. However, one cannot underestimate the reservations that are brought forward by one school against the other. The prejudices against Steiner from the one side as well as the ones against Jung from the other (albeit not quite so strong) are known.[10]

In view of all these difficulties, what justifies such a comparative study? Science, which represents the "religion of our time," according to Carl Friedrich von Weizsäcker, has not only produced an explosion of knowledge and an immeasurable, constantly expanding amount of data and facts. In our century, science has broken through the boundaries of

classical natural science in many fields, and has brought about what Jean
Gebser called the "transformation of the West." Gebser has demonstrated this in many separate domains of science. We are dealing here
with a transformation that is not limited to a single culture but has the
potential to revolutionize the thinking of all humanity. The tendency of
this transformation of scientific thinking is based on a general change in
consciousness that is more and more being recognized.

> The new position may be characterized as one that would over-
> come the supremacy of the intellect, yet would not signify a rever-
> sion to the magical or mythical, nor a stagnation in philosophical
> concepts. With these three latter components one could describe
> the whole development of humankind so far. This new position
> would require rising above the present state into a spiritual dimen-
> sion that is not in opposition to psyche or physical body, but rather
> constitutes a new form of consciousness for which humankind
> seems to prepare itself. This new spiritual dimension, inasmuch as
> it could be called a super-awake sphere, could, in a surprising way,
> bring us closer to the source and origin of our being. We may con-
> sider what constitutes thought according to the new scientific
> research. Its origin in the immaterial realm identifies it as belonging
> outside of space and time. [11]

With this we have entered new territory that cannot be opened up
simply by accumulating, storing, and utilizing new facts and information, in spite of the old faith in traditional science. The new territory
of consciousness-raising of which Gebser is speaking turns out more
and more to be the problem of the human being, and the confrontation with the self. For not only in the laboratories and on the proving
grounds of science are thresholds being crossed, but also in the human
soul and spirit.

But who is the human being? It is no coincidence that the ancient
riddle of the Sphinx, the demand of the old mystery priests: "Know
thyself!" as well as the core question of the creator God: "Adam,
where art thou?" are being voiced so insistently today. Arnold Gehlen

summarizes his observation of a deep shift in interest toward the human being: "Outside of religious institutions, in the sciences, even in philosophy, the human being is becoming the central theme."[12] Similarly, von Weizsäcker says, "The key we have lost is precisely the key to the human being."[13] Whoever is aware of the total and radical threat to humanity in our time senses what it means to lose the key to the human being, or to be in danger of losing it. The situation puts high demands on the humanities. A psychology like Jung's, which is able to shed light into the deep unconscious levels of the personal psyche and at the same time has discovered the connections within humanity's collective unconscious, is now being asked for help in restoring the lost image of the human being. Psychology is being asked how the individual and mankind can find the way to maturity and how, in the face of the threatening loss of soul, individuation, human self-realization, can be accomplished.

Spiritual science, which is what Steiner's method of research understands itself to be, wants to be primarily Anthroposophy—the wisdom of the human being. This means qualitatively more than just knowledge based on the accumulation of facts and data. For decades, Steiner's knowledge of the human being has been utilized in the above-mentioned fields, in spite of all the prejudices. Even fundamental critics of Anthroposophy cannot deny the value of what has appeared as the fruits of practical Anthroposophy.

We can approach our theme, the comparison of Jung and Steiner, from another aspect when we consider that in our rapidly shrinking world any monopoly of knowledge is becoming an anachronism. Humankind, even though it finds itself closer together in space, is all the more separated by ideological differences and prejudices. It urgently needs a "community of spirit" (to use the words of Sarvepalli Radhakrishnan) in the form of a newly practiced humanity. In the face of the manifold challenges of our time and the existential threat of one person against another, we need a concentration of spiritual forces that can help self-knowledge and world-transformation, even though they come from such divergent streams as Jung's analytic psychology and Steiner's Anthroposophy.

Steiner and Jung must not be seen in isolation. Their insights and experiences will have to be evaluated in the context of other insights gained in East and West by the greatest spiritual exponents of our century. Merely staring at the situation will not save us. In the face of the aforementioned dissociation of the individual and humanity there are already converging forces at work, which Pierre Teilhard de Chardin has brought into focus in his theological-scientific vision. Jung sees this process expressed in symbolism that unites the opposites. Sri Aurobindo, a representative of Eastern spirituality, while looking at what he called the unmasking of evil, has described the "descent of the spirit," of the "supramental," as an ongoing process of purification and salvation. Other wise teachers of the East, such as Ramana Maharshi, have recognized as real, and a process of far-reaching consequences, what Rudolf Steiner spoke of since 1910 as "the Christ-event of the twentieth century."[14]

It would be worthwhile to look at this "East-West conflict," as Steiner has called it on occasion. Steiner and Jung each saw, from his own standpoint, the problem of the contrast between East and West and tried to decipher it for Westerners. We must not be indifferent to what this answer looks like for Steiner and Jung in the dialogue of the "hemispheres of the spirit."[15]

The current great efforts to eliminate hunger and ensure peace for the world have to be supplemented by a corresponding effort to achieve psychological and spiritual renewal for humanity. In view of humanity's worldwide "extraversion," of human engagement in the political, social, and economic arenas ("engagement" has become a keyword of our time!), Christ's words "But one thing is needful" (Luke 10:42) take on new weight and importance. In the monasteries of the past, wisdom dictated a balance between the *via meditativa* and the *via activa*, between meditative religious practice and active engagement in world affairs. The old wisdom prescribed that meditative activity (introversion) should come *before*, not after, outer activity (extraversion). A reversal of this order must have dire consequences. Therefore contemplation and spiritual schooling cannot be called a superfluous luxury in which a few will indulge to the detriment of the majority.

Individuation is the responsibility and goal of *every* person. The number of those who, in the words of the prophet, "make straight in the desert a highway" is naturally small. Steiner and Jung belong to this active minority.

The present study must confine itself to a relatively small aspect of the problems that have been raised. The task here is to compare and contrast Anthroposophy and analytical psychology. The works of two men will be put face to face with each other. Each of these works has been created according to its own inherent laws. To begin with, one needs to see and acknowledge the differences in the two ways of cognition. These must not be obscured by attempts to harmonize the two and must not be played down by seeking parallels prematurely. However, one does not have to stop at the differences, if one can find some sort of common language and a common denominator. This is precisely what Steiner was concerned with when Anthroposophy began to be known beyond the circle of the original membership. Whoever reads the lecture notes of the years immediately after World War I that deal with the new social order knows that Steiner was very intent on finding the "right language," and on overcoming the "organized sectarian unkindness," as he called it, in certain anthroposophical circles. Whoever is unwilling to honestly study the language of the opponent, he said, creates prejudices and only exacerbates the condition of the ideological split.[16] One also cannot fail to hear the earnest appeal when he says elsewhere: "My hope is that out of the circle of our friends those will come forward more and more who are able to build the necessary bridges."[17] He means here the spiritual bridge-building between Anthroposophy and non-anthroposophical science. Steiner always rejected dogmatic fixation as well as idolatry of his own person, although these remain a problem even today. He knew that "in the theosophical [i.e., anthroposophical] movement the danger of injury through the worship of a personality cult and belief in authority is particularly great.... Personalities must be the bearers of revelation; yet we must take care not to confuse the one with the other." The personality must always be scrutinized.[18] Jung was also never in doubt about the provisional and pioneering character of his work. He once wrote in a letter: "It will be a task for my successors to systematically work up and clarify many of my thoughts that I only jotted down. Without such work there will be no progress in the science of analytic psychology."

These appeals by Steiner and Jung may arise from different motives, but they can still encourage us to continue the work. Since both Jung's and Steiner's methods of research reveal a universal tendency toward a total reality, a synopsis seems to be indicated. In the workshops of the "Internationale Gemeinschaft Arzt und Seelsorger" (International Society of Physicians and Spiritual Advisers), initiated by Wilhelm Bitter, the synoptic method has long been successfully used. Bitter, a physician and psychiatrist, and Adolf Köberle, a Protestant theologian, have defined the concept thus: "Synopsis does not mean synthesis, nor the sum of the different hypotheses and theories, nor does it indicate an amalgam like the one Schultze-Henke has attempted by merging Freud's and Adler's theories into his neoanalysis. Nor is it eclecticism or syncretism. Synopsis tries, as its Greek name indicates, to visualize together all the proven essential elements and in addition, to be open to new insights and innovations."

That representatives of different schools can report good results allows us to conclude there is some common ground.[19] Bitter is working on a synoptic psychotherapy.

In addition to Bitter and Köberle, the theologian Ulrich Mann practices the synoptic method. In his important work *Theogonische Tage*, he delivers an impressive example of synoptic interpretation.[20] In this connection it is interesting to note that both Mann and Köberle come from the Tübingen school of Karl Heims (1874-1958). There important work has been done, outside mainstream theological trends, to achieve a theology that would transcend the disciplines and tend toward a holistic view of reality and a universal Christology. "The religious legacy of the Swabian fathers," foremost among them the great theosophist of the eighteenth century, Friedrich Christoph Oetinger, who was a prominent follower of Jacob Boehme, is the spiritual source of Heim, Köberle, and Mann. With this we meet the eminently fertile stream of post-Reformation German mysticism. Both Steiner and Jung acknowledged their debt to this movement in many important points of their work. One of the most prominent key figures in the spiritual heritage of Central Europe, Jacob Boehme, influenced both the founder of Anthroposophy and the creator of analytic psychology directly as well as indirectly.

At the present moment, when a tortured humanity is experiencing turmoil and apocalypse as never before, there is need for a synoptic effort toward wisdom and knowledge. The forces of atomization and dissociation appear to be overwhelming. Where should we direct our attention in the midst of the tempests and jolts that plague our century? Emil Bock, the theologian and Anthroposophist, wrote in one of his essays on the Christian festivals: "In these times we have to learn two things: a sense for what is dying, so we can recognize it; and a sense for what is emerging, so we can cultivate it. The outer conditions of the world are doomed; everything transitory, everything time-bound, is essentially dying. But there are also signs of something new emerging. To see the first rays of eternity glimmer through the cracks and crevices of the bursting sense world: this gives us the strength to calmly give over to the abyss what is dying, and to welcome that which is arising."

2

A BIOGRAPHICAL COMPARISON

THIS AUTHOR IS NOT THE FIRST to notice that the life stories of Steiner and Jung contain many similar features. For instance, Fred Poeppig writes: "There are certain compelling parallels between Jung and Rudolf Steiner, the 'scientist of the invisible,' since both men saw their life's mission in exploring the world of the invisible."[1] Hans Erhard Lauer, one of the few Anthroposophists to have studied Jung in detail, points out: "We believe that we speak not from a favorable disposition toward Rudolf Steiner but from objective facts when we maintain that there are not many biographies of important, pioneering men of our time that have so many similarities and analogies as those of Steiner and Jung." Lauer qualifies this statement: "Of course there are, besides the similarities, also decisive differences." For our inquiry the first part of their lives will be of special interest. That is the time when both men were finding the direction their life's paths would take.

Lauer's qualifying statement is certainly justified. Aside from the parallels, both biographies show some significant dissimilarities that are important to recognize. It begins with the different socioeconomic status of their ancestry.

But first a remark about the biographical sources. In the case of Jung, practically the only source we have is his autobiography, which was written down by Aniela Jaffé, his private secretary during the last six years of his life: *Memories, Dreams, Reflections*. There may be a few unexpected revelations by friends or family, but they cannot signifi-cantly augment the picture Jung himself revealed shortly before his death. This can be attributed to the uniqueness of Jung's life and his biographical revelations. "My life is a story of a self-realization of the unconscious....What we are to our inward vision, and what a man

48

appears to be *sub specie aeternitatis*, can only be expressed by way of myth."[2] Only he himself was capable of relating this myth. Others, even close friends, family members, and relatives, could at best provide a context, enriched by anecdotal material. The "mythical" picture that is embedded in Jung's life would not be altered by these. Strictly speaking, his life did not fit into the conventional dimensions of history. This strange-sounding statement is corroborated by Jung's own judgment of himself. It is not surprising that Aniela Jaffé could not obtain any clear "outer" dates about his life from him. "He found only the spiritual essence of his life's events memorable and worth the trouble to tell."

Obviously the "myth of his life" was played out on a plane where outer events were so unessential to him that he did not remember them. He himself confessed:

In the end the only events in my life worth telling are those when the imperishable world irrupted into this transitory one. That is why I speak chiefly of inner experiences, amongst which I include my dreams and visions. These form the *prima materia* of my scientific work. They were the fiery magma out of which the stone that had to be worked was crystallized.

All other memories of travels, people and my surroundings have paled beside these interior happenings....Recollections of the outward events of my life have largely faded or disappeared. But my encounters with the "other" reality, my bouts with the unconscious, are indelibly engraved upon my memory. In that realm there has always been wealth in abundance, and everything else has lost importance by comparison.[3]

The confessions in this book, as well as corresponding statements in his letters and in the forewords to his scientific works, give us the clues to his essential character.

Rudolf Steiner did not have time before his death to write a complete autobiography, as Jung did in his eighties. Steiner worked on his autobiography until shortly before his death. The account ends with the events of the year 1913, when Steiner broke with the Theosophists and founded the Anthroposophical Society. It is not insignificant that this autobiography was first published in a magazine in seventy install-ments, in keeping with the contents of that publication. What the author has to report, his inner experiences, the outer run of events, as well as his encounters with people, blends well into the intellectual his-tory of Europe at the time. Accordingly, it is right to present Steiner "before the background of European history," as Friedrich Hiebel did.

Steiner, the founder of a modern form of initiatic knowledge, did not leave an autobiography reserved for an inner circle of initiates. Inner and outer events that had to be related are in perfect balance. In the terms of Jungian typology, one could speak of a balance of introversion and extraversion. In comparison, Jung's memoirs could be called rather esoteric and exclusive. Had he published these in the form of magazine articles, he might have run into many misunderstandings among his readers. The degree of openness with which these revelations from the unconscious poured out of him, almost like volcanic eruptions, can give the impression of something very strange, if not disturbing.

Steiner could also have given accounts of an esoteric nature. How-ever, he refrained from sharing these with a wider public. The one time that he gave an autobiographical sketch of an esoteric nature, he did it for a closed circle of friends, in answer to some outrageous accusations that had been launched against him. A few years prior to this, in 1907, he wrote an autobiographical sketch for Edouard Schuré, the French poet and esotericist. This was published for the first time in 1965, on the occasion of the fortieth anniversary of Steiner's death.[4]

Let us try now to juxtapose some of Steiner's and Jung's important milestones.

Steiner grew up in a family that was already marked by the work sit-uation of the modern era. His parents, who came from the Lower Aus-trian Waldviertel, a region north of the Danube, had to sever themselves from the traditional ties of family and village life. The father's modest employment with the Austrian railway forced them to move many times, as he was assigned posts in different station houses. They adopted this kind of life because their former landlord, whom they had served as forester and maidservant, would not give them his consent to marry. Individual freedom was gained for the price of a low-paying job and a sort of homelessness. This is the fate that played into the life of the young Rudolf Steiner. The parents had to move many times, and the home was mostly a small railroad station, up to Steiner's eighteenth year. Thus, in the 1860s and '70s, he was aware of the steady progress of the then-modern railroad technology.

Jung's familiar surroundings were a Reformed church parsonage in northern Switzerland. Among his ancestors on his mother's side there were seven theologians. Even though the parsonage was not a place of wealth, as Jung says in his memoirs, it was, together with the family and their numerous relatives, a place of security and stability, features that were highly valued in those days. The social gap between the Steiners and the Jungs was quite wide. Steiner's father, who, though born a Catholic, saw himself as a liberal thinker, and Jung's father, the Protestant pastor, would have had very little in common. While the Steiner family had left the traditional bonds of master and servant, the Jung family was certainly much bound up with tradition. The Jungs' far-reaching family tree also confirms this attitude.

Even more important for Jung must have been the inherited soul constitution that was laid into his cradle. It is mirrored in his dreams and thoughts, his deeds and sufferings.

Very little is known about Steiner's ancestors. He found it important to mention that although of German blood, he was born into the Yugoslav part of Austria, which was quite foreign to the milieu and customs of his own family. He told this once to a Russian audience in Helsinki, in the year 1912, during one of his lecture cycles. Marie von Sivers, Steiner's second wife and the most important collaborator in all his anthroposophical work, once characterized him thus: "Germanity immersed in Slavic culture, with a good measure of Celtic ancestry—these characteristics combined to give his evolving 'I' the flexibility and the fire that he needed to have a loving understanding for everything strange and different. He was capable of this to a large measure, and he used this talent of his to help people of great diversity to understand themselves and their destiny."

Steiner's biographer Fred Poeppig adds the following:

Only on this basis was it possible to live a life that was firmly rooted in the development of higher knowledge, without falling into the trap of abstract intellectuality that often is the mark of philosophers. His origins helped him to avoid this trap, and they gave him Austrian charm, Slavic flexibility, and cosmopolitan broadmindedness. He truly was a man of the world.[5]

Obviously, such statements cannot constitute a complete characterization of Steiner. We have to let his destiny as well as his life's mission speak to us in order to get a picture of the man. Some childhood experiences give a clue as to how his calling announced itself early on.

One of the first memories Steiner relates is a vision he had when he was four years old.[6] In the waiting room of the small Austrian railroad station in Pottschach the child saw a woman he had never seen before, who closely resembled one of his relatives. "This woman came through the door, walked to the middle of the room with gestures and words that can be described as follows: 'Please try to do as much as you can for me, now and in the future.' She remained there for a while gesticulating in a way that can never be forgotten, once you had seen it, then went to the stove and disappeared into it."[7] After some days it turned out that a remote living relative of the family had committed suicide just at the time of the boy's vision. The impression this made on the boy turned out to be especially profound and lasting.

Two factors deserve special mention here. One is that the child was utterly alone with his experience. In a lecture of 1913, given before a small circle of friends, Steiner mentioned this for the first time: "The boy had nobody in his family to whom he could talk about this, because even at this early age he would have had to hear the harshest words about his silly superstition, had he divulged anything about it." His father's daily routine, which fascinated the young Rudolf early on—for instance, the work with the telegraph—was hard to reconcile with visionary experiences. But even here we see the workings of destiny in the juxtaposition of modern technology and spiritual vision.

The question arose in the young boy's mind that was to occupy him in the future: "How can one gain certainty of the reality of a spiritual world without denying the world in which the laws of modern natural science and technology prevail?"

With this we already touch on the second factor, the access to a side of reality that is normally hidden from our perception. In this connection Steiner relates that from the time of his vision, "Life for the boy was such that it allowed him to see not only the outer trees, mountains, etc. but also those worlds that are behind these phenomena. All this spoke to his soul at the same time. And the boy lived with the nature spirits that are very much alive in such a rural environment, the creating beings behind the outer appearances, while at the same time the outer world spoke to his senses."[8]

From now on there were for Rudolf things "you see" and those "you don't see." One must not overvalue the gift of clairvoyance that nature had given to the boy Rudolf Steiner. This natural gift can be looked upon in anthroposophical terms as a last remnant of an ancient clairvoyance, a legacy from archaic humankind. For Steiner this gift in itself was not of great significance. Much more important for his further development was his attitude toward the gift and what he did with it. Especially in his endeavor to penetrate this mysterious phenomenon with clear understanding, Steiner distinguished himself from those visionaries who accept their visions in a more passive way. In this way the experience of the four-year-old becomes the *impulse to understand,* which gains in importance throughout his life. The other side of his nature let the boy take an intense interest in all the mechanical things that surrounded him at the railroad station. "My interest was drawn strongly toward the mechanical quality in that existence, and I realize that this interest always tended to obscure the deep bond of sympathy that my young heart felt with that charming and majestic natural world into which the train—always subject to the mechanical—disappeared in the distance." So he writes in the *Autobiography.*[9]

Just as the polarities nature/technology and spirit-world/technology posed riddles for the mind, so did the surrounding world present a wealth of problems for the young boy. The nearby textile factory, for instance, provoked many questions in him. Steiner observed carefully what raw materials were delivered to the factory and saw the end products emerging. But he was prevented from seeing the work that was going on inside. "I came up against 'the limits of knowledge.' And I was very eager to transcend those limits." The director of the factory was a riddle to him also. Then there were events at the railroad station. A car with combustible materials caught fire. The boy puzzled over how that could have happened. "As in other cases, the explanations of those around me failed to satisfy me. I had countless questions, but they remained unanswered. Thus I reached my eighth year."[10]

These and similar accounts show how greatly he longed to understand his surroundings. It is of crucial importance to see how these longings were satisfied eventually. Even though he only went to small country schools—for a while in Pottschach, from his eighth year on in Neudörfl, a small Hungarian village near the Austrian-Hungarian border—these simple schools were able to give him important insights. His way of learning took a direction that differed markedly from Jung's.

In the small room of the lay teacher at Neudörfl who provided extra lessons to a few children, Steiner discovered a geometry book. It fascinated him. He was allowed to take the book home, and he taught himself from it with great enthusiasm. "For weeks my soul was completely filled with the congruence, the similarity of triangles, quadrilaterals and polygons. I racked my brains over the question of where parallel lines actually intersect; the theorem of Pythagoras fascinated me.... I realize that I first knew happiness through geometry." The contentment that Steiner derived from geometry came from learning how "one can live with the soul in building forms that are seen wholly inwardly, independent of the outer senses."[11] Steiner saw later in his relationship to geometry the first inkling of a realization that had grown within him more or less unconsciously when he was very young. Around his twentieth year it became a definite and conscious conviction. In his *Autobiography* he describes his thoughts thus:

> I would have said that the objects and events seen by the senses exist in space, the space outside the human being; but a kind of soul-space exists within as the setting for spiritual beings and events. I

could not see anything in thoughts that was like pictures we form of things; rather they were revelations of a spiritual world on the stage of the soul. To me, geometry seemed to be a knowledge that we ourselves produce; but its significance is completely independent of us. Of course, as a child I could not have expressed this to myself clearly, but I felt that knowledge of the spiritual world must in fact be carried within the soul just as geometry is.

The spiritual world's reality was as certain to me as the physical world's reality.[12]

For Steiner this conviction was based on experience. But his problem thus far had been to find a way to justify what he saw and to find a foundation based on knowledge. There must not be an inner conflict between what one sees and what one does not see. "I would have experienced the sensory world as surrounding spiritual darkness if it had not received the light from that other world." Today we can read on a plaque at the railroad station in Neudörfl: "In this house appeared for the child the first inkling of the spirit world, 1869–1879." This same sentence is summarized in the *Autobiography*: "Through his geometry book, that assistant teacher at Neudörfl provided me with a confirmation of the spiritual world I needed then."[13]

Another influence of Steiner's childhood among the simple country folk was his participation in the life of the church. While his freethinking father stayed away, Rudolf was deeply involved in the rituals, as an altar boy and a member of the church choir. He later confessed that these had a profound influence on him. "My youthful soul gladly lived in the ceremonious nature of the Latin language and the cult."[14] Ultimately the instruction he received at school was augmented in many ways by the priest, whom Steiner greatly admired. From him he learned about such things as the Copernican world system and solar and lunar eclipses. He was interested in all this. In his first autobiographical sketch he confessed that he could not learn very much about religion from the priest. From this it becomes clear that it was not religion as such that gave him the answers to his intellectual questions. The ritual at the altar impressed him greatly, but it was not theory and dogma that he needed in order to solve his life's problems. His interest in geometry and in mechanical things pleased his father, who would have liked to see him become a railroad engineer. In this way the decision was made that he should go to the *Realschule*. (In Germany and Austria there were two branches of high school: the *Gymnasium* and the *Realschule*. The first was oriented toward the humanities, the second toward natural science and technology.)

Let us place next to this short overview of Steiner's childhood a few characteristic events of Jung's early years. His childhood memoirs reach very far back and are marked by a great wealth of experiences. We have to limit ourselves to just a few themes.

There is the familiar environment of the parsonage, which is located near the falls of the great Rhine River. The roar of the waterfall can be heard clearly in the house, especially at night when the child is sometimes visited by "vague fears."

> The muted roar of the Rhine Falls was always audible, and all around lay a danger zone. People drowned, bodies were swept over the rocks. In the cemetery nearby, the sexton would dig a hole— heaps of brown, upturned earth. Black, solemn men in long frock coats with unusually tall hats and shiny black boots would bring a black box. My father would be there in his clerical gown, speaking in a resounding voice. Women wept. I was told that someone was being buried in this hole in the ground. Certain persons who had been around previously would suddenly no longer be there. Then I would hear that they had been buried, and that Lord Jesus had taken them to himself.[15]

What a different picture is conjured up here! At first the memories are still in the realm of outer experience. But boundaries, riddles, and problems become visible. People you knew disappear into a pit at the cemetery, and your own father in his black gown is somehow involved in all this. A corpse is salvaged from the Rhine. One lays it into the washhouse of the parsonage. The curious boy, whom people tried to shield from these things, sneaks up to the washhouse and sees blood and water emerge from a drain. Carl Gustav is not even four years old. Another image appears: Carl Gustav's mother took him along on a visit to a friend who lived on Lake Constance. "The lake stretched away and away into the distance. This expanse of water was an inconceivable pleasure to me, an incomparable splendor. At that time the idea became fixed in my mind that I must live near a lake; without water, I thought, nobody could live at all."[16] For half a century Jung was to live close to the water. Not only did he build his home on the Zürichsee, but at the southern end of the lake he eventually built with his own hands his "tower," into which he withdrew now and then like a monk into his cell.

Reminiscing in his later years, Jung came across some strong, overwhelming memories. He vaguely remembers a fall down some stairs, when a wound on his head required stitches. His mother also told him he had had a dangerous slip on the bridge over the Rhine Falls. The child had gotten his leg caught under the railing, and his nanny came running just in time to prevent him from falling into the river below. Jung makes the following comment in his memoirs: "These things point to an unconscious suicidal urge, to a fatal resistance to life in this world."[17] There is no doubt that a borderline situation existed of which the child had no clear concept, but which he sensed nevertheless. The mysteries of death, the solemnity of the graveyard, open tombs, mourners in black garments, and so on, found expression in his soul as nightmares, and in connection with these was the picture of "Lord Jesus," who apparently snatched people away and made them disappear into a dark, unknowable region. The boy arrived at the sinister conclusion that "Lord Jesus" could not be trusted. This led to the "first conscious trauma."

At about the same time, just as Jung was four years old, he had his first significant dream, which he would remember forever, and which made him familiar with the realities of the deep unconscious. Jung was the same age that Steiner was when he had his vision in the waiting room of the Pottschach railroad station! I may also mention that the dream occurred in 1879, the same year that Steiner, then eighteen years old, became aware of the significance of the "I" experience, as described in his autobiography. Moreover, the hidden spiritual events of the year 1879 have given it a special significance for the anthroposophical worldview (see chapter four below). In the dream, which Jung describes in great detail in his autobiography, the child is led into an underground vault, where he sees a huge object, like a tree trunk, but of living flesh. The object has an eye at its crown. Much later, the psychologist interpreted this object as a ritual phallus, a "subterranean God 'not to be named'" that the dreamer suspected to be a powerful antagonist of the not quite lovable Lord Jesus. All his life Jung pondered about this dream: "Who spoke to me then? Who talked of problems far beyond my knowledge? Who brought the Above and Below together, and laid the foundation for everything that was to fill the second half of my life with stormiest passion?" Such were the probing questions of the eighty-year-old Jung. His answer is: "Who but that alien guest who came both from above and from below? Through this childhood dream I was initiated into the secrets of the earth. What happened then was a kind of burial into the earth, and many years were to pass before I came out again. Today I know that it happened in order to bring the greatest possible amount of light into the realm of darkness. It was an initiation into the realm of darkness."[18]

Let us pause here for a moment to compare the psychic experience of the four-year-old Steiner with that of the four-year-old Jung. In both cases something extraordinary happened. In both cases, pictures appeared before the inner eye of the child that pointed to a reality that could not be compared to "what we can see" in the ordinary sense. Even though neither child could at the moment understand or even sense what was happening, the event was so strongly engraved into the mind of each child that each—Steiner in his sixtieth year, Jung in his eightieth—considered the event to be the beginning of his spiritual biography. Interpretation is only possible for the mature spiritual scientist and psychologist. Steiner points out that with this moment a special soul-life had its beginning; Jung calls it his "initiation into the realm of darkness." He writes, "My intellectual life had its unconscious beginnings at that time."

It should not be necessary to repeat here that the experience itself, even though it seemed extraordinary, does not carry great significance. Such things happen more often than is generally recognized. What is decisive is what a person will do with the experience, how one tries to come to grips with it, whether one sees the symbolism in it, and whether one does something to demystify this sign that destiny has given. For initiation (from *initium*, "beginning") is not yet an end. It does not mean the completion but rather the beginning of a process, albeit one that takes a turn different from ordinary, outer events.

One indication of the significance of the experience is the feeling of loneliness that overcame each of these two afterward. There was nobody with whom they could talk about this very special event. It is typical that Jung, the son of the well-situated pastor, is no better off in this respect than Steiner, the son of a poor railway employee. On the contrary, Jung suffered immeasurably from loneliness and from the utter conviction that what he had seen was a reality, especially when it later clashed with the religious views of his family. There were six pastors in his mother's family and two more theologians, his uncles on his father's side. They all were supposedly "experts" in such problems. But the pastor's son had to confess that "everywhere in the realm of religious questions I encountered only locked doors. I felt completely alone with my certainties. More than ever I wanted someone to talk with, but nowhere did I find a point of contact; on the contrary I sensed in others an estrangement, a distrust, an apprehension which robbed me of speech.... I felt the singularity into which I was being forced as something threatening, for it meant isolation."[19] A few more unconscious themes in Jung's childhood warrant examination, for instance, water in connection with rivers, waterfalls, and lakes. In the dangerous situation of the slip on the bridge they are connected with the theme of falling. The longing of the child to live close to the lake one day is involved here. Unlike the uniform roaring of the waterfall, the lake speaks its own language in calm and storm.

In one as well as the other, dreamlike imaginations play into the child's consciousness. Here and there he senses something of the mystery that Goethe expressed in his poem "Song of the Spirits over the

Waters," which he wrote in contemplation of a waterfall in the Lauter-brunn Valley:

> The soul of man resembles the water.
> It descends from heaven,
> It returns to heaven,
> And down to earth it must return,
> Forever changing....
>
> Soul of man, how like the water!
> Fate of man, how like the wind!

It is as if the future psychologist needed the imagination and inspiration he found near the watery element. This seems to express itself subconsciously, even in the slip on the bridge, and in the early contact and longing to be near the water. Here I am thinking also of what Rudolf Meyer wrote in his subtle interpretations of German folk and fairy tales: "People who live near the water often retain a soul mood that has a dreamy quality and keeps them from living fully in a clear waking consciousness. To spend many hours, day in and day out, looking over the waves, widens and opens the soul; it gently withdraws the fine etheric element from the body."[20] So Jung develops, in spite of his thorough education in natural science and his gentlemanly intelligence, a soul configuration in which the imaginative element plays an extraordinarily large role. Jung has interpreted water as a symbol of the unconscious many times and from many different angles. Anthroposophy is in total agreement with these views. A spiritual interpretation of the Bible also recognizes the image of the lake or the sea as the region whence Christ comes to meet his disciples when they see him walking on the water. "To the height of the lake" he sends them to cast their nets. The sea and the archetypal flood play important roles in many myths.

Stimulated by nearness to a body of water, etheric forces can gently withdraw from the physical body. Knowing this, one might think of the repeated falls of the child Carl Gustav. Seen from an anthroposophical perspective, such connections can become clear. Traumatic experiences can cause a sudden loosening of the etheric body, which is what Steiner calls the aspect of the human being that carries the life forces. In a life-threatening situation one can experience the frequently reported panoramic life review, sometimes called the near-death experience. This sudden clairvoyance does not have to last long; it is in fact compressed into split seconds. It is the effect of this loosening of the etheric body. This etheric body, or body of formative forces, acts like a mirror, reflecting soul experiences. We are told that in certain situations the young Carl Gustav tended to have fainting spells in school. One can surmise that this was caused by a permanent looseness of his etheric body, which means an openness toward the dimension of imaginative pictures. This openness to the normally unconscious dimension shows itself when he tells about his "number two personality," with which he was in constant communication for many years of his life.

Steiner has alluded repeatedly to the possibility of the loosening of those members that carry the vegetative and soul life, or as they are called in anthroposophical terms, the etheric and astral bodies. He saw in this process the necessary prerequisite for receiving and understanding truths that originate from supersensible facts. While outer knowledge can be understood by the rational mind, knowledge that reaches into the depth of the human soul has to be received by the whole being: "Truths about the nonphysical world cannot be received in the same frame of mind as truths relating to the physical world. To take them in we must slightly loosen the etheric and astral bodies; otherwise we shall only hear words."[21]

Evidently Jung's particular psychic structure and disposition had to do with this ability to "loosen up" the etheric body. Thus can be explained his psychic and spiritual agility, which allowed him to pay close attention to his inner life and to important signals from his dreams and intuitions. Depending on the degree to which such a change in the structure of the psyche occurs, there can be quite a danger to the individual. Steiner has often warned of this fact when he discussed his path of schooling. It is known that Jung did not escape such

a severe upset of his inner equilibrium. After his break with Freud, he
went through a severe inner crisis. He even said of his experiences, "It
is of course ironical that I, a psychiatrist, should at almost every step of
my experiment have run into the same psychic material which is the
stuff of psychosis and is found in the insane."[22]

Finally, we must also consider the rich psychic inheritance that Jung
received from his maternal ancestors; I refer to parapsychological abilities, a few of which have been documented. Aniela Jaffé has related
them in the family history at the end of Jung's autobiography. It seems
that it was almost the norm in this family to have intimate conversations with entities from an extrasensory world. Jung told of his grand-
father Samuel Preiswerk that he always imagined himself to be
surrounded by "ghosts." If you synthesize all these factors, you get the
impression that for Jung, psychic constitution and outer events formed
a whole. There is a certain parallel here to Steiner's life. In both cases
events in early childhood become transparent as part of their destiny
inasmuch as they were a suitable preparation for the course of their
later lives.

And yet an important question arises in this connection: in what
way can we talk of a parallel between the two lives? What direction, for
instance, does the further development of each child take after the
aforementioned "initiation experience"? Is there an event in Jung's life
that could be compared to Steiner's elation when he discovered geometry? Is there a similar need for knowledge as it announced itself in the
young Steiner and was developed quite logically in the course of his
further life?

Looking at the pertinent passages in Jung's autobiography, one
finds, along with reminiscences of his early school years, frequent mention of nightmares, of premonitions, of an "inescapable world of shad-
ows" from which the child sought to protect himself with nightly
prayers. "But the new peril lurked by day. It was as if I sensed a split-
ting within myself, and feared it. My inner security was threatened."[23]
On the other hand, there are memories of a mysterious stone, and of a
little mannikin that he carved for himself out of wood. His interest in
rocks, plants, and animals was awakened. He experienced nature as very

much alive and filled with wonders. The boy was constantly in search of mysteries.

For the school years, there are hardly any parallels between Jung and Steiner. From the outset, their interests point in different directions. Steiner tells of his enthusiasm for mathematics and later for physics and chemistry, to the point where he tried much too soon to understand mathematical and scientific articles. He loved to make geometrical drawings with compass, ruler, and square, and soon he bought mathematical textbooks in order to have additional material for learning. He was intent on making progress in this field. Jung, on the other hand, found that mathematics caused him fear and horror in school. "All my life it remained a puzzle to me why it was that I never managed to get my bearings in mathematics....Least of all did I understand my own *moral* doubts concerning mathematics."[24]

Jung does not deny that from time to time he had problems with symptoms of neurosis, even though he was a gifted and diligent student. Later he noted: "From these I learned what a neurosis is." He especially points to his passion for solitude and his delight in it. Steiner, on the contrary, describes himself as a sociable student.

This much we can discover from a comparison of the childhood of the two men: both Steiner and Jung came at an early age to an experience of the invisible world. They made the acquaintance of powers and beings of whose existence their contemporaries seemed unaware. In this respect both were utterly on their own. Both had to find a path to the light that would solve these existential riddles for them. On the one hand, Steiner soon started to work systematically on the problem of epistemology, at first in the *Realschule* in Wiener Neustadt, then as a student of natural sciences at the Technical University in Vienna. Jung, on the other hand, gives the impression that at the corresponding time of his life he was increasingly haunted by "the inescapable shadow-world" that had plagued him since his childhood. "My whole youth can be understood in terms of this secret. It induced in me an almost unendurable loneliness. My one great achievement during those years was that I resisted the temptation to talk about it with anyone. Thus the pattern of my relationship to the world was prefigured: today as then I am a solitary, because I know and must hint at things which other people do not know and usually do not even want to know."[25]

The authorities who should have given him some guidance in his psychospiritual conflicts—the church and his father who stood in its service—proved utterly ineffective. What added to the boy's confusion was that he felt himself to be "divided into two different personalities": "One of them was the schoolboy who could not grasp algebra or understand mathematics and was far from sure of himself; the other one was important, a high authority, a man not to be trifled with…powerful and influential.…This 'other' was an old man who lived in the eighteenth century [and] wore buckled shoes."[26] Jung discovered himself as someone who lived in two different time periods, and whose number two personality was filled with an inexplicable nostalgia for the eighteenth century. His occupation with this second personality increasingly brought on depression, especially because the sources of information he depended upon did not yield anything. "I felt completely alone with my certainties. More than ever I wanted someone to talk with, but nowhere did I find a point of contact; on the contrary I sensed in others an estrangement, a distrust, an apprehension which robbed me of speech. That, too, depressed me."[27]

The only parallel we find between Steiner and Jung at this time in their lives is that each was alone with his certainty of a supersensible world. As a result, Steiner also led sort of a "double life." But unlike Jung, he did not experience a split into two personalities, one of whom lived in the present, one in the past. These number one and number two personalities had their roots in Jung's psychic structure itself, and were further reinforced by his introverted character.

It was different with Steiner. His two "diverging streams" sprang from his love for contact with others ("I longed for companionship") and his realization that all these dear friends did not have the slightest inkling of his special struggle to gain knowledge of the two different worlds. This was also the case with his beloved teacher at the *Technische Hochschule* in Vienna, Karl Julius Schröer, who introduced him to Goethe's cast of mind but could not understand Goethe's ideas about natural science at all.

Steiner's youthful friendships had interesting consequences for his later life:

> They compelled me to lead a kind of double inner life. My struggle with the questions of cognition—which then occupied me more than anything else—was always met with great interest by my friends but with little active participation. I remained rather alone in the experience of these enigmas. On the other hand, I participated fully in everything that involved my friends. Thus my inner life was divided; I followed one path as a lonely wanderer, the other as a lively participant with others whom I held in affection. But very often this second kind of experience, too, had deep and lasting significance for my development.[28]

This last remark shows how this double life was somehow kept in balance. This did not, however, eliminate the loneliness of the budding spiritual researcher.

It lies in the nature of the experiences described above that the feeling of loneliness for Jung as well as for Steiner was not merely a temporary condition limited to their years of puberty. During his time in Weimar in the early nineties of the nineteenth century, Steiner was, in his capacity as a Goethe scholar, in contact with many well-known representatives of German intellectual circles. Of these times he relates:

> I had to come to terms, entirely on my own, with everything related to my spiritual perception. I lived in the spiritual world; not one of all those I knew followed me there. My social interactions involved visits to the world of others. Nevertheless, I loved those excursions.... I received a good training in the art of lovingly entering with understanding whatever interested others, who nevertheless did not attempt to understand what deeply concerned me.
>
> This was the nature of my "loneliness" in Weimar, where I led an active social life. I did not hold it against others that they sentenced me in this way to loneliness. In fact, I saw that many of them felt a deep, unconscious need for a philosophy that could get to the roots of existence.[29]

What characterized both Jung and Steiner in their formative years was their relationship to the natural and spiritual sciences. For Steiner, his family steered him toward a career in technology and natural science. The choice of school was therefore the *Realschule*, and later the Technical University. Destiny later brought about a certain adjustment that saved Steiner from one-sided Darwinism. In any event, his broad interests in philosophy and the arts guaranteed him a well-rounded outlook on life.

It seems natural that Jung, whose father taught him Latin at the age of six, was predestined for the *Gymnasium*, which specialized in the humanities. It is interesting to see that he too did not want to be restricted by a one-sided education. Jung vacillated for a considerable time before he decided on his life's career. Both the humanities and natural science attracted him strongly. Both attractions existed because his number two personality was drawn to the past, to archaeology and philology. "Science met, to a very large extent, the needs of No. I personality, whereas the humane or historical studies provided beneficial instruction for No. 2."[30] Theology, the discipline that brought about the tragic alienation from his father, was evidently never considered as a field of study. Jung was so much a *homo religiosus* that he had no need to study theology. In the form in which it was presented to him it could have served no useful purpose for his later profession. Finally, Jung found in psychiatry the field where his number one and number two personalities could be reconciled. "Here alone the two currents of my interests could flow together and in a united stream dig their own bed. Here was the empirical field common to biological and spiritual fact, which I had everywhere sought and nowhere found. Here at last was the place where the collision of nature and spirit became a reality."[31]

As we know, it would take decades of hard work, studying the alchemical concept of the *unus mundus* as well as researching the phenomenon of synchronicity, to meld together nature and spirit, psyche and matter into a *coniunctio*.

It is also revealing to observe the different ways in which Steiner and Jung sought to bring light into the riddles of their lives. In addition to reading philosophical works, Jung turned to the parapsychological and spiritualist writings that were then available. He participated in séances and experimented with a medium within the framework of his medical studies. Steiner's search for knowledge took a completely different direction. He systematically followed the goal that apparently became clear to him at the moment when he discovered geometry in the book given to him by the lay teacher in Neudörfl.

> Mathematics remained significant for me as the foundation of my entire efforts for knowledge. After all, mathematics offers a system of mental images and concepts built up independently of all external sensory experience. Nevertheless, I repeatedly told myself that it is precisely these mental images and concepts that allows one to approach sensory reality and discover its inherent laws. One comes to know the physical world through mathematics, but to do this one must first let mathematics emerge from the human soul.[32]

Thus wrote Steiner about his academic years in Vienna. The initiative to understand knowledge came from himself. When scarcely twenty years old, he began to work out his own theory of cognition, in which the inner experience of thinking played an important role. He was attracted by the surety with which Hegel, for instance, moves from thought to thought.

It was different with Jung. One gets the impression that Jung's struggle for knowledge did not take the form of active thinking. His approach was more groping, experimental. Undoubtedly he preferred the intuitive approach. For Steiner, fateful events serve as tools to be used for a constructive end. The actual activity is centered in his own soul, which means in his thinking.

Initially the task was defined through this "collision of nature and spirit," as Jung expressed it. But the two part ways in their manner of dealing with this problem. Steiner, in his enthusiasm for mathematics, says, "I felt that I had to grapple with the phenomena of the sensory world in order to gain a perspective of the spiritual world that was naturally visible before me. I was convinced that one could come to terms with the spiritual world through the soul as long as thinking assumes a form capable of grasping the true nature of physical phenomena.

These feelings accompanied me during my third and fourth years at the *Realschule*. Everything I learned I mobilized in order to come closer to this goal."[33] At the bottom was always his conviction that thinking itself could be transformed into an instrument with which to perceive things and processes in the world. This conviction served later as the basis for his work on the theory of cognition. For Jung, who certainly explored philosophers as well as theologians, the world finally began to "show depth and background" when he discovered the writings of William James, F. Myers, Zoellner, Crookes, Eschenmayer, Passavant, C.G. Carus, J.J. Kerner, Görres, and Swedenborg as well as Kant's *Dreams of a Spirit Seer*. "The observations of the spiritualists, weird and questionable as they seemed to me, were for me the first accounts I had seen of objective psychic phenomena."[34]

In 1879, when Steiner, then eighteen, began his studies in natural science at the *Technische Hochschule* in Vienna, his immediate experience of spirit was transforming itself to the extent that he could transfer his inner visions into thought. In the same year that the four-year-old Jung received his "initiation into the realm of darkness," Steiner began to gain entrance into the realm of the "I" by studying Fichte's *Theory of Science*. The polarity between these two initiations is obvious. Up to that time Steiner had "tormented himself" with finding concepts for natural phenomena; now he tries to "penetrate through the 'I'" into "nature's workshop." This inner contrast in the quest for knowledge in Steiner and Jung is also revealed in the following.

While Jung, the future physician, was conducting parapsychological experiments—whose results he would utilize a few years later in his dissertation—Steiner experimented with his own thinking. "At that time I felt that I had the duty to find the truth through philosophy," he writes. The young scientist did not turn his back on his field of studies, but he felt he needed to acquire the necessary philosophical prerequisites first. Like Jung, Steiner was completely on his own in his search for truth. "No one wanted to hear about it. At most, someone would come forward with something spiritualistic; then I was the one who did not want to listen. To me, it seemed an absurd way to approach the spiritual."[35]

Here the contrast between Steiner and Jung apparently cannot be bridged. From Steiner's viewpoint, Jung seeks advice from people who are experimenting with atavistic soul forces, a method Steiner finds absurd. From Jung's standpoint, Steiner overvalues the rational function of thinking. Both these assertions, which are voiced from time to time by adherents of one camp or the other, miss the mark. One should keep in mind that Jung, aiming to be a physician, had to pay attention to parapsychological and psychopathological phenomena. He could not neglect them without leaving this often thankless pioneering effort to others. Here lay his life's mission. He was predestined for this work on the basis of his psychological makeup and his destiny. Correspondingly, allowances should be made for Steiner. Besides, his thinking cannot be categorized as a merely rational function of the brain, as Jung might have regarded it. This becomes clear when one gets deeper into Steiner's theory of knowledge and into the whole of his Anthroposophy.

From Steiner's biography, we learn of a typical episode from the time when he was studying Fichte and Hegel. He made the acquaintance of a simple man who collected and dried herbs, a man who had no knowledge of science or modern civilization but who possessed an ancient, instinctive folk wisdom. He shared some of his wisdom with the young Steiner, who felt that here he had met someone who was a "mouthpiece for spiritual contents that streamed down from hidden worlds."

Steiner remained a soul mate to this simple man; theirs was not simply a fleeting acquaintance. Steiner gave him a voice in one of his mystery dramas, written decades later; he appears there as a soul type. In addition, it may be worth mentioning that the encounter also points to connections of an esoteric-occult nature in Steiner's life, of which he makes only sporadic mention. It seems that this meeting helped Steiner to find his life's mission and bring it to fruition.

There is no doubt that at the core of both Steiner's and Jung's biographies lies an esoteric-occult element that found individual expression in each man. To understand what—for the uninitiated—lies behind a "wall of mystery," it is really not sufficient to merely acknowledge the accounts given by each of these men. Steiner confined himself to brief references, while Jung gave rather extensive descriptions. It would be better to undergo a similar process of initiation and then pay attention to how, in the context of the biography and the complete works, the underlying inner experiences have found expression in ideas. One reason for the often reserved and critical attitude toward Jung as well as toward Steiner can certainly be found in the fear that something mystical, frightening, something that causes uneasiness, lies in the background of Anthroposophy as well as analytical psychology. We are dealing here with the phenomenon of fear in the face of soul-spiritual reality. Steiner and Jung were fully aware of this in dealing with the public.

Now where do we find the occult-esoteric connections? After Steiner had made the acquaintance of the "herb-gatherer Felix," as he called the simple man from a village south of Vienna, he had another encounter that brought him into contact with the "Master." "My Felix was only a messenger, so to speak, of another personality who used him as a means to stimulate in the soul of the youth, standing as he was in the midst of the spiritual world, an interest in the regular, systematic things one has to know in that world." From Steiner's allusions in his autobiographical sketch of 1913, one can assume that he received certain spiritual-scientific instructions that later enabled him to write his fundamental anthroposophical works, such as *An Outline of Esoteric Science* (1910). "Those remarkable currents that flow through the spiritual world became visible to the youth at that time. You can only recognize them when you are able to perceive a double current, one down, one upward, flowing at the same time. This was the time when the youth had not yet read the second part of Goethe's *Faust*, when he was introduced to certain occult facts."[36] In his very first autobiographical sketch, which he made for Edouard Schuré in 1907, he mentions one significant insight that he received by occult means: "the absolute clarity about the concept of time. This insight had nothing to do with my studies and was guided entirely from my occult life. It was the realization that there is a backward evolution: the occult-astral evolution, which interferes with the forward evolution. This insight is the prerequisite for spiritual seeing."[37] The occupation with this problem, which touches anthropological-psychological questions, stayed with him for the rest of his life. It was important for Steiner to point out that he became an occult teacher only after he had reached sufficient maturity. "The time came toward the turn of the century when, in accord with the occult powers that stood behind me, I could say to myself: You have laid the philosophical base for your world outlook, you have shown an understanding of the two streams of time and you have treated them as only a true believer could treat them; nobody will be able to say: This occultist speaks of a spiritual world because he doesn't know the philosophical and scientific accomplishments of the time. I had also reached my fortieth year. Before that age nobody is allowed, according to the masters, to become a teacher of occultism."[38]

Anthroposophy can be viewed as the fruit of Steiner's occult development. If you try to find connecting links to other congenial streams in spiritual history, you encounter Rosicrucianism. In his numerous descriptions of this esoteric school, Steiner has made sure that there is no possibility of confusing other similarly named groups with Rosicrucianism. He wanted only a specific, clearly definable spiritual substance. That was why he was not interested in historical research about other Rosicrucian societies. A comparison he made in one of his many lectures on the theme, collected in *The Theosophy of the Rosicrucian*, is characteristic in this connection. Speaking in 1907, he said: "As little as the pupil who learns elementary geometry today is concerned with the form in which it was originally given to mankind by Euclid, as little need we concern ourselves with the question of how Rosicrucianism developed in the course of history. Just as the pupil learns geometry from its actual tenets, so shall we learn to know the nature of this Rosicrucian wisdom from its intrinsic principles."[39]

Steiner found Rosicrucian ideas not only in the original writings themselves, such as Johann Valentin Andreae's *Chymical Wedding of Christian Rosenkreutz* (to which he wrote a commentary), but also in a number of other works of the eighteenth and nineteenth centuries. One example is Goethe's *Fairy Tale of the Green Snake and the Beautiful Lily*, whose esoteric contents he recognized and described. One could call this a prelude

(written in 1889) for his anthroposophical activity that was to follow.[40] Rosicrucianism, as envisaged by Steiner, is primarily a path of
initiation, as is Anthroposophy itself. Students undergo a transformation of their inner being that leads them to a deeper understanding of
the Christ. By gaining a new understanding of nature and spirit, as well
as of themselves and the world, they are led to see everything as an
integrated whole. There is no teaching of abstract knowledge; spiritual
truths should reveal themselves through concrete life experience. Spiritual schooling does not rely on the authority of a teacher but develops
in full respect for the freedom of the individual. Manipulative intru-
sions into the (unconscious) life of the will are therefore taboo.

When we compare Jung's and Steiner's experiences, we have to
remember that Jung did not approach the problem with the same cognitive intention as Steiner did. They were unequally prepared for the crisis
that afflicted each of them in midlife, between their thirty-fifth and fortieth years. Steiner had struggled with the problem of cognition since
his early years, and not only philosophically. His academic studies were
augmented by his occult training; his efforts of reasoning were supplemented by a spiritual process. Therefore his description and evaluation
of the midlife crisis is different not only because the biographical material is quantitatively different. Steiner described his temporary identification with the Zeitgeist as a conscious "slipping into the skin of the
dragon" in order to conquer it from within. Steiner has described the
true meaning of his ordeal in the emblematic statement: "It was decisive
for my soul's development that I stood spiritually before the Mystery of
Golgotha in a deep and solemn celebration of knowledge."[41]

Jung was not at all prepared for the midlife crisis that hit him after
his separation from Freud and from psychoanalysis and pushed him
into a position of utter disorientation. In his autobiography he confesses this unreservedly. "From somewhere" he was forced into a psychic process whose outcome he could not foresee. However, his long
practical experience with psychotic patients had made him familiar
with the symptoms. A deluge from the unconscious swept over him;
hard-to-recognize fantasies, personifications of psychic phenomena,
visions, voices, and mysterious dreams assaulted him. In his house in

Küsnacht he was plagued by poltergeists. The condition of "bottomless abysses of ignorance" that the outwardly successful professor of psychiatry had to admit to himself is illuminated by the astounding sentence in his biography: "In my darknesses...I could have wished for nothing better than a real, live guru, someone possessing superior knowledge and ability, who would have disentangled for me the involuntary creations of my imagination."[42]

One must concede that a person with the knowledge and skill that Jung sought did exist, and was at work very nearby just at that time. He lectured in Zürich several times in those years, speaking about, among other things, Anthroposophy and psychology in 1917, before Jung's dark times came slowly to an end. But the potentially fateful encounter did not and could not occur. Apparently, their contrasting inner necessities spoke clearly in these two earthly lives, even though they were full of remarkable parallels. Perhaps an outer guru could not have been as effective as Jung's inner guru, who appeared to him at times to be "physically real." Who can judge?

The biographies of Steiner and Jung reveal further shifts in their inner development. At the end of World War I, Jung still had the realization of his professional life as a researcher ahead of him. The images and dreams that began in 1912-13 did not come to fruition till after his spiritual breakthrough.

During those years, between 1918 and 1920, I began to understand that the goal of psychic development is the self....

I hit upon this stream of lava, and the heat of its fires reshaped my life. That was the primal stuff which compelled me to work upon it, and my works are a more or less successful endeavor to incorporate this incandescent matter into the contemporary picture of the world. The years when I was pursuing my inner images were the most important in my life—in them everything essential was decided. It all began then; the later details are only supplements and clarifications of the material that burst forth from the unconscious, and at first swamped me. It was the *prima materia* for a lifetime's work.[43]

Thus Jung reflected at the time when, at about the age of forty-five, he had accomplished his breakthrough and saw his life's work spread out before him. What Jung calls the self is what Steiner began to see, in reference to Fichte's "I," when he was eighteen or nineteen years old. As I have already mentioned, this occurred for Steiner at the same time as the four-year-old Jung received his "initiation into the realm of darkness."

To what shores did Jung set out after his crisis, and what direction did his further research take? It was alchemy, a historical body of knowledge that offered him helpful "prefigurations" of his own inner experiences in text, pictures, and symbols. The fundamental ideas in alchemy are very much the same as those in Rosicrucianism, where Steiner found something like the "prefiguration" of Anthroposophy. However, here again the two men differ in approach as well as in ultimate aim. While Steiner is after knowledge, Jung has the diagnostic-therapeutic application in mind. Steiner does not bother with historical concerns, neither with the Rosicrucians nor with the alchemists. He saves himself the trouble of reading alchemical folios and collecting documentation, while Jung is intent on carefully deciphering the alchemists' writings. It goes without saying that he did not become a philologist and he did not take these texts literally. It is remarkable, however, that a modern psychiatrist of the twentieth century immersed himself in Rosicrucian and alchemical literature to the extent that Jung did. He also made use of it for his own psychological body of knowledge. He saw the alchemical opus as a spiritual-psychological prefiguration of the individuation process that he had discovered. The central goal of alchemy is, as we know, the "preparation of the stone," in which the *lapis* of the alchemists is identical with Jung's Self. If you compare this with Steiner's sevenfold path of Rosicrucian initiation, you will find in the center as the fourth step the one that deals with the "preparation of the stone."

In comparing Steiner's and Jung's biographical data, it is interesting to see how destiny placed each into a movement that allowed him to work for some time in preparation for his ultimate life mission. For Steiner, it was the Theosophical Society of H.P. Blavatsky and Annie

Besant; for Jung, it was Freud's Psychoanalytic Association. These movements gave them each a platform from which they could announce the results of their research to interested individuals. Within a very short time Jung and Steiner were each given leading positions. Steiner became the general secretary of the German section of the Theosophical Society, Jung, president of the world society of the Psychoanalytic Association. Both men knew that their connections—to the Theosophists on the one hand and to the then not fully acknowledged psychoanalysts on the other—represented an exposure that could hurt their reputations. And they felt the consequences. Steiner had made a name for himself as a Goethe scholar and thinker, Jung as the head physician at Burghölzli clinic in Zürich. Both had a reputation to lose. Steiner had already shown himself to be a nonconformist when he spoke for Nietzsche and Haeckel, when he moved in avant-garde literary and artistic circles, and when he gave lectures to monists, Marxists, and Theosophists.

It is remarkable that both Jung and Steiner understood their collaborations with these movements as only a temporary phase. For Jung, this phase belonged to the first part of his life, while Steiner, fourteen years his senior, had already found himself and his life mission when he connected himself with the Theosophists. This is an important distinction when comparing and evaluating the two men.

The following factors should also be mentioned. Jung was born in 1875. This was the year of the founding of the Theosophical Society. The foundations of the future psychoanalysis were laid by Freud and Breuer at about the same time as the philosophical and epistemological principles of Steiner's future Anthroposophy. This was in the 1880s and 1890s. In 1892, when Freud's first publication of the cure of a hysterical patient by hypnosis was published, Steiner's dissertation, *Truth and Science*, was released. He received his Ph.D. in 1891, ten years after Freud. In both instances, the elements of a future science of healing and a science of cognition were developed. In 1900, after having overcome his midlife crisis, Steiner became involved with the Theosophical Society, whose member and general secretary he became in 1902. He was the same age that Jung was when he severed his ties with

Freud's psychoanalytical movement. The break between Steiner and Besant occurred in 1912-13, again at the same time as Jung's break with Freud's Psychoanalytic Association. While Steiner's life crisis lay behind him at that time (he was forty years old), Jung, fourteen years younger, still had to face his after his break with Freud. "After the break with Freud a time of inner insecurity, even disorientation began for me. I felt utterly suspended, because I had not yet found my own position," Jung confesses in his memoirs.

We see that for Steiner and Jung, the year 1913 had an utterly different biographical significance. For Steiner, this year brought the founding of the Anthroposophical Society and the beginning of construction on the Goetheanum on Swiss soil. From then until his death in 1925, Steiner had only twelve more creative years before him. Jung's creative phase did not really begin until the 1920s. Only his *Psychological Types* was published while Steiner was still alive, in 1921. Steiner did not live to see the real pioneering discoveries of analytical psychology. Jung died in 1961, the same year that Steiner's one hundredth birthday was celebrated.

3

Jung's *Psychology of the Unconscious* and Steiner's Lectures on Psychoanalysis

When anthroposophical authors review the work of Jung, they refer again and again to Steiner's two "lectures on psychoanalysis"[1] and point out the judgments they contain about Jung. Therefore if one attempts a comparative study of Jung and Steiner one cannot ignore these two stenographed lectures from 1917. *The Psychology of the Unconscious* is the only one of Jung's writings that Steiner has commented upon in detail.

The Psychology of the Unconscious, published in 1917, the same year that Steiner gave the above-mentioned two lectures, is based on Jung's article, "New Paths of Psychology," which was first published in 1912 in Konrad Falke's *Rascher's Jahrbuch für Schweizer Art und Kunst*, volume 3. In the revised version of this paper Jung's intention was twofold. He wanted to describe the beginnings and aims of psychoanalysis and, after his break with Freud, to introduce his own analytic psychology, which was then at its inception. The book was written at a time in Jung's life that he himself described later on as a "time of great inner uncertainty," in which his literary output was comparatively small. In this book Jung gives us a glimpse into his workshop. And it is obvious from what he writes that he considers this work to be preliminary if not inconsequential. This study was one on which he would later work for decades without ever arriving at a clear conclusion. The frequent change of titles over the years reflects the unfinished, tentative character of the work. The third title reads: *The Unconscious in the Normal* and *Pathological Psyche* (1925). The fifth and last title, under which the work was included in the German *Collected Works*, reads: *The Unconscious in the Normal and Pathological Mind*. [In the English *Collected Works*, volume 7, the essay appears under the title *On the Psychology of the Unconscious*. — Ed.] Jung commented on each of the revisions and extensions in the foreword to each new edition.

Steiner, who followed all new literary publications with great interest, must have been referring to the edition of 1917, Jung's only publication of that year, when he spoke about psychoanalysis in Dornach on November 10–11. In those November days he also held several lectures in Zürich, among them four public lectures about his relationship to the theoretical sciences. The first of these was titled "Psychoanalysis and Spiritual Psychology."

What was Jung's intention with this book that Steiner criticized? He wanted to give "a beginning orientation" to the newest findings of his psychology of the unconscious. "I regard the problem of the unconscious as so important and so topical that it would, in my opinion, be a great loss if this question which touches each one of us so closely, would disappear from the orbit of the educated lay public by being banished to an inaccessible technical journal, there to lead a shadowy paper existence on the shelves of libraries."[2] Already at this point one could "enhance" Jung's foreword with a text by Steiner, who had realized during and immediately after the war that "in regard to important, even utterly important impulses in the development of mankind in our time there are some decisive things going on beneath the threshold of outer events. Because this is so, one has to look into the unconscious and subconscious in human nature in order to be able to draw the necessary and urgent conclusions for shaping the social conditions of the present time [1919]. What we have in our consciousness today does not tell us much at all about the future development of humankind, even though we live in the age of the consciousness soul…in our *unconscious* we have to find the most essential transitional forces for the *whole of humankind*, just as we must find in the *individual* the most important forces for the development of a *fully awake consciousness*."[3] Jung and Steiner obviously both agree about the plane on which decisive things are happening. Steiner especially urges that the "crossing of the threshold" (to the supersensible world) that was being prepared in the unconscious must be made conscious for humanity. On this point it should be possible to find common ground between Steiner and Jung; practical methods are a different matter.

Jung refers to the situation of the year 1917 when he continues: "The psychological concomitants of the present war—above all the incredible brutalization of public opinion, the mutual slanderings, the unprecedented fury of destruction, the monstrous flood of lies, and man's incapacity to call a halt to the bloody demon—are uniquely fitted to force upon the attention of every thinking person the problem of the chaotic unconscious which slumbers uneasily beneath the ordered world of consciousness."[4] Steiner's public lectures during the war expressed the same concern over the situation when, in his lectures at the Berlin Architektenhaus, he called on people not to forget the spiritual heritage of civilized Central Europeans.[5] Jung sees his task to be that of transforming the individual psyche. He felt that the intended "change in the psychology of the nation" had to begin with the individual.

Jung's following qualifications are important for our understanding of his *Psychology of the Unconscious:* "I do not want to claim that this work is in any way finished or sufficiently convincing. One would need extensive scientific treatises about each single problem that is touched on in this paper." When a year later a second edition of the work had become necessary, Jung stated once more that he was aware of the "extraordinary difficulties and new challenges of the material." Seven years after the end of World War I, the year of Steiner's death, the third edition appeared with "quite substantial changes and improvements." Again the author speaks of the risk involved in writing in popular terms about some "highly complicated material that is scientifically still in the birth process." Again he expects to encounter much prejudice, "but one should appreciate that the purpose of such a book as this can only be to give an approximate concept of its material and to stimulate thought. It cannot go into detailed consideration and proof."

Jung hardly takes back this qualification even in the fifth and last edition, published in 1942. Jung was sixty-seven by then, and although he had undergone a psychological maturation and had gained much important knowledge, he was still reluctant to speak freely about "such a difficult and complicated matter" as the psychology of the unconscious. True, he had been able to remove a great many inadequacies, but he still saw himself before an immense new territory "in which we proceed only with great caution; and it is only by way of detours that we find the straight path."

If one follows the long and arduous path of the depth psychologist just in relation to this one book, it becomes clear that Steiner's much-cited lectures about psychoanalysis can only be seen as documents of the time, not as a sufficient characterization or basis for critique. This becomes obvious when one considers that the full extent of Jung's work could not yet have been foreseen at the time of Steiner's death. One look at the publication dates of Jung's main works shows this clearly. Nevertheless I want to refer briefly to some points in the lectures.[6]

On the occasion of the above-mentioned lectures in Zurich, Steiner realized that one could not appreciate the cultural or spiritual life of that city without taking a look at "analytical psychology or psychoanalysis." Steiner at least uses the proper name for Jung's psychoanalytical work, even though he does not make a clear distinction between Jung's analytical psychology and Freud's psychoanalysis. Steiner always calls Jung "the psychoanalyst Jung, albeit one of the better ones." He accords him a certain measure of respect. Steiner also observes that even serious seekers are turning to psychoanalysis. One cannot ignore this movement any longer, "because the phenomena it takes into consideration about really present that this movement is addressing are without doubt a reality."[7]

Steiner not only admits that psychoanalysis recognizes certain undeniable facts, but he acknowledges: "This is one way people try to emerge from materialism, and to reach some knowledge of the soul." And further: "I can assure you that in terms of knowledge and study of the soul these psychoanalysts are far ahead of what psychiatry and psychology currently offer in the universities."[8]

Nevertheless, Steiner's rejection of Jung is clear in his critique. He did not doubt the existence of the psychical facts that psychoanalysis addressed. But, said Steiner, "it studies these processes with insufficient means...half-truths are, under certain circumstances, more harmful than complete errors."[9] In this connection he mentions Freud's sexual theory in particular. However, Steiner's two lectures lack a thorough epistemological exposition. Perhaps the lecturer was justified in forgoing a detailed explanation in view of the composition of his Dornach audience at the time. He merely warns of the "various serious errors" that could affect social life when psychoanalytical practices are applied.

Let us see how Steiner approaches some of the provisional results of Jung's research. To start with, he acknowledges that Jung does not find Freud's sexual theory and his theory of neuroses adequate.[10] He then turns to Jung's theory of types. (Jung's groundbreaking work, *Psychological Types*, did not appear until four years later.) He uses this work as an example to demonstrate the above-mentioned "insufficient knowledge." Even aside from the fact that a thoroughly substantiated representation of the two types could only be given in the book to come, Steiner's verdict about Jung's ideas of the two psychological types and their respective basic functions is disappointing. He introduces his short lecture with the words: "Here again a great scholar made an 'epoch-making' discovery, which actually every reasonable person can always easily make right in his or her immediate environment." Steiner admits that the division between extraverts and introverts is "scholarly...ingenious, brilliant, really descriptive, at least up to a point," but he then concludes: "Jung's theory is simply a paraphrase of the banal and trite division of people into feeling and rational types without adding anything to the facts." Steiner considered Jung's discovery to be a mere theory. "The researchers set up a theory about the subconscious, but with this they themselves agitate the subconscious."[11]

We can be sure what Jung's answer would have been had he heard Steiner's lecture. There are enough records. For instance, when he wrote the foreword to *Psychological Types* just three years later, in the spring of 1920, he opened with the terse sentence: "This book is the result of almost twenty years of work in the field of practical psychology."

Twenty years after Steiner's psychoanalysis lectures, when a seventh edition of Jung's book became necessary, Jung answered those of his critics who still had not quite understood the elements of his theory:

> The critics often fall into the error of assuming that the types were, so to speak, fancy free and were forcibly imposed on the empirical material. In face of this assumption I must emphasize that my typology is the result of many years of practical experience—experience that remains completely closed to the academic psychologist. I am first and foremost a doctor and practicing psychotherapist, and all my psychological formulations are based on the experiences gained in the hard course of my professional work. What I have to say in this book, therefore, has sentence for sentence been tested a hundredfold in the practical treatment of the sick and originated with them in the first place. Naturally, these medical experiences are accessible and intelligible only to one who is professionally concerned with the treatment of psychic complications. It is therefore not the fault of the layman if certain of my statements strike him as strange or if he thinks my typology is the product of idyllically undisturbed hours in the study. I doubt, however, whether this kind of ingeniousness is a qualification for competent criticism.[12]

Jung had to defend himself repeatedly against the accusation that he was merely theorizing. In a discussion during the Tavistock lectures of 1935 in London he said: "I must repeat that my methods are not based on theories but on facts. What we find indeed are certain facts that are arranged in a specific order, and we then name them on the basis of mythological or historical parallels. One cannot discover a mythological theme, one can only discover a personal theme, and this never appears in the form of a theory, but always as a living circumstance in a human life." Only from the apparent facts or phenomena can one then develop a theory.

Continuing his lecture, Steiner speaks about the content of the "suprapersonal unconscious." He believes the psychoanalyst starts from the premise that a man actually experiences, let us say, the Oedipus myth. One should remark here parenthetically that Jung insists on a decisive difference between the personal themes that appear and the mythological material that he then juxtaposes by way of amplification. Steiner's position shows the essential difference between the spiritual scientist and the psychiatrist. It is the problem of the "relationship to the gods," or rather the concept of God itself. Steiner's understanding of reality always includes the spiritual dimension, and he is always interested in the question of the underlying reality. Jung, on the other hand, focuses primarily on the alleviation of psychological suffering. Steiner concedes the latter to Jung; he expressly mentions this in his lecture. "Jung approaches the matter as a physician. It is important that patients are treated psychologically and therapeutically from that standpoint."[13]

Steiner, from his own spiritual-scientific viewpoint, considers some of Jung's psychoanalytical attempts at interpretation to be grotesque. He thinks Jung's interpretation approaches the problems but is not serious about the reality of the spiritual world. "Everywhere we find important facts that…can only be successfully dealt with...by spiritual psychology [i.e., Anthroposophy]. At least, psychoanalysis has made us aware that the reality of the soul is to be accepted as such.…But the devil is at their heels. By that I mean that they are neither able nor willing to approach spiritual reality."[14]

Meanwhile Steiner felt that what psychoanalysis had discovered would indeed be suitable "to lead them to a spiritual realm."[15] That is the other point Steiner makes in his second lecture on psychoanalysis, and it shows a far-reaching mutuality of interests between the spiritual scientist and the psychiatrist. Steiner here emphasizes:

> In our unconscious…we are connected with an entirely different world, which Jung says the soul needs because it is related to that world, but he also says that it is foolish to inquire about the real existence of that world. Well, that is how it is: as soon as the threshold of consciousness is crossed, the human soul is no longer in a merely material context or environment, but in a realm where thoughts rule that may be very cunning.

Jung is correct in saying that especially people of our time, the so-called people of culture, need to pay attention to these things.[16]

With this Steiner touches upon a group of questions that have to be mentioned in connection with other statements within his work. Let us summarize here what Steiner's lectures about psychoanalysis have shown in regard to our inquiry:

Steiner turns against analytic psychology, a discipline that is in its very beginnings. Seen from his standpoint, analytical psychology is very similar to Freud's psychoanalysis, even though the paper thus criticized contains admittedly quite substantial differences from Freud.

Steiner's verdict about Jung from the year 1917, which may have been to some extent influenced by his audience, can in no way be justly taken for an overall judgment about Jung's later work.

In addition, the two lectures of September 10–11, 1917, show that there must be a destiny factor at work in the relationship between Steiner and Jung. That is the only way to explain why Steiner appreciates the unquestionable merits of depth psychology on the one hand, but on the other cannot muster much understanding for Jung's pioneering achievement.

An overvaluation of the two above-mentioned lectures does no justice to Jung's work; nor do the lectures themselves show the true reasons that led Steiner to his negative stance. We will have to deal with this in other, larger contexts.

4

Spiritual Backgrounds

The more familiar you become with Rudolf Steiner's work, the more you realize that single statements in one particular lecture cannot really be appreciated and understood unless seen in their larger context. This makes it hard, if not impossible, for those unversed in Anthroposophy to make use of remarks Steiner made about some relatively limited subjects. This is especially true for those lectures that were given exclusively for members of the Anthroposophical Society; these were not meant for the public. Sometimes notes were taken, but often notes were not allowed. Later these notes were published with Steiner's consent, but he did not have time to review them. Thus the somewhat forbidding cautionary remark often printed at the beginning of each lecture cycle reminding the reader that only those with detailed knowledge of Anthroposophy would be qualified to judge the content of the lectures. This remark is certainly justified in regard to these particular lectures; it does not, however, apply to the books and public lectures.

In regard to Jung one runs into similar problems. People who simply want to look up quickly what Jung had to say about a certain subject find themselves in a difficult situation; this is even true of psychiatrists. In a discussion following his Tavistock lectures, given to physicians and psychiatrists in London in 1935, Jung pointed out how difficult it was to come to grips with certain criteria for his dream interpretations. "That is the great trouble: there is such a gap between what is usually known of these things and what I have worked on all these years. Only when you possess that apparatus of parallelism can you begin to make diagnoses and say that this dream is organic and that one is not. Until people have acquired that knowledge I am just a sorcerer. Special knowledge is a terrible disadvantage."[1]

In approaching the work of both Jung and Steiner, we need to think about a vast context. Both demanded of their pupils a special degree of patience, openness, and confidence. Jung has the comparative advantage in that he can point to known ethnological, cultural, historical, and spiritual facts to explain his psychological insights. I am referring especially to Jung's interpretation of and commentary on Eastern esoteric texts and alchemical writings and illustrations.

These tangible documents are often not available to Steiner. He often has to familiarize the reader with problems and phenomena that are not empirically accessible to most people. These things, being of an esoteric nature, are utterly unknown, and therefore seem to be even stranger than Jung's depth psychology. Verification of some of the results of spiritual-scientific research cannot be assured by simply quoting Steiner out of context. That is why the gap between what is generally known and what Steiner has to say is even greater than in Jung's case. Nevertheless, Steiner's accounts of his spiritual research must not be disregarded. They belong to their context, as do Jung's.

What, for example, is the background to Steiner's lectures about psychoanalysis? Certain esoteric connections to what is said there are laid out in lectures that preceded the Dornach lectures of November 10–11, 1917.

Steiner's attitude toward history is that he considers external dates, facts, and events to be symptoms of processes that go on beneath the surface of outer events. An inner event expresses itself in the outer. "Spiritual backgrounds" call for attention. The present stage of the evolution of human consciousness demands that we comprehend the revelation, or the "transparency," of the spiritual-supersensible world. "Men must realize that henceforth they will be unable to progress spiritually unless they open themselves to the new revelation of the supersensible world."[2]

Steiner wants to make us aware of the tendencies underlying the evolution of humankind, but also of the elements that stand in the way of our becoming fully conscious. This is a very important aspect of his work, because "behind the scenes of world history spiritual forces are at work, both in good and in bad ways." We read in a lecture held in

Zurich on November 6, 1917: "Spiritual deeds and happenings are to be understood only when the light of spiritual science can be shed into those regions which lie behind the scenes of life in the ordinary world of the senses."[3] At a definite point in time humankind is predestined to develop certain capacities of the will and cognition. These will enable us to recognize the reality of the spirit, and thereby we will attain full maturity of the soul. Steiner sees as one of the tasks for present humankind "that they should become conscious of certain facts that have so far been hidden in the unconscious, and that they master the situation revealed by these facts."[4]

In a cycle of fourteen lectures given between September 29 and October 28 in Dornach in the same year, Steiner describes what was going on in the course of the nineteenth century according to occult observation. He speaks of a decisive event that took place around the middle of the nineteenth century. This event was important for the whole Western world. The development of "materialistic knowledge" culminated at that time. Steiner means here an "intellectual knowledge" of utmost precision and scientific exactness that is well suited to the understanding of dead, external facts. This type of cognition, however, does not suffice for understanding living beings, and, contrary to its claims, is even less suited to understanding soul and spirit. For this mode of cognition, only quantitative measurements are valid.

For Steiner, such developments are the consequence of events in the spiritual world. He talks about a "battle among spiritual beings" that is supposed to have lasted from the 1840s until the year 1879. He clothes his descriptions in biblical and mythological terms: The opponents in this battle are the Archangel Michael and Ahriman, the representative of evil in its dark aspect (in contrast to Lucifer, who represents the opposite form of temptation). Chapter 12 of the Revelation of John speaks of the battle between Michael and the dragon. This story is of a symbolic nature, and Steiner asserts that similar events have taken place several times through history, always for specific reasons. "The late 1870s were a particular time when human souls became subject to ahrimanic powers with regard to certain powers of perception." This means that the satanic-ahrimanic impulses had a significant influence on the soul and the will life. "Before this they were more of a general property; now they were transplanted to become personal property. We are thus able to say that due to the presence of these ahrimanic powers from 1879 onwards, personal ambitions and inclinations to interpret the world in materialistic terms came to exist in the human realm."[5] Steiner employed the symbolic language of the Bible when he called this event "the fall of the spirits of darkness." This event has rendered the human psyche strangely susceptible to attacks from the satanic-ahrimanic realm of the spiritual world.

Jung was also aware of such influences on mass psychology. He speaks of "invasions of archetypal substance," of a "deadly embrace by the unconscious." In his 1936 essay "Wotan," he characterized the "Nordic god of storm and bluster who unleashes the passions and the warring spirit; he is the mighty magician and illusionist." Jung saw him overpowering Central Europe in the 1930s.[6] Steiner also sees these things not merely as stirrings in the individual psyche, but as eruptions that point toward a close interrelation between earthly and spiritual worlds. The symbols and images Steiner employs are not mere pictures. They point to an underlying spiritual reality or, if you will, to the spiritual dimension of the one reality. For "anything which happens in the physical world is really a kind of projection, or shadow, of what happens in the spiritual world, except that it would have happened earlier in the spiritual world."[7]

At the same time Steiner warns against nebulous talk about spirit in general terms that leads to nothing: "Mere speculation does not get us anywhere; it needs genuine spiritual observation."[8] This mode of observation must not be confused either with mediumistic or spiritualistic activities that had become so popular in Europe and America in those decades. Steiner opposes spiritualistic practices because they actually stand in the way of a true recognition of the spiritual world. The rapid spread of the spiritualist movement could perhaps be seen as an expression for the longing after deeper knowledge. It led to the founding of the Theosophical Society (in 1875, the year of Jung's birth); the Anthroposophical Society (1912-1913); and to psychoanalysis and Jung's analytic psychology (from 1912 on). If one compares the dates, one makes surprising discoveries. Steiner's insistence on clear, unequivocal differentiation is understandable as far as the method of cognition is concerned. He believed that the twentieth century demanded a high degree of wakefulness and spiritual clarity: "The most dangerous thing you can do in the immediate future will be to give yourself up unconsciously to the influences which are definitely present."[9] The immediate future brought Germany what Jung had characterized as the "unleashing of Wotan." Upon the "fall of the dragon" followed the "seed of the dragon's teeth": the First and Second World Wars and their aftereffects. Steiner uttered the warning about the "immediate future" just a few days before the outbreak of the Russian Revolution in November 1917.[10]

In this discussion one needs to include the viewpoint, mentioned above, that results from looking at the "spiritual background of outer events" and the "fall of the spirits of darkness" and its symbolic significance. It then becomes easier to understand why Steiner felt the need to carefully scrutinize everything that claimed to give a new direction or to have a healing influence on the culture of his day. He suspected depth psychology of trying to downplay the pressing problems of the time. Steiner did grant that the psychoanalysts had overcome the starkest materialism by recognizing the existence of the psyche as real. On the other hand, he could not agree with the basic assumptions and spiritual foundation that informed psychoanalytic research and therapy.

Two Images of the Human Being

Explaining the Terminology

Jung and Steiner spoke different languages. They held divergent views about the world, their own relationship to the history of the human mind, the tasks that each had set for himself, and the aim each was pursuing. Nor did they always use consistent terminology within their own work. They borrowed from other writers, gave some words new meanings, and coined entirely new terms. This is entirely reasonable, considering the complexity of their work and the evolution that both Anthroposophy and analytical psychology had to undergo.

Thus a scrutiny of Steiner's older anthroposophical writings reveals that while he was a member of the Theosophical Society, he used its terms and phrases to describe his image of the human being and the world. During that time he preferred Indian, or rather Sanskrit, terminology. Up until 1913 the name he used for his Anthroposophy was Theosophy. The same name is used in one of his basic books, in several lecture cycles, and in single lectures. It is obvious that changes he made in his terminology later served only to make his meaning more precise.

The relationship between Theosophy and Anthroposophy was defined in the lectures Steiner gave at the 1909 general meeting of the German section of the Theosophical Society in Berlin. At this point, as his wife Marie Steiner said, the movement that he inaugurated had to be given a firm foundation for the first time. These lectures demonstrate that in starting point as well as in outlook, Theosophy and Anthroposophy are of different natures. According to Steiner, the Theosophist maintains a more "elevated" level from which to view the world, which allows him or her to judge reality as if from a "higher plane." Anthroposophy, on the other hand, wishes to stand "at the halfway point, looking both down and up." According to this description, Anthroposophists do not feel themselves above exploring the "lower world," the physical plane, with the same devotion as the "higher worlds." Theosophy wants to let the "god within us" make assumptions about reality. The danger in this, said Steiner, is that one may entirely overlook the phenomena of the physical world that are, after all, spread out around one's feet. "Anthroposophy...may be characterized as the wisdom spoken by us as human beings when we are between God and nature, and allow the human being in us to speak of what is shining into us from above and of what is projecting into us from below. *Anthroposophy is the wisdom that human beings speak.*"[1]

Steiner's original followers did not understand his characterization as well as he had hoped. Wallowing in a mixture of fantasy and irrational spirituality was easier for many who preferred to avoid the strict discipline of the thought exercises that stand at the entrance of the anthroposophical path. But the person who is conscious of his or her "I" and strives constantly to enhance "I"-consciousness is the one Steiner placed increasingly at the center of his teaching. To create spiritual knowledge in human beings, and to act out of this knowledge, is the aim of all anthroposophical work. One must also not omit the "heart" of anthroposophical esoteric teaching, which is typically missing in Theosophy: it is he who in the Christian tradition is known as Jesus Christ, the one who called himself "the son of humanity."

We know from the history of depth psychology that a clear demarcation line has to be drawn at the point when Jung separated from Freud. Steiner's departure from the Theosophical Society seems analogous to these events. The separation of Jung and Freud was apparently not only a matter of the personal destiny of the two scientists, but was also based on technical and scientific factors. Psychoanalysis followed a course of development during which Freud had established, step by step, a solid foundation for his analytical theory and his therapeutic method. Considering this, one can imagine what it meant for Jung to make fundamentally new statements that took him beyond Freud's position.

For well-known reasons, Jung could not always, or at least not entirely, accept the terminology that had been established by Freud. The facts and processes he discovered were established under different conditions, and they had to be adequately named. Jung's concepts were in the beginning quite fluid and remained so for a long period of time, because his work led him to different results and was never a finished product. Moreover the object of his studies, the ever-fluctuating life of the soul, with all its processes, transformations, and upheavals, demanded great flexibility of interpretation.

The name "analytical psychology," which Jung chose for his new method of work to set it apart from Freud's psychoanalysis (which was similar to what Steiner intended with his new name "Anthroposophy"), was not chosen merely for practical reasons. Jung did want to honor Freud's accomplishments in the field of depth psychology. His new psychology and therapy could still be called an "analytical method." It had to use analysis because it dealt with the unconscious realm. However, analytical psychology did not merely aim to analyze the soul in the sense of investigating its parts. This had to be clearly emphasized to counter certain prejudices that exist regarding the word "analytical." One example of tragic misunderstanding is the outstanding anthroposophical scholar Emil Bock, who could not see the true nature of Jung's analytical psychology, even though Jung's intentions were quite similar to his own. Bock wrote: "We don't need psychoanalysis, we need psychosynthesis. The human soul is a thousandfold treasure, carrying much that is precious, but also much that is problematic and tragic. It must not be split up by constant analysis. We must see it as a whole that must be unified, ordered, and harmonized. The all-encompassing consciousness needed to do this is not the same as the faint flicker in our heads that we nowadays call consciousness."[2]

Jung would have unequivocally agreed with Bock's statement. His whole body of work was dedicated to just this goal: to achieve psychic wholeness. Like Bock, he might have called it psychosynthesis.

At this point it seems appropriate to quote Wilhelm Bitter, who recognizes Jung's psychology as a valuable therapeutic method encompassing much more than just "analysis": "In Jung's analytical psychotherapy synthesis takes center stage. The contrast between conscious and unconscious—like that within the unconscious—is bridged by the 'synthetic function' and merged on a higher level. This function is effective, whether it is achieved by psychoanalysis or happens autonomously. The process aims at human wholeness, at Self-realization."[3]

Steiner's Image of the Human Being

For a detailed description of the anthroposophical image of the human being, one would have to refer to the appropriate literature. However, I will give a short overview here in order to make a comparison possible.

We are reminded of ancient anthropological ideas when we learn about Steiner's emphasis on the importance of the threefold nature of the human being: body, soul, and spirit. Steiner recalls that Goethe's views "draw our attention to three different kinds of things: first, the objects we constantly receive information about through the gateways of our senses, the things we touch, taste, smell, hear, and see; second, the impressions they make on us, which assume the character of liking or disliking, desire or disgust, by virtue of the fact that we react sympathetically to one thing and are repelled by another, or find one thing useful and another harmful; and third, the knowledge we 'quasi-divine beings' acquire about the objects as they tell us the secrets of what they are and how they work."[4]

Thus the human being discovers that humanity is connected to the world in a threefold way. Steiner does not, however, wish merely to revive old ideas about the human being. He points to the phenomena themselves, which can be experienced as clearly now as ever. Steiner's statements can also be distinguished from the merely traditional in that he only maintains that which can stand scrutiny by modern science. Every time his Anthroposophy had to answer to the demands of scientific questioning, he declared that he was in full agreement with the scientific thinking of his day, insofar as it was applicable. On the other hand, Anthroposophy strives to gain an objective and exact knowledge of the supersensible world. This is to be achieved by a rigorous, exacting training of the inner faculties that slumber in everyone. Such training results in the capacity to see phenomena of the supersensible world, including our own soul-spiritual organization. These can be seen in as exact a way "as a mathematical problem appears to a mathematician."[5]

In the introduction to an essay, "Philosophy and Anthroposophy," which is based on a lecture given in 1909, Steiner writes: "By Anthroposophy I mean a scientific exploration of the spiritual world, taking into account the one-sidedness of mere observation of outer nature as well as of traditional mysticism. Before attempting to enter into the supersensible world, Anthroposophy must develop the forces inherent, but not yet functioning, in our ordinary consciousness and in ordinary scientific thinking. Without such training it is not possible to enter the spiritual world in a meaningful way."[6]

We will have to come back again later to this important point in order to clearly distinguish Anthroposophy from depth psychology.

Steiner's spiritual science, aiming as it does at scientific exactness, leads to the following distinction: The human being is not only an organism composed of body, soul, and spirit; as a unique, distinct individuality, it is a participant in each of the three realms of reality: the physical world, the soul world, and the spiritual world. We are not merely the sum of these three; rather we constantly create ourselves anew within them. We use the physical and the soul realm to build up the physical body that we need to live on this earth. We clothe ourselves with a body as with a garment; we live in it like in a house. This comparison itself is very old. The Bible also speaks of the "house of the body that will have to be disassembled one day," or of the "glory in which the stars are clothed" (I Cor. 15:41). What is new, however, is the recognition of the individuality. The thinkers of Central European idealism were led to this idea. With Steiner it appears as the "I," the fourth human principle that incarnates into the three aforementioned "garments." It is this "I" that belongs forever to the spiritual world. In the "I," the core of the human being, the spirit is individualized and able to become aware of itself.

Thus, as human beings, we are constantly linking ourselves to the things of the world in a threefold way. (We should not read anything into this fact at first, but simply take it as it stands.) It shows us that there are three aspects to our human nature. For the moment, this and only this is what will be meant here by the three terms *body, soul,* and *spirit....*By *body* is meant the means by which the things in our environment...reveal themselves to us. The word *soul* designates the means by which we link these things to our own personal existence, by which we experience likes and dislikes, pleasure and displeasure, joy and sorrow. By *spirit* is meant what becomes apparent in us, when, as "quasi-divine beings," to use Goethe's expression, we look at the things of the world....

In this way the soul sets itself up as something personal and private in contrast to the world outside. It receives stimuli from the outer world, but constructs an inner private world in accordance with them. Bodily existence becomes the basis for soul existence.... Nature subjects us to the laws of metabolism, but as human beings we subject ourselves to the laws of thought. Through this process, we make ourselves members of a higher order than the one we belong to through the body. This is the spiritual order.[7]

What Steiner wrote above, at the beginning of his anthroposophical work in 1904, was reformulated in his *Anthroposophical Leading Thoughts,* written toward the end of his life (1924–25):

Man is a being who unfolds his life in the midst, between two regions of the world. With his bodily development he is a member of a "lower world"; with his soul-nature he himself constitutes a "middle world"; and with his faculties of Spirit he is ever striving toward an "upper world." He owes his bodily development to all that Nature has given him; he bears the being of his soul within him as his own portion; and he discovers in himself the forces of the Spirit, as the gifts that lead him out beyond himself to participate in a Divine World.[8]

To prevent misunderstanding, it should be said here that this participation in the divine world is to begin with far from perfect. It must be striven for and can only be achieved by a substantially enhanced consciousness. The "I" is certainly the starting point for these efforts to gain knowledge of higher worlds, as will be shown in more detail later in this book.

The degree of wakefulness required here is that of clear thinking. But spirit cannot be equated with reason alone, just as the "I" is not yet the ideal form the spirit can take in the human being. Steiner does characterize thoughts as "real beings" when he says: "We are surrounded by thoughts as we proceed on our way, but these thoughts are *real beings*."[9] Human beings participate in the true reality of the world through their thinking, even when their thoughts pertain to physical objects. These are only an aggregate of spiritual realities.

> Only because sense-perceptible things are nothing other than condensed spirit beings can we human beings—who can lift ourselves up in thought to the level of spirit beings—think about and understand them. Sense-perceptible things originate in the spirit world and are simply another manifestation of spirit beings; when we formulate thoughts about things, we are simply inwardly directed away from their sense-perceptible forms and toward their spiritual archetypes. Understanding an object by thinking about it is a process that can be compared to melting a solid body so that chemists can study it in its fluid form.[10]

Yet according to Steiner, the "I" and our normal thinking relate to the spiritual world like shadow play to the real thing. "We might also say that the thought activity of physical human beings is a shadowy image, a reflection, of the true spiritual being to which it belongs. During physical life, the spirit interacts with the earthly material world by using a material body as its basis."[11] Only when someone leaves the physical sphere and enters the spiritual world, be it through death or through the enhanced consciousness described above, does he or she get to know the "spiritual archetypes" that form the basis of all life. That which is merely thought while we are in the physical body can then be experienced as full reality. "The thought appears to us, not as a shadow hiding behind the things, but as a living reality that creates the things. We are in the thought workshop, so to speak, where earthly things are shaped and formed."[12]

These words indicate that Steiner does not grant ultimate importance to thinking. He does point out that "healthy discrimination" is needed when it comes to receiving messages from the spiritual world. This healthy discrimination, however, does not suffice for actually experiencing spiritual facts. For this, special schooling is necessary.[13]

Steiner has further refined this four-dimensional character of the human being in order to do justice to minerals, plants, and animals, which exist in the world along with human beings. Everyday observation shows that the human physical body (which, strictly speaking, is no more than a corpse) cannot be directly connected to the soul or spirit worlds. To understand the connection clearly, we need another concept that plays a role when we compare the lifeless mineral to the living plant organism. Even though the plant consists of mineral substance, there is something else at work that makes the plant sprout, grow, blossom, and produce seeds. This "something" is what Steiner calls the formative, life-giving forces. These are what plant, animal, and human have in common, each in a specific and different way. In particular, the plant is distinguished from the mineral because of these forces. Steiner calls this specific combination of living forces the "life-body," sometimes also the "body of life forces," when describing its function. When he speaks of the substance of this "body" he calls it the "etheric body." The etheric body cannot be seen with physical eyes and cannot be studied by conventional scientific methods. One can detect it thorough its effects on the life processes. It becomes directly observable in plants, animals, or humans only when the spiritual senses are developed. The way to develop these senses is through Steiner's occult path of schooling, which he describes in detail in his writings. Even though the physical realm is an expression of the spirit, according to Steiner, the etheric forces are supersensible and cannot be seen by the physical eye. Again, to study them one needs enhanced spiritual senses.

When we turn to the soul world, Steiner makes further distinctions. Pain and joy have their seat in the soul or astral body. The animal has a soul-body because it can feel pain as well as joy. The animals' soul-body is not the same as that of the human because the animal does not have an individual "I." Rather the soul of animals is what Steiner calls a "group soul." They act out of instinct as guided by this group soul.

Basic anthroposophical works contain detailed descriptions of the fourfold human being. They also make further distinctions regarding the relationship of physical, etheric, and astral body to the "I." According to its ability to have sensation, intellect, and consciousness, the soul is differentiated into the sentient, intellectual, and consciousness soul. This arrangement could be called the *static* aspect of the soul.

The *dynamic* aspect is found in the fact that the human being is capable of transforming the physical-psychic being by receiving impulses from the spiritual world. "Within the human soul, the 'I' flashes up, receives the impact of the spirit, and thus becomes the vehicle of the spirit body [*Geistmensch* or 'spirit man']. Thus we each take part in three worlds—the physical, the soul, and the spiritual worlds. We are rooted in the physical through the material-physical body, ether body, and soul body; we come to flower in the spiritual world through the spirit self, life spirit, and spirit body, but the stem, which roots at one end and flowers at another, is the soul itself."[14] As one can see, in the anthroposophical scheme the human being is not just the sum of its parts. Therefore, the human can never be defined as a complete being. On the contrary, we are forever changing. We manifest as a spiritual-psychical process that also includes the physical aspect. Here is anticipated what in theology is called eschatology.

A further dynamic is present in the idea of karma and reincarnation. Human destiny is thought to be the result of many earthly lives. The present life offers the chance to influence one's future destiny by developing and maturing the human "core," the individual "I," in a conscious way. The "I" is the spiritual principle of the human being. It is immortal and goes from incarnation to incarnation. Anthropogenesis (which Jung called "individuation"), is seen not only under the aspect of one lifetime between birth and death, but far beyond, into prenatal existence as well as in the life after death. Thus new perspectives open up that are missing in traditional depth psychology, which Steiner criticized with the harsh words: "dilettantism squared."

What emerges from all that has been said in this chapter is the tremendous, far-reaching importance of the human "I." Human beings do not only experience themselves through the "I" in their physical and psychological being. The "I" becomes the vessel that receives contents from the spiritual world, the sphere where all creativity has its roots, the source of manifold revelations. This is the world we ultimately come from, the world that gives our life its ultimate meaning.

As we have seen in the biographical sketch, Steiner was inspired to think about individuality not only by the "I"-philosophy of the German idealists. The problem of the "I" had existential importance for him. This becomes clear from his philosophical and epistemological works as well as in his writings on Anthroposophy and spiritual science. Steiner sees in the "I" the possibility for human freedom and for continued development. The model for human freedom and for self-realization is Jesus Christ: the "I AM." We might say with Klaus von Stieglitz: "While the philosopher saw self-realization and freedom mainly as the aim of Western intellectual history, [Steiner's] Christosophy sees it as the ultimate mission of all humankind. Self-realization becomes part of cosmic history."[15] Worldwide horizons open up. But as already noted, this does not refer to the everyday, still-undeveloped ego. A human being is not what she seems to be, but rather what she is able to become.

Jung's Image of the Human Being

With Jung's model as with Steiner's, we will have to limit ourselves to the most important elements of his teaching.[16] Jung's contribution to the subject is concentrated on the psyche, which, for him, is reality itself. One of the fundamental characteristics of Jung's psychology is that he conceives of an objective psychic reality that follows its own laws. Steiner, incidentally, recognized this special feature of Jung's psychology, even though Jung had not yet refined his system to the extent that it is known today.

This "reality of the psyche," namely, the realm within which one can find empirical evidence of immaterial forces, is divided into the conscious and the unconscious. In the conscious we encounter the *ego*, which is determined mainly by the fact that it is conscious. In *Psychological Types*, Jung defines consciousness as "the relationship of psychic contents to the ego in so far as this relation is perceived as such by the ego. Relations to the ego that are not perceived as such are unconscious. Consciousness is the function or activity which maintains the relation of psychic contents to the ego. Consciousness is not identical with the psyche...because the psyche represents the totality of all psychic contents, and these are not necessarily connected with the ego, i.e. related to it in such a way that they take on the quality of consciousness."[17]

The everyday waking consciousness does not constitute a totality but is of a partial nature. Accordingly, the ego is also of a partial nature. In *Psychological Types*, Jung describes the ego as a complex of ideas "which constitutes the center of my field of consciousness and appears to possess a high degree of continuity and identity. Hence I also speak of an ego-complex. The ego-complex is as much a content as a condition of consciousness."

Connected to the conscious ego, yet different from it, is the *persona*, the part of the psyche that is turned toward the outer world. It fulfills the function of adaptation. Mindful of the original function of the mask in the theater of antiquity, one could call it the masklike side of the ego (indeed the Latin meaning of *persona* is "mask"). It mimics true individuality inasmuch as it represents name, profession, title, social status, lifestyle, and so on. Depending on circumstances, character, and surroundings, a person can slip more or less completely into his or her persona, like a mime into a mask.

These entities that function within the psychic and physical field of consciousness, however, are only part of an individual's personality. In Jung's conception, the ego is not yet the real individual, which is only realized when one succeeds in integrating the conscious and unconscious into a complete whole. Jung calls the result of this process *individuation* (becoming a Self). The Self in Jung's terminology can be understood as the goal as well as the path to the goal.

One factor in the unconscious is the *shadow*, which constitutes the negative, reluctantly acknowledged, and thus for the most part unconscious traits of our character. The inferior character of the shadow asserts itself as a consequence of an underused or insufficiently developed soul function. The relation of the shadow to the unconscious is such that the shadow's negative traits are denied to the point of seeming nonexistent, both to the outside world and the inner self. (If consciousness becomes aware of the shadow at all, it often sees it as "projections" from the darker side of the psyche without realizing what it really is.) The persona that is presented to the outer world could be called, on the other hand, the façade of the ego.

Strong identification with the persona (if, for instance, a person pretends to totally *be* his or her role in life: the servant, the boss, the official) is just as problematic as total identification with the shadow. The latter is lived out when a person takes on the victim role and considers what are really his own shortcomings to be "bad luck." On the one hand, an individual can never completely give up the persona, since it is not possible to live a life of total honesty and inwardness. On the other hand, total negation of the shadow results in an overvaluation of one's ego and shows a lack of realistic self-evaluation and self-knowledge.

While the shadow that belongs to the ego often lives in the unconscious, recognizable in the way it manifests itself, another layer of unconscious content exists in the psyche that does not belong to the individual alone. It is Jung's great pioneering achievement to have studied this layer in a scientific manner. He called it the *collective unconscious*. He encountered a baffling parallel between descriptions of healthy (as well as sick) individuals on the one hand and mythological or symbolic tales on the other. The name he chose to give the form in which the collective unconscious presents its contents was the *archetypes*.

"The archetype is essentially an unconscious content that is altered by becoming conscious and by being perceived, and it takes its color from the individual consciousness in which it happens to appear."[18] In a footnote the author adds for clarification: "One must, for the sake of accuracy, distinguish between 'archetype' and 'archetypal ideas'. The archetype as such is a hypothetical and irrepresentable model, something like the 'pattern of behaviour' in biology." One could say in Jung's sense that the archetypes, while remaining unobserved themselves, cause

archetypal representations that show up in the human field of awareness. Archetypes are in truth the precondition for these representations. To put it differently, archetypes can be called factors and motives
that have the ability to arrange psychic elements into certain images or
pictures, in a way that can only be recognized by their final effect. They
exist preconsciously and may well constitute the dominant structures
of the psyche altogether. While the archetype itself rests, unobservable,
deep in the unconscious, the archetypal picture of the individual person is recognizable.

Jung clearly distinguishes the ego from the *Self*, which in its greater
expanse unites the whole psyche, conscious and unconscious, into a
whole. "As an empirical concept the Self designates the whole range of
psychical phenomena in man. It expresses the unity of the personality
as a whole. But insofar as the total personality, on account of its
unconscious component, can only be partially conscious, the concept
of the self is in part only *potentially* empirical and is to that extent a postulate. In other words, it encompasses both the experienceable and the
inexperienceable (or the not yet experienced)."[19] Jung has shown how
this Self has archetypal character, and how it can assume the form of a
hero, a leader, or a messiah in dreams, myths, and fairy tales. Or it can
show itself in the form of symbols of wholeness, such as the circle,
cross, or square. Considered in this way, the Self is not only the center
but also the periphery that encompasses both conscious and unconscious. Jung contrasted the Self as center of psychic wholeness with the
ego as center of consciousness.

Analytical psychology is certainly more than analysis and more than
the description and interpretation of what is found in the psyche. All analytical and therapeutic work aims at change and transformation. The goal
is wholeness of the Self, or Self-realization. How is this accomplished?

Jung's answer to this question points to a process of psychic development: the birth of the Self or individuation. It is the dynamic
aspect of his psychology. "Individuation means becoming an 'individual,' and insofar as 'individuality' embraces our innermost, last,
and incomparable uniqueness, it also implies becoming one's own self.
We could therefore translate individuation as: 'coming to selfhood' or

'self-realization.'"[20] The purpose of this psychic transformation—
which has been consciously achieved, according to Jung, by only a very
few individuals—is the following: to free the individual on the one
hand from the constraints of the persona, that is, the masklike collective psyche that only mimics true individuality, and on the other hand
from the compulsion of the unconscious archetypal images.

Jung also speaks of the "integration of those psychic contents that
are capable of becoming conscious," whereby ego-consciousness is still
not identical with the Self. Even, so he mentions "certain remarkable
but hard to describe consequences for the ego-consciousness" in the
individuation process. Jung defines this process thus: "Individuation is,
in general, the process by which individual beings are formed and differentiated; in particular, it is the development of the psychological
individual, as a being distinct from the general, collective psychology.
Individuation, therefore, is a process of differentiation, having for its
goal the development of the individual personality. Individuation is a
natural necessity inasmuch as its prevention by leveling down to collective standards is injurious to the vital activity of the individual."[21]

Placing the sketches of Steiner's Anthroposophy and Jung's depth
psychology side by side gives rise to some questions. What is the relationship between soul and spirit for Steiner and for Jung? How can one
compare the dynamic aspect of the image of the human being and of the
psyche from the standpoint of both seekers? Before we tackle these questions, we will have to deal with the problem of consciousness, for psychic
processes and facts must always be seen in the context of consciousness.

It should not be necessary to point out that placing the individual
chapters in this book side by side is of necessity a stopgap. With material that is not composed of fixed and easily defined elements but has
to do mostly with processes and transformation, one cannot avoid
anticipating things that should follow later. In other words, some
important aspects should be introduced before they are dealt with.
The reader of anthroposophical and psychological literature of this
kind has to adopt a special attitude. It will not do just to acknowledge
facts, hypotheses, and assertions. Credulous acceptance of everything
that is said is just as inappropriate as rigid skepticism. What is needed

is constant watchful consideration, where critical distance and an open mind, as well as a certain amount of goodwill, counterbalance each other. The often-voiced prejudice that Steiner and Jung have nothing to offer but mysticism, metaphysics, and ideology blocks from the outset the possibility for a fruitful discussion. In both cases a great deal of awareness is needed as well as a willingness to attempt some measure of personal experience. A person who is afraid of opening herself up to spurious suggestion by considering the unknown has no trust in her own awareness and critical thinking. On the other hand, one who blindly accepts Anthroposophy remains equally blind to Steiner's true intentions. Enthusiastic verbal confessions, membership, and so on cannot cure such blindness. One who acts in this way merely constructs, to quote Hermann Poppelbaum, "a pseudo-'I' of anthroposophically formulated illusions, that is, one deceives oneself. Such a person may talk about 'knowledge of higher worlds' when he or she may be better off undergoing psychotherapy."[22] It might be in order here to mention something Steiner said in 1911: "I beg you not to give credence to these things because I say them, but to test them by everything known to you from history, above all, what you can learn from your own experience....In this age of intellectualism I do not appeal to your belief but to your capacity for intelligent discrimination."[23] Jung was perhaps even more frank than Steiner when he confessed: "Work in this field is pioneer work. I have often made mistakes, and had many times to forget what I had learned. But I know and am content to know that as surely as light comes out of darkness, truth is born of error....Not the criticism of individual contemporaries will decide the truth or falsity of my discoveries, but future generations. There are things that are not yet true today, perhaps we will not dare to find them true, but tomorrow they may be."[24]

6

STEINER'S "SECOND SELF" AND
THE UNCONSCIOUS

IN HIS LECTURES ON PSYCHOANALYSIS (discussed in chapter 3), Steiner
did not limit himself to mere criticism of psychoanalysis and analytical
psychology. He went on to discuss a field of research that is relevant to
both Anthroposophy and depth psychology.

In view of Steiner's negative judgment of psychoanalysis, one could
conclude that he underestimated the importance of the unconscious as
such, which he always called the "subconscious." One could think that
his efforts were exclusively directed at raising and broadening consciousness. And one could assume that he was so intent on gaining knowledge
of "higher worlds" that he ignored the reality of the abyss of the human
soul and neglected the subconscious and the unconscious altogether.

This is not the case, as readily becomes clear from the second of his
two lectures on psychoanalysis. Steiner never left any doubt about the
character of his spiritual science, whether he was merely delineating his
method of research or taking a stand against certain methods of an inferior occultism. There is just as little doubt, however, that his spiritual
research always kept the depths of the so-called subconscious in mind.

One has to follow the connecting line that Steiner himself drew,
leading from the Dornach lectures on psychoanalysis in 1917 back to
the three lectures in Copenhagen in 1911. These were titled (in
English translation) *The Spiritual Guidance of the Individual and Humanity*,
and he had them published the same year, which was not his usual
practice. This was done "because I have reasons for allowing this work
to be published at this time," he wrote in the preface. For just these reasons he had to forgo a more in-depth treatment of this theme. Instead
he returned to it several times in later lectures.

The text begins: "If we reflect upon ourselves, we soon come to realize that, in addition to the self we encompass with our thoughts, feelings, and fully conscious impulses of will, we bear in ourselves a second, more powerful self. We become aware that we subordinate ourselves to the second self as to a higher power. At first, this second self seems to us a lower being when compared to the one we encompass with our clear, fully conscious soul and its natural inclination toward the good and the true. And so, initially, we strive to overcome this seemingly lower self."[1] Steiner has described this "other self" and its "lower nature" in many other lectures. Some examples of this may be given here, before we go into the anthropological and Christological connections that he points up in the printed edition of the Copenhagen lectures.

Let us start with texts of the same year, 1911. In April, Steiner gave a paper at the fourth international philosophy congress in Bologna entitled "The Philosophical Foundations of Anthroposophy." He intended to make clear what Anthroposophy meant by cognition and to identify cognition as something "fluid, capable of evolution." He explained that "beyond the horizon of the normally conscious life of the mind, there is another into which we can penetrate." To avoid being confused with pseudo-occult practitioners, Steiner points out that the soul realm he is talking about is not the same as the one presently called the subconscious. This "subconscious" may be the object of scientific study; it can be studied with the present methods of science. "But this has nothing in common with that condition to which we are referring, within which the human being is as completely conscious, possesses as complete logical watchfulness, as within the limits of ordinary consciousness."[2] He follows this with a description of his method of cognition according to his chosen theme.

In his lectures in Munich in August, 1911, titled *Wonders of the World, Ordeals of the Soul, Revelations of the Spirit*, he returns to the statements he made in Copenhagen and once more describes the "expansive soul life" that is much larger than what our common consciousness allows. Steiner amplified this description by mentioning figures from Greek mythology, Persephone and Demeter, as representatives of this deep-seated element of the soul. The old clairvoyant forces of humankind have descended into Persephone's realm, and they present an analogy to the present state of the human soul. It was formerly the task of these forces to make human beings clairvoyant. At present they stand in the service of strengthening the "I." At the same time, Steiner also sees in Demeter a "still older ruler, both of the forces of external Nature and of the forces of the human soul." Whether one may see here a connection to Jung's collective unconscious cannot be said with certainty. On the other hand, Steiner sees in the myth of the abduction of Persephone a phase in the evolution of human consciousness: "In the course of the historical development of humanity, the rape of Persephone has been brought about by soul-forces which lie deep in the subconscious, forces which in outer Nature are represented as Pluto." As lord of the underworld, Pluto represents the forces that are active in nature as well as in the human soul. According to Steiner's description, the gods withdrew from the forces of nature. The abduction of Persephone is also an image of this event. Consequently, the old atavistic clairvoyance came to an end and the guidance of humankind through instinct had to take on a new form. From now on, spiritual guidance had to come from the place where the sacred, soul-transforming drama was performed: the ancient mysteries: "Originally the gods bestowed morality upon men along with the forces of Nature; then the forces of Nature more or less withdrew, and later the gods substituted a moral law in a more abstract form through their messengers in the Mysteries. When man became estranged from Nature he needed a more abstract, a more intellectual morality, hence the Greeks looked to their Mysteries for guidance in their moral life, and in the Mysteries they saw the activities of the gods, as previously they had seen their activity in the forces of Nature. For this reason the earliest Greek period attributed the moral law to the same gods who were at the back of the forces of Nature."[3]

For Steiner, something else is significant as well. He mentions in the same connection the "etheric body," that is, the part of the human being that mediates between the physical body and the soul or astral body. Functioning like a mirror, it reflects the pictures that arise in the soul—in Jung's terms, the "creations of the unconscious"—and makes them visible: "It is the ether body which brings to the point of vision, to perception, the images called forth by the astral body. What man perceives of the goings-on in his own astral body is what is mirrored from him by his ether body. If all our inner astral processes were not reflected by our ether bodies we should of course still have the astral body's activity within us, but we should not be aware of it, we would not perceive it. Hence in the whole picture of the world that the human being makes, the total content of his consciousness is a reflection of his ether body. Whether a man knows anything of the world depends upon his ether body. This was so in the old clairvoyant days, and it is still so today."[4] Here indeed is a key to recognizing the world, including the activities of the unconscious. Later we will say more about this aspect of Steiner's view of the human being. For now, it is clear that from the anthroposophical viewpoint, the sphere of the unconscious can be understood as a phenomenon that lets us connect mythological picture content with anthropological facts.

Beyond that, Steiner describes the living pictures of Greek mythology as having once had educational and soul-strengthening functions. These functions have undergone some change, since the Christ event brought about a new development of consciousness. This change is to be seen primarily in the birth of ego-consciousness. To the degree that ego-consciousness grew stronger, the old, more instinctual perception and the mythical creation of pictures containing profound wisdom faded away. They were "abducted" by the underworld.

In the last lecture that Steiner was able to give abroad (in 1924), he returned once more to the theme of the Persephone-Demeter myth in connection with the activity of nature spirits and the path to the spiritual world. Marie Steiner speaks in the foreword to these lectures, entitled *True and False Paths in Spiritual Investigation*, of the "alchemy of the human soul-being that, having been obscured by the body and robbed of its most precious organs, can recreate them anew by transubstantiation of all that is earthbound."[5]

In the fourth of the above lectures, where Steiner deals with the metamorphosis of consciousness, he once more brings in mythical pictures. While the upper world represents everyday waking consciousness,

Persephone, living in the underworld, symbolizes, together with Pluto, the activity of the physical and etheric bodies during sleep. What we nowadays quite abstractly call "nature" was once a living participation in Persephone wisdom, albeit in a more dreamlike fashion.[6] Jung and his school have looked at these facts from many different aspects. Here one must refer to the far-reaching work of Erich Neumann and M. Esther Harding.[7]

From the standpoint of spiritual history, it is remarkable that the world of images has not been buried forever. It presses again toward the light of day in a twofold way: in the form of depth psychology, and also as spiritual science. (Another symptom is modern humanity's hunger for pictures.) Of the "old knowledge, the knowledge aroused by those impressive pictorial images of the Greeks," Steiner says, "what was submerged in the depths of the soul is coming to the surface again for the life of today in the form of spiritual science."[8] Depth psychologists can confirm similar facts from their own experience. However, the way these contents of the soul's depth are interpreted and used are different from Steiner's.

We must not lose sight of another important aspect here: Steiner, like Jung, knew that a new way to the Christ could be found. "And the force which penetrates into human souls in order to lead them up again to clairvoyance—or I could also say in order to bring down clairvoyance to them—is the force which was first prepared as conscious thought in the old Jahve civilization, and then reached its full development through the coming of the Christ Being, who will become ever better understood by men."[9]

This Christ force, as Steiner calls it, is what carries the impulses that will once again make conscious what has been submerged in subconscious depths in the course of our development. Steiner speaks of the "greatest event in human inner development." He means here the return of Paul's Damascus experience, namely, the beholding of the risen Christ. This experience, according to Steiner, was not a single event, but is a process of long duration that will enable humanity to become aware of the reality of Christ's presence (see in appendices: "Unus Mundus and the Cosmic Christ"). Steiner's aim in developing his spiritual science was to facilitate this "progress of the human soul" (not to be confused with modern concepts of "progress"). In this he saw his mission.

It is no accident that Steiner brings his comments about the importance of the unconscious soul forces into close connection with his Christological communications. One example is the cycle of lectures, held in Karlsruhe in 1911, *From Jesus to Christ*. This cycle was introduced with a public lecture. Here we find further explanations of why today (meaning since the appearance of the Christ) "a new way needs to be found to the 'divine foundations of the world' different from the one that existed at the time of the ancient mysteries. In those ancient times Demeter and Persephone, Isis and Osiris, Dionysus, and the Persian Mithras were personifications of an inner process in which each human soul was a portal that allowed the gods to enter and to influence human development on earth."

In the Karlsruhe lectures Steiner took great pains to avoid any misunderstanding about all that he had to say about the unconscious realm, which he once called the "living depths of the soul-ocean." He was concerned that misunderstandings could lead to misuse of the information. He acknowledged that human beings receive powerful positive impulses for their spiritual and moral life from these deeply unconscious regions. And he emphasized: "All conscious life is rooted in unconscious soul life. Basically, one cannot understand the whole evolution of humankind if one does not reckon with the unconscious life of the soul....Therefore, one has to acknowledge the unconscious as the second element in the soul, besides the conscious one. That is one side of the coin. The other is that this region, which is normally not accessible to observation, must be protected very carefully from intrusion. The unconscious is the seat of the will, and even though it is not directly accessible it can be manipulated by certain practices." As an example, Steiner mentioned the spiritual exercises of the Jesuits, which, he said, touch the roots of the will forces. Steiner said in this connection: "When we meet another human being and enter into the most varied relationships with him, it is in the realm of conscious spiritual life that understanding should be possible....On the other hand, we must recognize the will element, and everything in another person's subconscious, as something that should on no account be intruded upon; it must be regarded as his innermost sanctuary....The only healthy way to gain influence over another person's will is through cognition."[10] Steiner felt justified in calling the unconscious the "innermost sanctuary" because the risen Christ "worked up from the unconscious soul powers of the disciples into their soul life."[11]

Without a doubt there is an inner correspondence between this short but important statement of Steiner's and what analytical psychology has to say about humankind's acceptance of the Christ.

The historian can only register the fact that Christianity was accepted surprisingly quickly in the first centuries A.D. Jung's explanation for this has found very little recognition up to now. He said, somewhat similarly to Steiner, "Christ would never have made the impression he did on his followers if he had not expressed something that was alive and at work in their unconscious. Christianity itself would not have spread through the pagan world with such astonishing rapidity had its ideas not found an analogous psychic readiness to receive it."[12] Gerhard Zacharias, who devoted a study to this subject, called this remark "a highly significant fact for Christian theology."[13]

Jung's concept of the archetypes is extremely helpful here. In *Aion*, Jung seeks to show in detail "the kind of psychological matrix into which the Christ-figure was assimilated in the course of the centuries. Had there not been an affinity—magnet!—between the figure of the Redeemer and certain contents of the unconscious, the human mind would never have been able to see the light shining in Christ and seize upon it so passionately. The connecting link here is the archetype of the God-man, which on the one hand became historical reality in Christ and, on the other, being eternally present, reigns over the soul in the form of a supraordinate totality, the self." Jung points at the psychological efficacy of the fish symbol, and he continues:

The noncanonical fish symbol led us into this psychic matrix and thus into a realm of experience where the unknowable archetypes become living things, changing their name and guise in never-ending

succession and, as it were, disclosing their hidden nucleus by perpetu-
ally circumambulating round it...the fish symbol is a spontaneous
assimilation of the Christ-figure of the gospels, and is thus a symptom which shows us in what manner and with what meaning the symbol was assimilated by the unconscious....The image of the fish rose
up from the depths of the unconscious as an equivalent of the historical Christ figure, and if Christ is invoked as "Ichthys," this name
referred to what had come up out of the depths. The fish symbol is
thus the bridge between the historical figure of Christ and the psychic
nature of man, where the archetype of the Redeemer dwells. In this
way Christ became an inner experience, the "Christ within."[14]

On the basis of this interpretation, one can understand Christ-
knowledge as a sort of re-recognition. Something essentially human
expresses itself in Christ. In a different, more spiritual sense than that
of Ludwig Feuerbach, Christology is fundamentally anthropology. In
Christ Jesus the *deus incarnatus* is revealed as simply man himself. The
dictum of Pontius Pilate: "*Ecce homo*—this is man," takes on a truth that
has to be realized by each individual in his or her own cognitive development.

Jung can best describe this cognitive act by describing the psychological side of the process, for instance by naming the "psychological
acceptance systems" that are prepared in the unconscious for receiving
the Christ. He can explain why the man from Nazareth became a "collective symbol" that was anticipated by the collective unconscious of
his time. But each individual must open himself to the Christ encounter. Every single person must be shown the way by which Christ can be
found.

Steiner started out where the psychologist necessarily comes to an
end. Steiner saw it as his special task to describe, in his Anthroposophy, the steps of Rosicrucian schooling. He did this in a number of lecture cycles[15] as well as in his basic books. While the psychologist
purposely limited himself to the interpretation of the important phenomena, the spiritual scientist attempted to "lead spirit seekers to the
path of inner development."[16]

How can one judge the efficacy of the unconscious? What merit does it deserve, according to Steiner? In the Karlsruhe lectures of 1911, Steiner says that the "second, more powerful self" could be thought of as a "lower being when compared to one we encompass with our clear, fully conscious soul," that one would strive to overcome. The rational modern Westerner in particular has the tendency to think that way. Steiner does not agree with this attitude at all. On the contrary, he points out that "we would not get very far in life if we had to do everything in full consciousness, rationally understanding the circumstances and ramifications in every case."[17]

When we look back on our lives, we come to a point where we can tap into our very earliest memories of the time when we still had a rather weak ego-consciousness. What lies before that, the first three or even four years of life, is not accessible to our memory. Again we stand before what Steiner called the "subconscious soul regions." According to Steiner, a great deal of important work is being done there to build up the human being. He lists the fruits of this work: the attainment of equilibrium, speech development, and the unfolding of brain activity. This is why he accords the subconscious formative forces a great deal of wisdom which the rational mind does not possess at any point in life. For our comparison of Steiner and Jung it is now meaningful to consider how Steiner answered the question: "How is it possible that such important work is being done in those depths of the soul that lie outside our consciousness?" Steiner's reply:

Because in the first years of our lives our souls as well as our whole being are much more closely connected with the spiritual worlds of the higher hierarchies than is the case....We work on ourselves with a wisdom is that is *not* in us, a wisdom that is more powerful and comprehensive than all the conscious wisdom we acquire later....The wisdom at work in children does not become part of our consciousness in later life. It is obscured and exchanged for consciousness. In the first years of life, however, this higher wisdom functions like a "telephone connection" to the spiritual beings in whose world we find ourselves between death and rebirth. Something from this world still flows into our aura during childhood. As individuals we are then directly subject to the guidance of the *entire* spiritual world to which we belong. When we are children—up to the moment of our earliest memory—the spiritual forces of this world flow into us....

The spiritual forces from this world flow into us, enabling us to develop our particular relationship to gravity. At the same time, the same forces also form our larynx and shape our brain into living organs for the expression of thought, feeling, and will.[18]

The information Steiner gives here is important because in the comparison we are attempting here, we need to find differences as well as correspondences that allow us some conceptual bridge building. We see that the Anthroposophist occupies himself with the "spiritual world" that is the ground of all existence much like the analytical psychologist, who works with the realm of the unconscious in order to draw conclusions about the reality of the soul. Consequently, we have to ask whether and to what extent Steiner's "spiritual world" corresponds to Jung's "unconscious," especially the collective unconscious. In the passage above, Steiner has given an answer that clearly seems to imply a correspondence between the spiritual world and the unconscious. Even so, it is unquestionably true that the central concepts of the Anthroposophist and of the depth psychologist do not overlap in any simple way.

Consider Steiner's statement that the "spiritual worlds of the higher hierarchies"—not merely some relatively minor spirits—"reach into the soul of the child and, out of their wisdom, give form to the physical body of the growing human." Obviously we are dealing here with creative forces that are of an archetypal nature insofar as they guide the "becoming" of a human being. This is done out of a wisdom that is not only far superior to normal consciousness but is unknown to it. Of this wisdom Jung says, "The unconscious is the ever-creative mother of consciousness. Consciousness grows out of the unconscious in childhood just as it did in primeval times when man became man."[19]

In respect to the analogy between the development of consciousness of the individual child and that of humanity as a whole, there is a wealth of similarities between Anthroposophy and depth psychology. We have plenty of empirical material to prove this theory. Jung noticed, by the way, that the very early dreams of children, when they are remembered, contain astounding archetypal pictures that have parallels in the spiritual history of humankind. In Jung's opinion, the investigation of the collective unconscious in children should not pose a practical problem for the physician, because for the child the important development lies in the process of adaptation to the environment, which means becoming conscious. For this reason the unconscious should not be emphasized too much in the case of children. This advice certainly agrees with the direction taken by the development of consciousness in general. It originates in prerational, dreamlike, mythical depths and leads to the awakening of the ego-consciousness.

Both Jung and Steiner put high demands on the educator. According to Jung, the child's unconscious (which Steiner calls the "inner sanctum") one should not make too much of. Jung wants to avoid awakening an unhealthy curiosity in the child that may lead to abnormal precocity and self-centeredness. He does, however, emphasize the importance of psychological self-knowledge on the part of the educator, because she influences the child not only by the knowledge and skills taught, but also through her psyche, including all its conscious or unconscious shadow sides. For his part, Steiner insisted in 1919: "In the future all instruction will have to be based on psychology developed from an anthroposophical understanding of the world."[20] Whoever is familiar with the spiritual and pedagogical basis of the Waldorf schools, founded by Steiner, knows that this demand has been realized in a method and pedagogy, in regard to the pupil-teacher relationship, that can be seen as a practical psychosophy.

Let us return now to the themes of the Copenhagen lectures, where Steiner added some remarks in which he quite agrees with the findings of depth psychology. He states that the unconscious spiritual and psychic forces play a certain role still in later life.

All that we can produce in the way of ideals and artistic creativity— as also the natural healing forces in the body, which continuously compensate for the injuries life inflicts—originate not in our ordinary, rational minds but in the deeper forces that work in our early years on our orientation in space, on the formation of the larynx, and on the development of the brain. These same forces are still present in us later. People often say of the damages and injuries we sustain in life that external forces will not be of any help and that our organism must develop its own inherent healing powers. What they are talking about is a wise, benevolent influence working upon us. From this same source also arise the best forces that enable us to perceive the spiritual world.[21]

Of decisive importance here is an additional remark of Steiner's to the effect that knowledge of the higher worlds cannot and should not be sought in an instinctive, unconscious manner. This would lead back to an atavistic clairvoyance that was characteristic of ancient mankind and its stage of consciousness. The subconscious forces themselves should be sought and understood through a conscious relationship to the spirit world. Steiner has given the necessary instructions for this in his basic books. We will come back to this later.

Further on in this lecture, Steiner explains in detail that the formative forces at work in early childhood also have a Christological component. For "to know the forces at work in early childhood is to know the Christ in us."[22] It is possible to find the Christ "without recourse to any historical documentation." In the lectures in Munich mentioned above, Steiner said that ancient humanity could instinctively trust the guidance of the gods. In these lectures he speaks expressly about the "spiritual guidance of the individual and humanity" that the Christ provides, and the Christ is to be understood as "the way, the truth, and the life," as he is called in the Gospel of John. "Words such as these about the way, the truth, and the life can open the door to eternity for us. Once our self-knowledge has become true and substantial, these words will resound in us from the depths of our soul. What I have presented here opens up a twofold perspective on the spiritual guidance of the individual and of humanity as a whole. First, as individuals we find the Christ in us through self-knowledge. We can always find the Christ

in this way because, since his life on earth, he is always present in us."
Here a parallel suggests itself with Jung's words about the spontaneous reception in the psychic matrix. One can also think of the *anima
naturaliter christiana* (the "naturally Christian soul") of the Church
Fathers. Steiner continues: "Second, when we apply the knowledge we
have gained without the help of historical documents to these documents, we begin to understand their true nature. They are the historical expression of something that has revealed itself in the depths of
the soul. Therefore historical documents should be regarded as part
of that guidance of humanity that is intended to lead the soul to
itself."[23]

With this the Christ is once again seen as simply the man. Neither
Steiner nor Jung, however, saw him as identical with the historical rabbi
Jesus of Nazareth. Nor does Steiner believe in the slogan of the "simple man of Nazareth." On the contrary, he wants to show the impulse
that has taken hold of humankind in the course of evolution and keeps
driving us on. "Thus, the next higher world of the spiritual hierarchies
guides the entire evolution of humanity; it works both on the individual in childhood and on humanity as a whole. The angeloi, or superhuman beings of this realm, are one level above us and reach directly up
into the spiritual spheres. From these spheres they bring to earth what
works into human culture. In the individual, this higher wisdom leaves
its imprint on the formation of the body during childhood, and it
formed the culture of ancient humanity in a similar way."[24]

Based on this, Steiner gives new meaning to the concept of inspiration that has experienced a dogmatic narrowing in Protestant orthodoxy and has been eliminated by rationalism as incomprehensible. He
does this by seeing the Evangelists as people "who wrote out of the
higher self that works on all of us in childhood."[25] Considered in this
way, the Gospels are writings whose spiritual origins are rooted in the
same wisdom that, although unconscious in the psychological sense,
builds the developing human body.

If this is true, then biblical exegesis is inadequate if it passes over
the reality of the spiritual world, ignores the spiritual dimension of
reality, and deals exclusively with the creations of the rational mind.

This is what happens in the philological and hermeneutic methods of our present schools of theology. The same right that is granted philology in Bible interpretation should also be given to a spiritual interpretation.[26]

In connection with the question of spiritual guidance, Steiner points to the example of Socrates, who claimed that he was inspired by a *daimon* in the original meaning of the word. The soul mood of "Socratism" has played a role in preparing the ground for Christ's message. For instance, the mission of Paul owes its success on Greek soil to Socrates' followers. Jung as psychologist arrives at an amazingly similar conclusion. He sees in Socrates' *daimon* the personification of an objective psychic power that we, in our present situation, see as unconscious, "having become so bashful in matters of religion, that we correctly say 'unconscious,'" says Jung, "because God has in fact become unconscious to us."[27] Only real experiences of "the abysses and peaks of human nature give us the right to use the word 'daimon' in its metaphysical sense," said Jung in an exchange with Martin Buber. Jung spoke about the "archetypal god-man who became historical reality in Christ but at the same time is forever present in the human psyche as its dominating whole or Self." This can be seen in the context of Steiner's words and of Jung's comment that "Christ would never have made the impression he did on his followers if he had not expressed something that was alive and at work in their unconscious."[28]

7

NATURAL SCIENCE AS A
STARTING POINT

BOTH STEINER AND JUNG REGARDED themselves as natural scientists. Both saw the value of the exactness of scientific investigation and applied it to their own work. Since they had gone past the Cartesian horizon of understanding and would not be satisfied with recognizing only what can be measured, counted, and weighed, they ran into skepticism from their contemporaries. Although accused of mysticism and psychologism, Jung always insisted that he was an empiricist and that all his psychological theories were based on actual experiences with his patients. That this assertion was no empty assertion is proved by all his individual studies, in which he uses the strictly inductive method of investigation. He always starts by recording the personal experiences of the patient, which are related to him as dreams, associations, and fantasies; these are the creations of the individual unconscious. He then adds the comparative material that the therapist brings in to help clarification. His final hypotheses concerning his discoveries of the unconscious, individuation, and synchronicity were never stated or published before they had been tested for years, sometimes for decades, and found to be reliable.

Jung thus found himself in a similar situation as Steiner, who never tired of claiming that the anthroposophical way of thinking was in accordance with that of natural science. Jung had to prove himself as scientist in the face of contemporary academic psychology and psychiatry; Steiner was concerned with establishing Anthroposophy as a science. He could not afford to popularize it too much in the beginning. In a lecture on January 24, 1918, he confessed: "I envision for the future a form of spiritual science that can be simple, popular, and understandable for every simple soul. ...Today spiritual science is still remote from mainstream science. In order to be recognized, spiritual science has to be expressed in such a way that it can stand up to the scrutiny of the recognized scientists."[1]

Thus, even in his first anthroposophical books, Steiner is eager to show that "one can faithfully follow scientific philosophy and still seek out the paths *to the soul*, into which mysticism leads, *when properly understood*. I go even further and assert that only those who understand spirit in the sense of true mysticism can fully understand the reality of nature. But people must beware of confusing true mysticism with the 'mysticism' of muddled heads."[2] For Jung, too, mystics are "people who have especially vivid experiences of the phenomena of the collective unconscious. Mystical experience is the experience of the archetypes."

Steiner's basic book *Christianity as Mystical Fact* begins with the assertion that he was guided to write this particular book in order to reach those whose thought life had been deeply influenced by contemporary scientific thinking. He says that "scientific ways of thinking" contain a power "that convinces the observer that here we have something that cannot be ignored if we are to form a modern conception of the world....To act in the spirit of natural science would be to study the spiritual evolution of humanity impartially, as the naturalist observes the sense-world." This positive attitude towards natural science can be found in many of Steiner's statements. But he continues: "That would lead in the domain of spiritual life to a method of investigation as different from purely natural science as is geology from theoretical physics, or evolutionary theory from advanced chemical research. It would lead to higher methodological principles, which would certainly not be identical with those of natural science, but would be in agreement with all that we really mean by scientific inquiry. Thus we can modify or correct the one-sided views deriving from scientific research by means of an added perspective. In doing so we are not betraying science, but advancing it."[3]

At this point it becomes clear why the spiritual scientist assumes this standpoint. He does not do so merely to conform to the prevailing thinking of the time, but to show that his method of spiritual investigation has grown quite naturally out of natural science; it constitutes a metamorphosis of scientific thought.[4] This becomes evident when one sees that for Steiner there is no unbridgeable gap between material nature and spirit. Spiritual reality cannot be identified with "another world." As Steiner has shown using the example of Goethe, the spiritual must not be sought "behind" the outer appearances. For the attentive observer, it manifests *within* them. The observation that spiritual science is, or wants to be, a continuation of natural science is very important, because all too often one meets with the misconception that Anthroposophy is either a "modern gnosis" or a pseudomystical mixture of certain theosophical ideas, or even a Western variation of an Eastern syncretism. But as I will explain later on in this book, Anthroposophy is not a modernized version of ancient occultism.

What is Jung's standpoint? In 1926 he says of himself: "I am no philosopher but merely an empiricist. All difficult questions I try to decide from my experiences. If there is no experiential foundation I would rather leave a question unanswered." He has a positive relationship to religion as well as to biology, and also "to scientific empiricism as a whole. Science seems to me to be a mighty effort to understand the soul from the outside in, while religious Gnosis, in contrast, is the equally gigantic attempt by the human spirit to gain knowledge from within." This shows that this statement, from the end of the 1920s, is already contemplating the *unus mundus*, the *one reality* that would play such a big role in his later work. Jung continues: "My worldview comprises a great outer world as well as a great inner world, and for me man stands between these two poles, turning either to the one or to the other; according to his temperament and constitution, he considers either the one or the other to be the absolute truth and tends to deny or to sacrifice the one for the other."[5]

Whoever writes such a sentence does not do so merely to distance himself from the dogmatic one-sidedness of Freud's psychology. He writes this way because, much like Steiner, he is not satisfied with a one-sided view of reality. Just as modern natural science sees itself as obliged to reach past traditional empirical methods into the metaphysical by interpreting some physical phenomena using seemingly antilogical hypotheses, so it was necessary for Jung to go beyond habitual realms of experience. In the beginning he believed he was doing traditional science in the best sense. He stated facts, and observed, classified, and described causal and functional connections. Finally, he discovered that he entertained thoughts that led him far beyond generally accepted science into philosophy, theology, comparative religion, and the history of the human mind. This puzzled him. Yet he felt that the course he was taking was unavoidable.

In his field Jung had made a discovery similar to those of other scientists: that the traditional concept of reality had become obsolete. It did not suffice any longer. Natural science had established a worldview that was as limited in its one-sidedness as Western humanity itself. "Restriction to material reality carves an exceedingly large chunk out of reality as a whole, but it nevertheless remains a fragment only, and all around it is a dark penumbra which one would have to call unreal or surreal."[6]

The psychologist sees phenomena that are undoubtedly real. But when he tries to describe them, he is unable to do so to someone who only recognizes a conceptual, logically defined way of thinking. Jolande Jacobi points to the difficulties in Jung's psychology: Jung never gave up the empirical method, but he ended up in a sphere where the usual expressions became inadequate to describe his experiences. Yet this does not make Jung a metaphysician, which he never claimed to be. Some biologists and physicists have encountered the same problem. It is the phenomena themselves that demand a transcendental approach.

The terms that have to be used for the description of such psychological facts, missing as they do a certain unequivocal clarity, indicate that a "threshold" is being crossed beyond which there is need for a different way of thinking, a different way of knowing. Apparently it is not merely a problem of language or hermeneutics. What we have here is of a symptomatic character inasmuch as it points to the need to ask deeper questions. Steiner also encountered this problem, but he approached it differently than Jung. Steiner did not work merely empirically. Mere observation cannot give answers to questions of recognition. Initially Steiner approached the problem by thinking. To avoid misunderstandings here, we have to point out that Steiner differentiated between abstract thinking and "pure thinking." For Steiner, pure thinking is a step towards spiritual recognition and can help one to understand the world on a deep level, according to *Intuitive Thinking as a Spiritual Path* (1894), his authoritative philosophical work. "My search finds firm ground only when I find an object the meaning of whose existence I can draw out of itself. As a thinker, I am myself such an object. I endow my existence with the definite, self-reposing content of thinking activity." And further: "In thinking, we have a principle that exists through itself. Starting with thinking, then, let us attempt to understand the world. We can grasp thinking through itself." And further: "The highest stage of individual life is conceptual thinking without reference to a specific perceptual content."[7]

On the basis of his autobiographical writings and his studies in the history of philosophy (*The Riddles of Philosophy, The Riddle of Man*) we know how highly Steiner regarded those thinkers who prepared and founded philosophical idealism. He did not stop there, however; he could not simply identify himself with them. On the other hand, he saw the necessity of building bridges between Hegel's pure experience of thinking and Goethe's intuitive experience of the idea behind the phenomena of nature. Here we find the beginning of a new understanding of the thinking process, which we will have to address later on. By activating a sense-free thinking, Steiner finally sought to cross the boundaries that had been drawn since the nineteenth century by Kant's theory of knowledge.

In contrast to Steiner's high respect for thinking, we find that Jung made statements that may sound strange to someone who takes the above position. In his "theoretical considerations about the essence of the psyche," Jung explores historical connections and then speaks about the attempts made in the last three centuries to understand the psyche. Better understanding of nature had led to an enormous expansion of knowledge of the cosmos. On the other hand, it was quietly assumed that everyone knew what the soul was.

With the discovery of an unconscious realm of the soul the opportunity opened up for an exciting adventure of the spirit, and one would have expected that people would seize such an opportunity with passionate interest. As it turned out, not only did this not happen, but on the contrary, a general resistance against this hypothesis arose. Nobody came to the conclusion that, should there be indeed an unconscious area within our instrument of knowledge, namely the soul, then all our conscious knowledge must be imperfect to an unknown degree. The validity of our conscious knowing was threatened by the hypothesis of the unconscious to a much higher degree than by the critical considerations of the usual theory of knowledge. The latter did set certain boundaries to human knowledge as such, from which German idealistic philosophers after Kant tried to emancipate themselves. Natural science and common sense, however, accepted this without difficulty, if they paid attention to it at all.

The philosophers, however, fought the idea of the limits to human knowledge, favoring instead an antiquated claim that the human spirit should be able to scramble over its own head and to see things that are obviously beyond the reach of human reason. Hegel's victory over Kant constituted a grave threat for reason as well as for further spiritual development, at least for the German thinkers.[8]

Only the influence of the late Schelling, Schopenhauer, and Carus could release forces that could compensate for this unfortunate development. Continuing in this train of thought Jung decidedly rejects Hegel. Hegel "set in motion the identification and inflation, practically the fusion of philosophical reasoning with the spirit. Thus he created the hubris of the rational mind which led to Nietzsche's Superman and the catastrophe in Germany."

An anthroposophical critic, Josef Hupfer, who concerned himself thoroughly with these statements by Jung, maintains that Jung did not ultimately uphold these views.[9] He sees in them, however, a sign of how little of value Jung saw in philosophical work. Hupfer rightly insists that the philosopher not only must have intuitions, but must also be capable of grasping them with his thoughts and of formulating their structure in clear concepts.

It would be convenient here to focus on the discrepancies between Steiner and Jung and assume that there is no way to build bridges between the two. But now we have to ask what each of them meant by *thinking*.

Jung was neither a philosopher nor a historian of the mind. He did not attempt any detailed study of how in the development of modern consciousness (which Steiner called the birth of the "consciousness soul"), thinking increasingly separated itself from a living connection with the world of Platonic ideas and ended up in abstract rationality. Thus, beginning with Descartes, philosophers had created an efficient tool to understand inorganic nature around them and to subdue it with the help of technology. Optimal exactness was achieved. This abstract thinking, however, was of little use in understanding life, soul, and spirit.

Jung could not approve of this absolute rationalizing of consciousness, because he saw that purely rational thinking led to a dangerous one-sidedness. Therefore he saw in this kind of thinking only *one side* of the soul's function, which would have to be compensated for by others.

In Jung's scheme of the four basic soul functions, feeling stands opposite thinking. Both these "rational" functions are complemented by two "irrational" functions: sensing and intuiting. Thus thinking is for Jung merely one of four basic functions of the soul organism. One must not conclude from this that he undervalues thinking. Rather one could say that Jung wanted to avoid an *overvaluation* of rational thinking. In his *Psychological Types*, Jung distinguishes between, on the one hand, a psychology that serves the rational needs of science and could be recognized as exact natural science, and, on the other hand, a "psychology as irrational practice," as it is called by Alice Morawitz-Cadio,[10] in which the intellect becomes the *ancilla psychologiae*, the handmaiden of psychology. "The intellect remains captive within itself as long as it cannot sacrifice its primary position and acknowledge the worthiness of other purposes. It shies away from taking the step beyond its limitation and from surrendering its universal supremacy. Everything else it declares to be just fantasy. Has there ever been anything truly great that did not start out as fantasy? By this way of thinking the intellect, having its only purpose in hard science, cuts itself off from the source of life."[11]

Aside from the fact that Steiner saw fantasy as a creative, inspiring force in human beings, he shared Jung's skepticism towards the intellect. Like Jung, he saw the need to avoid one-sided intellectualism and rationalism. He showed possible approaches to overcoming hardened, abstract thinking. What is decisive, however, is the direction that these approaches take. Steiner categorically rejected a return to precritical, irrational methods. He did not want to abandon what the great German idealistic philosophers, whom he considered his mentors, had achieved. He also admired the achievements of modern natural science in regard to the mathematical exactness of its conclusions. "We need a way of looking as exact as that of mathematics with which to penetrate into the higher processes of the outside world.... Eventually, when it is realized how, from the spirit of modern knowledge of nature, knowledge of spirit can be gained, this spiritual science will be found to be justified precisely from the standpoint of our modern knowledge of nature. It has no wish to run counter to the important and imposing results of natural science."[12]

As mentioned before, Steiner could not rest on the achievements of philosophy or science either as thinker or as scientist. What he had in mind he called "the transformations and metamorphoses of human soul life."[13] He told himself: "With the attitude of soul that we have here in the sense world, which is suitable for living and acting in that world, we could never gain entrance to the supersensible world."[14] On the one hand, Steiner trusted the soundness of "pure thinking"; on the other hand he knew that this thinking could and would have to be transformed into an organ of higher perception with the help of "metamorphoses of human soul life." (Working with Steiner's theory of knowledge, one learns that it takes perception *and* thinking to arrive at true knowledge.) Whatever is valid for natural science has its counterpart in spiritual science. In any case, as Steiner emphasized early on in his anthroposophical activity, spiritual knowledge is not attained by deductive thinking. "The power of the intellect chases away the spirit, but if the power of the intellect itself can be developed to become the faculty of Imagination, then we can approach the spirit once more."[15]

On the whole, knowledge gained by spiritual research is just as hard to describe as that which the depth psychologist has to say about certain subjects, for instance the archetypes. These resist accurate definition and clear description, just as the meaning of a symbol cannot be exactly defined. Jung has often emphasized and justified the necessity of different interpretations of his findings.[16] "Nothing is accomplished with definitions. Usually one doesn't see the inadequacy of each definition."[17] These words of Steiner's could also have been written by Jung. They show how much both men agree on this point.

In a 1919 lecture, Steiner pointed out that the forces that drive the human development have to be found in the unconscious, or rather the subconscious. "Basically our language today is made to express the life of the soul in the outer sense world. This language makes it hard for us to adequately describe things that don't belong to the sense world but to the supersensible realm." The following sentence of Steiner's reminds us of Jung's method of amplification, his way of "augmenting" the material brought up by the patient from his unconscious with similar elements, perhaps from the realms of mythology, fairy tales, or religion, in order to arrive at the meaning. Steiner says: "Oftentimes one has to resort to comparisons...of one life situation with another one, so that the one may throw light on the other. When such comparisons are made, one has to understand that only a flexible thinking that will not press the definition and the exact words can arrive at a correct understanding of the matter described."[18]

For the same reason, Steiner demanded in another lecture that a multidimensional reality should be taken seriously. Even though it may be more convenient to work with "mere corpses of ideas," one has to learn to think "in accord with reality." "For reality doesn't exist in templates, reality lives in constant metamorphosis.... Our way to see the world will have to arrive at the essence of things once again. One only can see the essence of things by seeing the world in a spiritual way."[19] Steiner was also thinking here of the artistic sensibility.

Steiner, whose entire work can be seen as one great pedagogical mission, was realistic enough to give, out of his intuitive knowledge of the human being, specific practical advice for developing healthy intellectual thinking in the child (see the relevant written work about Waldorf pedagogy as well as the working methods of modern Waldorf schools). One time he expressed his view of the unwholesome effect of certain habits of thought in these words: "Thus we are able to say that tubercular and bacillary diseases come from a similar source as the materialism which has taken hold of human minds."[20]

These examples, which could easily be rounded out by others, may suffice to show that the misunderstanding between analytic psychology and Anthroposophy regarding thinking does not need to exist. It is only that Steiner and Jung dealt with the problem from different points of view.

Jolande Jacobi, who writes about the double vision of modern analytic psychology and compares Jung with the masters of "paradoxical thinking," Pascal and Kierkegaard, means by this term a way of thought that allows for abstract thinking as well as living experience. It is remarkable that Jung studied Goethe extensively but was not touched, so it seems, by the latter's theory of knowledge. Steiner was the first who actually formulated Goethe's theory of knowledge. Yet it is Goethe's view that could bridge the gap between Jung and Steiner on this question. As Steiner was able to show as a result of his decades of study, Goethe had a deep antipathy for abstract thinking and "thinking about thinking."[21] Jung shared this antipathy. He also refused to search for the spirit in "another world." Without saying it or defining it philosophically, he knew of the *unus mundus* from personal experience. "Goethe sought the spirit so much in the things of this world that he had to reject the idea of finding it in some other world. Even the notion that one had to leave this world in order to find the spirit, seemed to him utterly devoid of spirit."[22] With this Goethe called forth the opposition of his contemporary scientists, and he was not the only one. His way of thinking lead him to practice "recognition through observation" (*anschauende Urteilskraft*), which led him to understand the natural phenomena as symptoms that point to the underlying

Urphänomen or archetypal phenomenon. There was no need for him to look for it "beyond" the appearances. This method of observation was possible because Goethe's gaze was not directed at mere details, but the world presented itself to him as a harmonious whole, expressing the spiritual in nature.

At this point one is reminded of the remarkable conversation that took place between Goethe and Schiller in July 1794, as they were leaving a lecture at the Jenaer Naturforschende Gesellschaft (Society for Nature Studies) in Jena.

They both agreed they could not accept the atomistic view that broke the whole of nature up into countless fragments that had just been presented by the lecturer, Professor Batsch. In his journals Goethe wrote, "I presented to him [Schiller] in vivid detail the metamorphosis of plants and painted before his eyes a symbolic plant with some characteristic pen strokes. He listened and took it all in with good understanding; yet, when I was finished he shook his head and said to me: 'This is not an experience; it is an idea.' I was puzzled and a little annoyed, because the line that divided us was thus clearly drawn. I did pull myself together, though, and said: 'It pleases me very much that I have ideas without knowing it, and that I can even see them with my own eyes.' ...If Schiller took for an idea what I called an experience, then something must exist that connects these two and relates to them both."

This episode, which has since become part of philosophical history, contains something of an archetypal nature. It shows the polarity of two views; each has validity for one of the partners in the conversation. Steiner writes in his *Autobiography*, describing his student years in Vienna in the early 1880s, when he himself had to live with these problems: "[Goethe] *saw* the whole *spiritually*, just as he saw its details physically. And there was no fundamental difference between the spiritual and the physical observation—only a transition from the one to the other."[23]

In order to find the spiritual, the whole, a metamorphosis of the cognitive forces is needed. Goethe speaks of "spiritual eyes" and "spiritual ears" that allow "perceptive thinking." In other words, for Goethe thinking does not mean manipulating abstract concepts that, in their logical clarity, are effectively dead and incapable of further development. One can sense from Goethe's "metamorphosis of plants" that he practiced a kind of thinking that was flexible enough to let him, for instance in botany, follow and visualize inwardly the metamorphosis of the leaf in a growing plant. This thinking does not in itself stand in opposition to scientific knowledge. Rather it can be seen as a further development of the thinking that mechanistic science has so successfully employed to explore inorganic nature, but which is insufficient for the understanding of living things and of the soul. It has only limited application. To this point, which should be of interest both to the spiritual researcher and the psychologist, Steiner says: "The methods of cognition that are rightfully used in natural science cannot suffice when we want truly to understand the realms of life and of the soul; we only have the choice to either stand still and remain in the inorganic realm, admitting that life and the soul cannot be understood at all, or to turn to different ways of cognition than those that can be employed only to understand the purely physical or chemical."[24]

Within the framework of the same lecture cycle in which he introduced Goethe as "the father of spiritual investigation," Steiner added, "whoever has a rigid way of thinking and is only capable of forming sharply contoured concepts will form a clear picture of a green leaf, for instance, or a flower, but he cannot move from one concept to the other in his thoughts. When he does this, nature falls apart for him into unconnected details. Because his concepts don't have inner mobility, he is not able to penetrate into the inner mobility of nature. When you consider this, you can try to enter into Goethe's soul and come to the conclusion that, for him, cognition is altogether different from that of many others. Whereas for many cognition means the assembling of concepts that they have formed separately, for Goethe cognition means submersion into the world of archetypes, observing there what grows and comes into being, continually changing and reforming itself.... Goethe brings into inner motion what otherwise would be merely thinking."[25]

Steiner developed his understanding of Goethe's worldview well before his anthroposophical period. He laid the foundation for it when he wrote the introductions to Goethe's scientific writings in *Grundlinien einer Erkenntnistheorie der Goetheschen Weltanschauung* ("Outline of a Theory of Knowledge in Goethe's Worldview," 1886) and in *"Goethes Weltanschauung"* ("Goethe's Worldview," 1897). In *Goethe Studien* of 1900, Steiner summarizes the results of his investigations. He once more makes clear "the merging of observation and thinking" in the cognitive process. Objective outer perception and subjective inner thought life are not separated by an abyss. The truth appears *within* the human mind as it approaches the world *observing* as well as *thinking*. For "man cannot ask for any other knowledge than the one he brings forth of himself. Whoever looks 'behind the things' for their real meaning has not made it clear to himself that any quest for meaning in the world stems only from man's need to penetrate with his thoughts what he perceives. The phenomena speak to us, and our inner being speaks when we observe the phenomena."[26]

As far as Jung is concerned, we have seen that he claimed, on the one hand, to proceed strictly empirically, according to the rules of natural science and that, on the other hand, he had found to his amazement that his findings and the new tasks he set for himself had led him far beyond the usual limits of scientific investigation. Steiner's descriptions of Goethe's view of nature can throw light on Jung's dilemma. From reading *The Theory of Knowledge Implicit in Goethe's Worldview* one can conclude that it is possible to adopt an attitude towards cognition that allows the empiricist to remain what he is and yet lets him go beyond the old boundaries without having to fear that he may have stepped beyond reality.

This was precisely Jung's problem, to which he denied himself the solution. He claimed to be "no philosopher," and he also was held back by his Kantian prejudices. Like Goethe, Jung did not need a formal theory of knowledge; he was content with a living observation of the phenomena that the daily contact with his patients as well as the steady communication with his own unconscious provided for him. Through all this Jung, again much like Goethe, developed a thinking that forced open the rational straitjacket and shed the hulls of abstract concepts. As he himself confessed, he was intent on "reducing abstractions to their empirical content, to be reasonably sure that I knew what I was talking about." Since, the psychologist confessed, he didn't know "what spirit itself" was, he concerned himself with life as a "criterion of the truth of spirit." For Jung, "life" is not something abstract to be defined, but something concrete that can be characterized. When Jung defines something, he makes a concession to the natural sciences, which he has already left behind in many important ways. It is much more compatible with his style to point to the phenomena as part of the whole, for instance when it comes to describing dream sequences, and to interpret them cautiously. In this process it is not relevant for the patient whether the therapist has any theoretical knowledge beforehand. Anything that is rationally knowable is of little use to the soul process, which is gradually evolving according to its own inherent rhythms and laws.

This is the reason for Jung's ambiguous way of expressing himself. He could not tolerate rigid concepts, since he was dealing with the unique laws of the unconscious. "Clear definitions are useful only in fact-finding, but not in the interpretation," Jung said. This statement is in essence a prescription for the method and *modus operandi* of the analytic psychologist. Again and again the analytic psychologist needs to practice flexibility, insight, and visionary thinking. Goethe has said of these qualities: "If we can perceive the eternal workings of nature, we become worthy of spiritual participation in her productions." Like Kant, he saw in this activity an adventure of the mind that made him search, at first unconsciously and instinctively, for the typical, the archetypal in nature. It finally enabled him to describe living nature in adequate terms.[27] This sentence could well have been written by someone who had occupied himself with modern psychology of the unconscious and was acquainted with the archetypes.

The similarity between Jung's and Goethe's mental attitudes is often astounding. Steiner gave a description of Goethe's singular mental constitution that could to a degree also apply to Jung: "It was possible for Goethe to bring his thinking, his emotions, and his entire soul into such motion that he would not only observe outer things and arrive at normal, intelligent conclusions about natural laws, but could at the same time observe the inner life of the natural phenomena and their metamorphoses."[28] This characteristic describes a natural gift that allowed the poet-scientist such a mobility of soul. It was an instinctual gift insofar as it was not developed by a path of schooling in Steiner's sense. The same holds true for Jung, when appropriately adjusted to the frame of mind of the psychologist. Goethe himself called it an "unconscious drive" in his essay about "seeing discernment" (*anschauende Urteilskraft*). It enabled him to immerse himself in nature and to experience how "ever-changing nature, ever proceeding from metamorphosis to metamorphosis, can be followed by an inwardly active soul." This flexibility of soul goes hand in hand with a flexibility of thinking and an ability to conceptualize that goes beyond those concepts that apply only to inorganic nature.

If we stay for a moment longer with this juxtaposition of Jung and Goethe, we have to add a word about the psychological types or at least attitudinal types. Steiner says: "Goethe was by his special constitution attuned to nature. Because of this strong bias he did not use his gift for the observation of the life of the soul. One can, however, apply Goethe's way of seeing the world to the life of the soul itself."[28] No doubt Steiner's remark was aimed at something different. Understood psychologically, it can be taken as a hint that Goethe's attitudinal type was clearly the extravert. The following remark of Jung's appears to prove the point: "I have sufficient reason to believe that Goethe belongs to the extraverted type rather than to the introverted one."[29]

Here I will pick up once more the train of thought that brought us to the psychological peculiarity that showed itself in Goethe as the ability to submerge himself in nature and to see the archetypes at work there. It enabled Jung to discover the archetypes in the depth of the soul. Whoever comes from Anthroposophy to Jung and misses a thorough clarification of his theory of knowledge is in the same situation the young Steiner found himself in when he became acquainted with Goethe's scientific writings. He felt the need to design a theory of knowledge for Goethe's work that had previously been missing. The anthroposophical or philosophical reader of Jung's works could also see a severe flaw in this lack of a theory of knowledge. Steiner remarked on the "insufficient methods of research" in his lectures of 1919. It is quite interesting to see that Steiner was extremely tolerant towards Goethe in this respect. In no way did he denounce Goethe's aversion to "thinking about thinking." He respected Goethe's reservation, even though he himself, in his theory of knowledge, considered "thinking about thinking" to be one of the basic requirements in overcoming abstract conceptual thinking. That is why Steiner, in *Intuitive Thinking as a Spiritual Path*, declared this form of thinking as "the absolute last as well as the first need" of any philosophical endeavor. Steiner's respect for Goethe's aversion arose when he realized that intense occupation with thinking would only have taken away from "those things that were Goethe's greatest strengths for his worldview."

According to Steiner, all criticism should cease here, "since one can get quite a deep insight into the configuration of Goethe's spirit." The *thinker* must not adopt Goethe's attitude, since he has to develop the ability to get hold of his own thoughts and transform them first into "sense-free thinking" and finally into organs of perception for the spiritual. Goethe would have cut himself off from his own wellsprings that enabled his soul to "go forth in its own instinctual way." The amiable discussion with Schiller illustrates once again that Goethe had to remain the "seer," Schiller the "thinker," in order for each of them to cultivate his special way of knowing. This is why in Schiller philosophical thought has more weight, while Goethe's work is more visual.

Jung's life and work can only be properly evaluated when it is understood, as he himself expressed it, "as the self-realization of the unconscious." He showed a new way into the world of imagination. It should be possible to extend Steiner's respect for Goethe to Jung as well, because here too "pale thinking or forced learning is transformed into imagination, into seeing in pictures." In both cases spirit is revealed, if not illuminated, by theoretical knowledge. In each case a natural scientist is at work. Both the therapist and the spiritual researcher did their work claiming to be scientists. It has been stated repeatedly that this claim was justified for Steiner.[30]

To sum up, one could say: For both scientists *experience* was the foundation of their work. Both men looked at their work *critically*, either by accounting for their method or by testing their hypotheses against their practical results. (The fact that Jung did not perfect a theory of knowledge to the extent that Steiner did for his own as well as for Goethe's work has been stated previously.) Both Steiner and Jung have described their subjective experiences in *objective, systematic terms.* They made an effort to offer their results in a language appropriate to the special character of their work. Neither left any doubt about the *provisional* and *unfinished* character of their work. For this reason both Steiner and Jung emphatically distanced themselves from any dogmatic interpretation of their insights. Their teachings were not to be taken on authority; Steiner and Jung encouraged *personal experience.* For this reason the path of education is of decisive importance for Steiner. For Jung, the physician, the activation of conscious and unconscious healing forces in the patient has more weight than a spiritual-scientific path.

In order to illuminate the scientific validity of Steiner's path and while showing how far Steiner has gone past both Jung's and Goethe's positions, we have to go a step further and explore the path that leads from natural science to spiritual science.

8

FORMS OF CONSCIOUSNESS

Multiple Dimensions of Consciousness

BOTH STEINER AND JUNG HAVE ENRICHED our knowledge of human consciousness to a high degree. Their contributions must be called pioneering, although both have had predecessors, especially among philosophers. Long before Freud and Breuer penetrated into the depth of the psyche and were able to make the concept of the unconscious the basis of their practical research, the notion existed that the human psyche must be far greater than the reach of normal consciousness would indicate. Freud was able to uncover the depth of the personal unconscious. To Jung we owe the discovery of the transpersonal, collective unconscious, even though there was earlier speculation about the subject.[1]

Unlike Jung, Steiner did not have to rely on esoteric Eastern literature to know about several possible levels of consciousness. As we know from his biography, he occupied himself from his early youth with the search for knowledge and the problem of consciousness. This took the form of practical experience as well as philosophical and epistemological pursuits. He took his starting point from Goethe, and organized Goethe's views into a theory of knowledge that remained the basis for his own research for the rest of his life.[2] Nevertheless, the multidimensional character of human consciousness only became clear to him after intensive research. It revealed itself to him to such a high degree that he was able to lead others in a gradual change of consciousness. He prepared a path of schooling that leads from everyday consciousness to stages of higher knowledge.

Starting from his own inner experiences, Steiner paid careful attention to the way other thinkers dealt with the problem of consciousness, either in theory or speculation. This is why Steiner returns time and again to the theories of his contemporaries, such as Wundt, Fechner, and Franz Brentano, and to Eduard von Hartmann's "philosophy of the unconscious." He does this more frequently and more thoroughly than he analyzes the psychoanalysis of Freud and Jung. This is why von Hartmann's *philosophical* concept of the unconscious receives more attention than Jung's *psychological* concept, a fact that makes it harder to compare Jung and Steiner.

Steiner's sole concern was to develop Anthroposophy, "a path of knowledge to guide the spiritual in the human being to the spiritual in the universe.... For a right development of the life of the human soul, it is essential for man to become fully conscious of working actively out of spiritual sources in his being. Nonrecognition of this impulse of the spirit working in the inner life of man is the greatest hindrance to the attainment of an insight into the spiritual world. For to consider our own being as a mere part of the order of nature is in reality to divert the soul's attention from our own being. Nor can we penetrate into the spiritual world unless we first take hold of the spirit, where it is immediately given to us, namely, in clear and open-minded self-observation. Self-observation is the first beginning in the observation of the spirit. It can indeed be the right beginning, for if it is true man cannot possibly stop short at it, but is bound to progress to the further spiritual content of the world."[3]

Here Steiner sets out an important aspect of the problem of consciousness. He demands that we expand what is normally called our waking consciousness and move into a "higher" condition. Of course, Steiner does not stop at this but develops a method of research and reveals the results that can be obtained with its help. He himself attained these higher stages of consciousness. A small group of his pupils attained them to a certain degree.

What stages of consciousness, then, exist? Steiner gave many answers to this question, which are scattered throughout his work. We have chosen here the one source that gives the clearest general classification.[4] Further answers are possible depending on the standpoint from which the question is asked.

We all know the everyday *waking consciousness* in which all people find themselves, although the degree of wakefulness can differ according to one's personal makeup. We spend the greatest part of our life within this consciousness; we are awake and aware of our ego, we perceive, think, plan, and are active.

Dream consciousness is known to be distinct from waking consciousness. Here we have to do with images that the dreamer receives passively. They only rarely remind us of our waking consciousness; they are remote from "real" experiences and often have a darkly symbolic character. (We disregard here dreams that are triggered by bodily functions.)

In addition to these, Steiner has identified one that he called—borrowing a term from Goethe—*imaginative consciousness*. It is different in character from the waking condition as well as from the dream. It is open to certain perceptions that are typically quite rich and differentiated, as we will show later. These perceptions do not come from the sense world, however. The sense organs are quite inactive in the *imaginative consciousness*. Accordingly, what is perceived in this state is of a super-sensible nature. The metaphor "higher" is appropriate here because the *imaginative consciousness* is clearer and reaches farther than ordinary consciousness. A region "higher" than the one ordinarily seen reveals itself to the *imaginative consciousness*. This is the dimension of reality that Steiner has called the *spiritual world*. It was very important for him to distinguish his method of research from those practices that mingled sense perceptions and supernatural phenomena in a mediumistic way or in the form of hallucinations. True anthroposophical research is done entirely free of the bodily senses. The soul forces that make this work possible have to be activated first, however. Steiner has given the proper instructions for this. At one point he formulated what he had in mind and how he distinguished his method from others:

"By Anthroposophy I mean the inquiry into the spiritual world that avoids the one-sidedness of mere nature study as well as that of ordinary mysticism. In order to be able to penetrate into the spiritual world in this manner, one has to first develop the necessary capacities in one's soul. These capacities are not yet active in our ordinary consciousness and are not used in conventional nature study."[5] We will show that this statement does not constitute a rejection of natural science, whose value Steiner acknowledged in his philosophical as well as in his anthroposophical writings. But Anthroposophy cannot stop short at natural science. Steiner sees his work as its continuation. "To be able to accomplish for the spiritual world what natural science has accomplished for the sense world, spiritual science has to develop different cognitive skills than those required for natural science." The skills required for the development of imaginative consciousness lie "absolutely in the line of development of the ordinary human psyche today." Steiner continues: "To be able to penetrate into the spiritual world man has to develop his soul capacities with the help of spirit-soul exercises beyond the stage to which they develop naturally by themselves."[6]

There is a distinct difference between imaginative consciousness and dream consciousness. The dream lies *below* ordinary waking consciousness in lucidity, even though it is often possible to recall it quite clearly after awakening. Steiner emphatically talks of "provinces of the soul" that lie "underneath" the normal consciousness. These are not accessible to the voluntary influence of the ego, so they are outside our consciousness.

Jung would say that here we are dealing with the realm of the *unconscious*, which is spread out beneath the so-called ego-complex as the personal as well as the collective unconscious. Steiner also uses the term "unconscious" several times, but always reluctantly and with reservations. "It is actually not correct to speak of the unconscious. One should say *superconscious* and *subconscious*."[7] Steiner justifies this statement by pointing out that the term *unconscious* merely has reference to ordinary consciousness. In this sense he uses it frequently, always with the nuance of *subconscious*, if not as a synonym for this term. Thus in Steiner we find neither a consistent concept of the unconscious as such nor a full congruence with the term *unconscious* as Jung employs it.

It has been frequently pointed out that "unconscious" is a flawed concept. "Both meaning and content are too negative and too confining. It does not allow for the concept of 'growth' that is emerging in our time."[8] Yet it is a key term in depth psychology that has taken shape, evolved, and transformed itself during its history. For Jung, the unconscious is simply the unknown that escapes empirical exploration, or at least tries to do so: "Theoretically, no limits can be set to the field of consciousness, since it is capable of indefinite extension. Empirically, however, it always finds its limit when it comes up against the *unknown*. This consists of everything we do not know, which, therefore is not related to the ego as the center of the field of consciousness. The unknown falls into two groups of objects: those which are outside and can be experienced by the senses, and those which are inside and are experienced immediately. The former group comprises the unknown in the outer world; the second the unknown of the inner world. We call this latter territory the *unconscious*."[9]

The profusion of descriptions Jung has lavished on the personal as well as the collective unconscious undeniably makes it hard to find a satisfying definition. This is due first of all to the peculiar character of the unconscious itself. In some ways it manifests and "creates" itself; in others it is "open to exploration." On the one hand, it seems to call for a definition that has to do with the past of the individual as well as with the collective soul life of humankind. Then again, it has aspects that can be formulated in a final theory. The unfathomable nature of the unconscious can be threatening, but it is also the matrix, the ground, of all human creativity. One can interject here that many important aspects of what Jung calls the unconscious are identical with what Steiner describes as the spiritual world. One certainly could say with Steiner: the spiritual world, namely, everything that requires imaginative consciousness and organs of supersensible cognition, is "unconscious" for ordinary awareness. This remains a fact as long as human beings are not yet in the position to incorporate the "unconscious" part of reality in their field of vision. Merely stating that something is either unconscious or part of a spiritual world does not make much sense. That is why Steiner's interest lies in transforming the soul forces needed to observe and explore the physical world into those that can also grasp the spiritual world. "Before one can comprehend the true reality of the world one has to create a soul condition that can relate to the supersensible.... Only the transformed consciousness can see into the world where the human lives as a supersensible being, a being untouched by the decay of the physical organism." While Steiner penetrates into the "unconscious world" with the help of imaginative consciousness, Jung chooses a different, more indirect way. He allows the "creations of the unconscious" to speak to him and compares them by means of so-called amplification with similarly motivated phenomena of religious and spiritual history.

At first sight it must appear that Jung's indirect approach would be a rationalistic, speculative undertaking, since direct insight into supersensible reality is not possible without the help of imaginative consciousness. But appearances are often deceptive. It is true that Steiner has described the requirements and the path that lead into the supersensible world. However, it cannot be denied that analytic psychology is able to touch empirically upon unconscious facts that slumber in the depth of the psyche. This has nothing to do with speculation and theorizing. It is *true individual experience.* The analytical process has proven this many times over. It is this experience of confronting heretofore unconscious factors in one's psyche that makes analysis so valuable. Psychological knowledge alone is neither more nor less valuable than any intellectual knowledge. The experience during analysis comprises much more than just what "dawns upon you," or what frightens you when you become aware of things you have repressed, such as your "shadow." Often there is a component of destiny—coincidences, hindrances, and solutions that occur during the analytical process. This shows clearly that there is a prevailing wisdom in your life that is beyond anything that rational thinking could ever devise. Your unconscious shows itself to be far cleverer and wiser than your rational mind. These experiences occurred a thousand times over both to Jung and his patients.

These facts in no way contradict many of Steiner's statements. At this point it is not the observed reality that differs, but the terminology and the thought pattern underlying the terms ("unconscious," "subconscious," "superconscious"). Jung has reservations about the terms "subconscious" and "superconscious" that are similar to those that Steiner has about "unconscious."

Yet it is remarkable that Jung thought it possible that "our ego-consciousness could be enclosed, like a smaller circle in a larger one, by a larger, complete consciousness." Still, he is unabashedly skeptical about the possibility of a "higher consciousness." He asks: "How can anybody know whether the unconscious finds itself *below and not above* ordinary consciousness?" Jung objects here, as so often, against the prejudices of a shallow psychology of consciousness (*Bewusstseinspsychologie*) that is trying to deduce the unconscious from the conscious state and judge the former solely by the standards of the latter. Needless to say, Steiner cannot be accused of such an attitude. He not only speaks of higher worlds but describes them in detail, and shows the way to know them. He also on occasion has used the metaphor "the depth." In addition, Steiner knows not only the ego of the waking consciousness, but also the unconscious "higher Ego," the "other Self," that can become conscious under special circumstances.

What does Jung have to say about the question of a "higher consciousness"? "Even if the possibility of a higher consciousness were needed to explain certain psychic facts, it would still remain a mere hypothesis, since it would far exceed the power of reason to prove the existence of a consciousness other than the one we know. It is always possible that what lies in the darkness beyond our consciousness is totally different from anything the most daring speculation could imagine."[10] Such an answer is disappointing, particularly when Jung writes at the conclusion of this article: "I don't know at all how we could ever prove the existence of a higher, or even a further, consciousness than the ego-consciousness we possess. But if there were such a thing it would interfere painfully with the ego-consciousness." Jung just barely considers a "further," but not a "higher" consciousness.

From Jung's point of view, such statements are entirely justified. He bases his thinking and his soul research on the assumption that consciousness is unalterable. This is in stark contrast to Steiner's spiritual science. Later we will have to speak about the *individuation process*, which can be seen as an equivalent to *the path of initiation*. We do not want to speculate here about the parallels between the two. In regard to the objection that a "higher consciousness" is impossible, one can only say that this assertion is only tenable as long as one does not have a clear picture of what imaginative consciousness is and how it can be obtained. In analytic psychology, there are different possibilities for inducing and accompanying the individuation process, but there is no path of schooling equivalent to Steiner's. This statement can best be proven by Steiner's descriptions. Jung's claims that "the most daring speculation" could not imagine transconscious things or that it "far exceeds the power of reason" to do so presents no serious challenge to Steiner's imaginative consciousness: Steiner's recognition of a higher reality is not based on thinking alone or on the exacting methods used by natural science to explore the sense world.

Philosophical thinking arrives at abstract concepts that are not yet the spirit or the spiritual world as such. The natural scientist knows the outside of reality, the mystic its inner side. Anthroposophists do not deny the dimension that is accessible to the mystic, but they need more clarity, more exactness. The same standards as those used by the thinker and the natural scientist have to be applied to spiritual science in order to assure the reliability of the results. As Steiner says in *Philosophy and Anthroposophy*, "For Anthroposophy, the process of cognition becomes a true inner experience that leads beyond the everyday consciousness. Natural science's logical judgment and its conclusions about the outer material reality are based on the everyday consciousness. Mysticism, on the other hand, is a deepened inner life which nevertheless remains within the confines of everyday consciousness." This is why Steiner starts with the ego and with thinking, but devises exercises suitable for enhancing and expanding consciousness without interfering with the integrity of the ego. Indeed it is the ego itself that enters the cognitive path. "With the help of the expanded consciousness brought about by spiritual schooling, the 'I' enters the spiritual world. The schizophrenic processes of separation, dissolution, and hardening remain in the sphere of the physical body." This is the assessment of the anthroposophical physician Rudolf Treichler.[11]

Jung's concept of the unconscious, as far as one can speak of a clearly defined concept at all, is understandable from his point of view as a scientist. He had "only indirect proofs that there is a mental sphere which is subliminal." The statement that a creation of the psyche (for instance a dream) has been formed unconsciously is not a hypothesis; it is a concrete fact. Such a product does not originate in a conscious decision; it has not been planned by an ego that is awake; it is simply unconscious. In accordance with his unique relationship to reality, Jung avoided theorizing about the unconscious revelations of the psyche. He did not want to press them into a rational framework, though he admitted that there definitely was an unconscious. Even though it is the job of the depth psychologist to make certain things conscious and to shed light on the hidden workings of the psyche, Jung never felt the need to bring his findings about the unconscious into any systematic order. We must remember that any attempt to express experiences of the unconscious or, for that matter, of the supersensible world, in the form of ideas is of necessity inadequate. That which is not accessible to direct experience has to be described in the form of picture language or of a story.

Anything described in this way must not be confused, however, with the underlying reality (that which is "at work" in the unconscious). The archetypal picture can be made conscious, but not the archetype itself. This remains in the unconscious, and its existence remains hypothetical, according to Jung. Something similar can be said about the relationship between reflective thinking and spiritual reality in Anthroposophy. Spiritual reality can be described in thought form, but it cannot be explored with thinking alone, as long as the thinker has not acquired imaginative consciousness. This comment of Steiner's should be helpful in dismantling Jung's skepticism in regard to the possibility of a "higher consciousness." Complete assurance, however, is attained only on the path of schooling itself—in other words, through personal experience.

Steiner was very keen on identifying what is unconscious, wherever it occurs, in order to differentiate it from what he intended to be the path of spiritual science. He wanted to avoid having "remnants of an archaic consciousness," or rather, fragments of archaic pictures, rise up in the psyche without the possibility of being understood. These can have chaotic effects on the psyche. Nobody could better understand this inundation of the psyche with unconscious contents than Jung, the experienced psychiatrist. He knew it well from his psychotic patients, and sometimes called it "inflation." The danger also exists that certain symbols from the unconscious cause what is known in the field of occultism as "occult imprisonment."[12] If the reality behind the symbol is not understood, such symbols can influence and alter the psychic structure of a person. The overwhelming numinosity of religious, occult, and even political signs and symbols can have great power while circumventing the conscious mind. Because, according to Steiner, the present time is right for the emergence of the "consciousness soul," he questions everything that is based on earlier spiritual practices. Therefore he is very cautious with the use of symbols. In his spiritual science, the only starting point is clear consciousness. All content has to be understood. Everything else is a backsliding into magic, into an obsolete form of consciousness that needs to be overcome. On this point Jung and Steiner are basically in agreement.

Higher Levels of Consciousness

Anyone who becomes intimately acquainted with Eastern spirituality and goes beyond the practice of yoga postures and breathing exercises is once again confronted with the problem of consciousness. There is more than one imaginative consciousness; in fact, the "higher" levels of consciousness are richly differentiated. The pertinent literature describes a whole system of centers of consciousness, which it is the task of the student of Eastern esoteric disciplines to activate. As long as Western readers do not understand the essence of this higher consciousness, they feel themselves to be in an illusionary, magical land when reading Asian religious texts or descriptions of the Buddha's enlightenment. The Eastern mentality remains foreign to them.

There is another way of acquiring higher levels of awareness than to follow Eastern practices. This is the way of meditation. While the philosopher's way of thinking happens on the level of day consciousness, the meditative process opens up the possibility of attaining higher levels. In Indian yoga we find the classical description of these possibilities. If one becomes acquainted with anthroposophical exercises, one realizes that Westerners do not need to make the detour through ancient Eastern esotericism in order to learn of these things. We have seen that Steiner does not take his starting point from Eastern traditions, but primarily from Goethe. The expression "imaginative consciousness" also points in this direction. Goethe applied the idea of metamorphosis in his observations of plant and animal forms. He was thereby able to "see" the spiritual archetype in his mind's eye along with the physical phenomenon. Steiner has applied Goethe's way of thinking to his own view of soul life. Here we also find metamorphoses. They are metamorphoses of awareness. This is not a fictitious analogy but concrete fact, even though the facts can only be verified when the appropriate stage of consciousness is already present or has been achieved by training. As long as this is not possible, one has to be content with a sort of conceptual picture. The underlying supersensible fact can only be described as an abstract concept. This concept seeks to express supersensible reality in a language that is really only suited to describe observable facts and the abstract thinking process.

What are we dealing with here? We could compare it with the moment of awakening. Just as in the morning a man wakes up out of his sleeping and dreaming state and gains the necessary awareness to allow his ego to become active, to think, to plan and carry out his daily tasks, imaginative consciousness is the result of an awakening. Waking consciousness is enhanced. This must not be confused, however, with an enhanced sensory awareness. The view that is now open to him is of a supersensible nature.

Steiner principally distinguishes three stages of higher consciousness:

IMAGINATION, a sort of picture-consciousness.

INSPIRATION, in which the spiritual world manifests in a quasi-audible form.

INTUITION, which may be described as an equivalent of the sense of touch in the spiritual world. Here the exchange is more intimate than in imaginative and inspirational consciousness.

These basic descriptions need further clarification.

Steiner speaks of an imaginative consciousness whereby the soul is filled with pictures that have a relationship to a supersensible reality but are not yet that reality itself. It is a weaving and creating of pictures that have to do with the thoughts the person is thinking, but not with mere hunches or fantasies. One is definitely in touch with a higher reality. "Whoever forms images of which the corresponding sensory objects do not actually exist lives in fantasy," said Steiner.[13]

When the seeker arrives at a picturelike perception that does not resemble a physical object, it has to be an object of a different nature. To avoid potential misunderstanding, Steiner has differentiated this first (imaginative) stage of cognition in a twofold way. The object of this imagination must not be confused with images that arise in a mentally disturbed person. That is why he wants to differentiate imagination from the visionary experience. For Steiner, a vision is similar to a hallucination; in both cases, the pictures produced arise from the physical organization. By contrast, imaginative consciousness is by its very nature a supersensible experience independent of the physical body. "We have to be certain to distinguish everything that happens in an unconscious way, in the form of visions and the like, from what spiritual science calls *imaginative consciousness*. This is characterized by the fact that one is fully present and awake while seeing the weaving pictures. One is able to think one's thoughts step by step, quite clearly. There is no chance to enter the spiritual world properly in any other way than by beginning with clear thinking, right from the start. The only difference is that our ordinary thoughts are shadowlike and dim. They all refer to outer objects or memories, while what is meant here by imagination is woven by the soul herself in the moment when it appears."[14]

On the other hand, imagination should not be confused with fantasy. By fantasy Steiner means creations that arise from the unconscious in a state of reduced awareness.

He is concerned solely with the ability to survey fully and clearly what is perceived in the imaginative state, and to see it as "objective reality."

To guarantee this, and to preclude any errors, the anthroposophical path of schooling starts with a certain discipline of thought. To begin with, one has to distinguish two different "attitudes" toward cognition in waking consciousness. There is the untrained, naïve form of consciousness in which we live our daily lives. We take in our surroundings rather indiscriminately and form our thoughts and words according to what happens to us. Distinguished from this is a disciplined form of thinking in which the objects of our thoughts are not outer impressions or memories, but in which thinking itself becomes the object. Already in his early work *Intuitive Thinking as a Spiritual Path: A Philosophy of Freedom*, Steiner writes: "The one who observes his or her own thinking lives, while doing it, directly within a fully self-contained spiritual activity. Yes, one can say that if one wants to experience spirit in the form in which it presents itself to the human being firsthand, one can do it by this kind of thinking." With this kind of disciplined thinking, the human being participates in the life of the spiritual world. Here we have the starting point that leads to higher stages of consciousness. Wherever Steiner describes the method of research he has developed, he demands clear thinking and mathematical exactness.

Such exactness, which needs to be constantly cultivated and tested, is also the prerequisite for the next higher stage of consciousness. Steiner called this stage *inspiration*. Here the spiritual world begins to "sound," as it were. For this stage another metamorphosis of the soul life is required. While *imagination* is achieved by the fusion of thinking and the ability to remember (although imagination is not identical with a memory picture, it resembles one in that it has a pictorial character), *inspiration* requires an awakening and enhanced awareness of one's feeling life. Entrance into the spiritual world can never be forced.

We could compare the more or less clear presentiments or hunches and the "voice of conscience" in ordinary life with the character of the inspirational stage. The context makes it clear that inspiration cannot merely be deduced speculatively from waking consciousness. It is not the objects of the sense world that begin to "sound." The spiritual world reveals itself inspirationally. When Pythagoras spoke of the "harmony of the spheres"; when Goethe writes in *Faust*: "The sun intones, in ancient tourney with brother spheres, a rival air"; when the Revelation of John speaks of the sounding of the seven trumpets after the seven seals have been opened, they all speak out of inspirational consciousness. Of course, in each case one has to distinguish: Did the philosopher still speak out of ancient, instinctive clairvoyance? Did the poet reach into the sphere of inspirational consciousness? In which way did the seer John receive his supersensible impressions? In any case, the great documents of the history of the human mind abound in imaginative and inspirational elements. Steiner's differentiation between the various levels of consciousness is helpful here.

The third level, *intuition*, is not to be confused with the vague statement: "I have found this out intuitively." What Jung calls "intuition" is an irrational psychic function and has nothing to do with Steiner's concept. Intuition as the third stage of a higher consciousness is the result of a fusion of thinking and willing. Steiner describes this stage as being within the spiritual world rather than being the observer of it. The distance between subject and object has disappeared. We find an important parallel in ordinary life: the experience of our own "I." This is what we identify with, and it is what distinguishes us from others and from external objects.

> In the same way, in intuitive cognition one lives in all things. The perception of the ego ["I"] is the prototype of all intuitive cognition. Thus to enter into all things one must step outside oneself, one must first become "selfless" in order to become blended with the self, the I, of another being.[15]

Like *imagination and inspiration, intuition* can be viewed in different ways. For instance, one could say that intuition is a process of soul-spiritual communion in which the individual becomes one with his or her own higher being as well as with the spiritual world. This requires love, which is transformed into a cognitive force.[16] The love that is meant here corresponds to the agape of the New Testament, because it strives toward *communio* in a selfless way. No doubt we are touching here on what the apostle Paul calls the great mystery of the union with Christ (Eph. 5:32). The apostle called this "being-in-Christ" the leitmotif of the whole Christian teaching. Therefore *intuition* in Steiner's sense is of sacramental character. On another level, we encounter the same reality in its psychological aspect of uniting two opposites in

Jung's *mysterium coniunctionis*. It is no coincidence that Jung was able to work with this theme, which touches on the very deepest human mysteries, only in his very last creative period. But it is still not identical with Steiner's stage of intuitive consciousness.

If one searches Jung's work for comparative terms, one must keep in mind that unlike Steiner, he was not primarily concerned with the question of "higher consciousness." This is evident from his rejection of the terms "subconscious" and "superconscious." No doubt this is due to his stated goals. His study of the unconscious does not aim to acquire higher knowledge of the kind that Steiner as well as Sri Aurobindo considered important for the further development of humankind, and which was also the aim of ancient Eastern paths such as yoga.

It seems as if Jung was not interested in human spiritual growth, even though he always insisted on introspection and on insight into the essence of the human being. Jung does not deny the existence of different levels of awareness, just as he does not deny the possibility of the chakras as centers of consciousness. The question of consciousness expansion is not without problems when it comes to Jung's psychology. It is true that his work aims at expanding the field of consciousness, at integration of unconscious content into consciousness; all his psychoanalytical work as well as his process of individuation constitute consciousness expansion. But we must not ignore certain statements Jung made that call for critical inquiry. In one of his last letters, which deals with the future fate of humankind, he writes: "The very thought that mankind ought to make a step forward and extend and refine consciousness of the human being seems to be so difficult that nobody can understand it, or so abhorrent that nobody can take up his courage. All steps forward in the improvement of the human psyche have been paid for by blood."[17]

These words make one wonder. Should all of Jung's former statements—in which, referring to immediate experience, he acknowledged "many degrees of brightness" of consciousness, and spoke of higher and highest stages "capable of unlimited expansion"—be disregarded? Perhaps we could understand this pessimistic-sounding passage as an attempt to protect himself from a euphoric and illusory assessment of those evolutionary possibilities that he did not have any reason to doubt. He did see a task for humankind in the progressive expansion of general consciousness. This was the only way in which he could find any meaning in the world.[18] In any case, the above statement is no reason to halt our comparative study.

In fact, it is remarkable that Jung penetrated into the soul-spiritual realm to such a degree that a study such as this is called for. Jung's main scope of work—dreams and dream analysis, and the exploration of the personal and collective consciousness—led him into a realm of pictures that are themselves based on ancient, original soul pictures, the so-called "archetypes." These archetypal pictures are manifestations of the unconscious and are in essence, as far as their content is concerned, nothing else but imaginative elements. Jung himself uses this term when he describes one of his analytical practices, known as "active imagination." (We will come back to this when we compare the paths of Anthroposophy and depth psychology.) Imagination as Steiner understands it is woven of "such stuff as dreams are made on," to borrow one of Shakespeare's famous lines. Imaginative content expresses itself in dreams, in visions, and in all the products of fantasy. These are picture-creating processes. The material that Jung is working with is essentially the same as what is active in imaginative consciousness, but we must not overlook the difference between dream and imaginative consciousness. The dream is received in a state of consciousness *below* that of waking. The ego is not involved; it has no control over the dream. This is why the dream is so eminently suited to serve as the royal road to the unconscious. By means of the dream, the depth psychologist seeks to find out what the conscious individual is rejecting, either voluntarily or unconsciously.

Imagination, in Steiner's sense, is completely different, since it is a higher, seeing consciousness. Here the ego is active. The gaze of the observer is not directed toward objects that can be seen with ordinary senses in the outer world, but toward *supersensible objects.* Here it becomes clear why Steiner insisted on the difference between the subconscious and the superconscious, while Jung, who was not concerned with this cognitive aspect, could be satisfied with the term "unconscious."

One could not do justice to the dream work that is practiced in analytic psychology without explaining what is at stake here, at least in broad outline. Dream work is necessary precisely because the dream stems from an unconscious region of the soul (unlike Steiner's imaginative consciousness). The dream itself can be of great value for the individual dreamer, especially those "great dreams" that nobody could invent or construct consciously. The wisdom hidden in a dream "knows" the right time for the dream picture to occur, since the purpose is to bring the psychic economy into balance by means of compensation. It is of decisive importance that the meaning, and therefore the spiritual content, be brought to light in a conversation between the patient and the therapist. Together they take in, so to speak, the entire soul-spiritual situation; they contemplate the dream, consider, ponder, and seek a connection between the dream sequence and the patient's field of waking consciousness. Only this intimate conversation about the dream, the contemplation and imagination in dialogue form, can open up the meaning and bring conscious recognition of the dream's symbolism. It is important that the patient "gets it," that he or she understands the meaning of the dream. Remarkably, even the experienced analyst is unable to interpret his or her own dreams adequately. Jung honestly admitted his inability in this respect. The partner is essential for "it" to happen. This "it" presents itself as a quasi-"third being" into which the hidden, unconscious soul-content is transformed and made conscious.

The History of Human Consciousness

Metamorphosis of consciousness is not only a phenomenon involving the single human being. For an understanding of human history in retrospect as well as of future evolution, it is a very important element to consider. In the light of metamorphosis of consciousness, history proves to be more than just a jumble of unrelated outer events. Both cultures and historical epochs will only be seen in their true significance when we can determine the prevailing configuration of their consciousness. Often this factor is not even addressed. We come across historical writings, especially in church and religious history, whose authors quietly assume that the level of human consciousness has always been the same. This erroneous assumption is fostered, for instance, by the existentialist interpretation of the Bible. This view holds that human existence itself is all-important. Therefore the question of an evolution of consciousness does not even occur. Yet a cursory look at the findings of ethnological research should suffice to show that even in today's world there are many "unequal stages of consciousness" among people who are contemporaries. This difference may not be so clearly observable among the industrialized nations, but in those regions of the Third World where "civilized" and indigenous peoples live close together on the same continent, the dissimilarity of consciousness is obvious. (Often the utilization of modern technology is not in keeping with the consciousness of native peoples.)

Steiner was not the first to consider the problem of consciousness, especially among ancient people. Others before and after him have concerned themselves with the same question, from different perspectives. Despite this, and despite the fact that we do not have a complete account of this subject by him, we owe Steiner a great deal for interpreting history as a history of human consciousness.

We may think here of Spengler, Frobenius, Dacqué, and Jean Gebser, and of anthroposophical authors like Emil Bock, Sigismund von Gleich, Hans Erhard Lauer, and Guenther Wachsmuth. Jung's special contribution, one might say a by-product of his depth-psychological research, has been made productive by his pupil Erich Neumann.

About five thousand years of recorded history can be seen as a process of human self-realization that expresses itself in a growth of awareness. For Steiner's Anthroposophy, one would have to add that his accounts cover a far wider field. Sometimes they sound rather hypothetical. He speaks, for instance, of many ancient cultures on the earthly plane for which there is no documentation, as well as of extraterrestrial cosmic history.[19]

We can limit ourselves here to the statement that from the anthroposophical viewpoint, human development can be seen as a process of incarnation. To begin with, the individual is completely embedded in greater collective connections. People do not yet experience themselves as free, self-reliant individuals. Thus early humanity lived in a dream consciousness. Where today we have clear, concise concepts, people formerly lived in mythical pictures. The path from myth to *logos* stretched over many centuries. There are, however, indications for the appearance of an independent thought life. In his *Riddles of Philosophy*, Steiner uncovers these connections. "One will gradually come to recognize," he said, "that in the course of the evolution of mankind a transformation of the human organization has taken place. There was a time when the subtle organs of human nature, which make possible the development of an independent thought life, had not yet been formed. In this time man had, instead, organs that represented for him what he experienced in the world of pictures."[20] This dreamlike picture consciousness enabled early human beings to see into the spiritual world that surrounded them, governing their lives and actions. Theirs was not the clear, rational mind we now possess, but a much dimmer consciousness.

In the ancient traditions we find certain references to the former significance of the "third eye," located in the middle of the forehead, and to the eye on the crown of the head. Both signify preconscious organs of perception. The strange horns that crown Michelangelo's famous statue of Moses are characteristic of this connection.[21]

Emil Bock writes in the foreword to his impressive *Beiträge zur Geistesgeschichte der Menschheit* ("Contributions to the Spiritual History of Humankind"): "The tablet on which Clio's stylus writes is human consciousness. If we try to read and describe history as the history of human consciousness, we gain insight into the aims of the gods, as they are woven all through history and are progressively realized. The transformations of consciousness that mankind has gone through are stations of God-willed advancement. In those we may recognize the meaning of history."

Human beings awaken only gradually to an awareness of the outer world. Like an unknown continent, the world of clear consciousness arises out of the slowly subsiding twilight of the soul. Only gradually do we become aware of the "I." To the degree that this happens, the old soul capacities fade, including the ancient clairvoyance. A characteristic feature of Steiner's view of spiritual history, which Emil Bock has applied painstakingly to the Old and New Testaments, is the central position of Jesus Christ. In a moment of historical importance "when the fullness of time was come" (Gal. 4:4), the Christ-Logos incarnated in the man Jesus of Nazareth. He united himself with the whole earth. At the same time, as the "Son of Man" he is also the archetypal human, the "second Adam." For human consciousness it is of the greatest importance that only the "I am" of the Christ makes human "I"-consciousness possible. ("'I'-consciousness" for Steiner means approximately the same as the "Self" does for Jung). To connect oneself with this Christ-Self is a task that could be called the "individuation process" of humankind. (This must not be confused with the "world mission" of the church!) This "entering of Christ into the world" means that the "I" or Self will "gain complete governance over the world."

Thus, in Steiner's lectures on the Gospel of Luke, we read, "In the Luke Gospel's account of his life, Christ Jesus clearly indicates that the new element of 'I'-consciousness has entered human evolution. We must simply understand what we read. The Christ tells us that in earlier times, the spiritual world did not flow into the self-aware human 'I', but only into human physical, etheric, and astral bodies. In other words, a degree of unconsciousness was always necessary for divine-spiritual forces to flow into human beings. This state of affairs, however, was meant to change."[22]

According to Steiner, the further development of consciousness has necessarily led to a distance from the spirit, to materialism and atheism. This movement toward a human crisis, in which our consciousness still finds itself, was necessary in order for us to develop full "I" or Self-consciousness and to reach maturity. It was also necessary, however, to achieve a clear mind, whose shadow is modern humanity's one-sided intellectualism, bemoaned by Jung and Steiner alike.

In the course of the process of incarnation outlined above, the human being has just now arrived on the earth, so to speak. This era in no way marks the end of the development of human consciousness, for evolution goes on. The task is to activate the slumbering psychic possibilities in human beings. The lost spiritual world has to be gained anew. The "loss of soul capacity" (Bitter, Jung) has to be overcome. The emphasis is on the word "anew." It will not do to artificially reactivate old capacities, which would lead to pathological conditions. In fact, the so-called mentally ill are basically those who frequently have spiritual experiences, who have grandiose dreams, but who cannot orient themselves in their conscious ego. For the Anthroposophist, the only way to find a path into the spiritual world is to start with clear ego-consciousness. Steiner had dedicated himself entirely to this task. Anthroposophy seeks primarily to serve as a guide to this path.

Out of the knowledge that an intimate contact with the spiritual world provides, a wealth of practical means is available to address the problems of our time in many different areas.

Steiner urged that humankind, while gradually expanding its soul capacities, should dare to take the step from mere global consciousness to a cosmic consciousness. In a time when interplanetary travel is being contemplated, this demand takes on new meaning. Obviously Steiner meant primarily the expansion of consciousness from the sensual-physical plane into the supersensible, spiritual one. That is why he answered a question put to him once in 1919: "Can one get off the earth?" as follows: "Yes, you can do this, but it is not the same as getting off a train....To get off the earth means to enter into your innermost soul. If you really do this, and find what is there in your soul, you have gotten off the earth."[23]

Human beings had to emancipate themselves from their old soul inheritance. They had to sacrifice the seemingly inexhaustible wealth of mythical pictures in order to acquire the clear consciousness and freedom of the personal self. This is what a study of the history of consciousness reveals. The wealth of pictures and of ancient clairvoyance that was lost in the process of emancipation will have to be replaced by something else: by a forward-looking effort to understand what the future brings. Steiner put it like this: "What we need, and what Anthroposophy seeks to provide, is a renewal of the mysteries in the appropriate way for our time."[24]

As already mentioned, Jung did not leave a detailed contribution to a history of consciousness, even though his books are full of material that could be interpreted and utilized for this purpose. He focused his attention on the individuation of the single individual, which means personal maturation. Depth psychology does not directly consider the consequences of individuation for the whole of humanity. So far, there are only a few studies that have addressed this theme. One is Erich Neumann's *Origins and History of Consciousness*.[25] A comparison between Steiner and Jung on this particular aspect is therefore not entirely possible. However, there are certain passages in Jung's work that do not exclude his thinking of a further development of human consciousness.

Even Freud's motto "Where there is 'it,' there will be 'I'" is already pointing in the direction of such concepts. Jung, for example, mentioned once that "the different mental layers in a person" correspond to the "developmental history of humanity." He did not mean this primarily in the historical sense, however. For Jung, the concept of the collective unconscious is always in the foreground. Everyone participates in this as in a common heritage. Jung saw this heritage of the collective unconscious as a complete whole that cannot be cut up.

There is no real parallel between the Self in Jung's sense, which can manifest in the archetypal form of Christ, and the Christ concept in Anthroposophy. Anthroposophy sees the Christ as the *central figure* in human development. In spite of the high esteem accorded in Anthroposophy, for instance, to the Buddha or Zarathustra, the Christ figure ranks qualitatively higher in importance for the development of humankind.

It is different in analytic psychology. Here archetypal images of the Self as symbol of psychic wholeness can also appear as the Buddha or as other great spirit representatives. Here we encounter significant difficulties for the study of developmental history. A comparison of Buddha consciousness with Christ consciousness shows marked differences, even though there can be no doubt about the Buddha's unique and exalted state. In his early work, *Christianity as Mystical Fact* (1902), Steiner pointed out how the Christ's life "contains more" than the Buddha's life. "The Buddha's life ends with his transfiguration, whereas the most significant part of Christ's life begins after the Transfiguration," namely with the passion and death on the cross.[26] Christ demands loyalty not only up to the culmination of a spiritual-religious development, but "unto death." Christ does not teach withdrawal from life in order to eliminate the cause of suffering in the physical incarnation. He teaches the affirmation of life as a means of overcoming suffering. Incarnation in the Christian sense is the expression of God's love for the world: "God so loved the world that he gave his only begotten Son" (John 3:16). Forgoing further proofs, we can say briefly: "With Christ the history of human evolution has taken a great step beyond Buddha."[27]

It follows that an equal application of the principle of Self to Buddha and to Christ does not tell us anything about the history of consciousness. It is true that Wilhelm Bitter and Marie-Louise von Franz have shown that self-realization will always lead to love of one's fellow humans and thereby proceeds into the social dimension. But this does not say anything yet about an evolution of humankind. Jung's manifold communications about the process of individuation in the single person do shed light on a possible individuation process of humankind as a whole. During his last period of creativity, Jung made some observations that contemporary theologians have not yet sufficiently appreciated. He said that his "psychology of the unconscious may be considered to be a vessel" with which to receive the Christ-Logos, since he is at work in the realm above the psyche.[28] These words certainly express a concern with humankind as a whole. The Christ in the form of the Holy Spirit, as he announced in the Gospel of John, points way beyond the historical Jesus. There is an *incarnatio continua* that happens "where and when God wills it." This is the event of which Wilhelm Bitter speaks when he writes about a "continuing permeation of the world by the pneumatic Christ." In this highly significant recognition, Jung and Steiner are in agreement.

For Steiner, it is the continuously creative, self-renewing power of Christ, the "Christ impulse," or the "Christ principle," that is effective once more in our time.

Anthroposophy has been created in order to prepare humankind for the "Christ event of the twentieth century." The cosmic Christ can be experienced in the depth of every person's soul independently of

Christian religious documents. For "we find the Christ, the guide in us, through self-knowledge. We can always find the Christ in this way because, since his life on earth, he is always present in us. Second, when we apply the knowledge gained without historical documents to these documents, we begin to understand their true nature. They are the historical expression of something that has revealed itself in the depths of the soul."[29]

Seen in this way, Christianity is not at an end, as one might expect when looking at the situation of traditional churches everywhere. On the contrary, it stands at the threshold of a promising beginning that points into a future as yet undreamed of.

Considering the transformation of consciousness that is occurring in our time, one would have to say: The consciousness that has evolved during the era of science and technology, which has proven itself well in conquering the outer side of reality, does not suffice for grasping the reality of soul and spirit. The misuse of drugs does not lead anywhere, but constitutes a betrayal of the new soul disposition. An imaginary expansion of consciousness that is achieved without the transformative effort of soul-spiritual training ends in illusion. Human beings must become spiritually active in order to stand up to what meets them from the spiritual world. Jung writes: "Since the stars have fallen from heaven, and our highest symbols have paled, a secret life holds sway in the unconscious...our unconscious, on the other hand, hides living water, spirit that has become nature, and that's why it is disturbed."[30] Because of this conviction, Jung considered coming to terms with the unconscious to be something of vital concern for the human being. The unconscious is obviously not only the matrix of human creativity for man, but also the matrix that brings forth the "Son," according to Revelation 12. This is the *puer aeternus* of the alchemists, the "spirit child in the depth of soul" (Rudolf Steiner), the Christ consciousness. The mutation of consciousness that is the task of humankind for our time is addressed in the challenging words of John the Baptist: "Change your soul's attitude, for the realms of the heavens have come close to you!"[31]

9

SOUL AND SPIRIT

Respective Positions Seen in the Context of Spiritual History

THE SUBJECT OF SOUL AND SPIRIT as understood by Jung and Steiner poses a difficult problem. Once again it becomes clear how much the paths as well as the goals of the two researchers differ in very important respects. As we have already mentioned, early in his life Steiner had a precise objective regarding spirit knowledge. There is no real break between Steiner's anthroposophical activity (after 1900) and the so-called "pre-anthroposophical period." All the insights gained from his Goethean studies, his ideas of how knowledge is acquired, and his philosophy of freedom were systematically and continuously applied, always mindful of the supersensible world. Steiner's spiritual viewpoint was established from the moment when he showed the way to "pure thinking," thinking seen as spiritual activity, in his *Intuitive Thinking as a Spiritual Path* (1894). Even his earlier publications point in the same direction. We must not overlook the fact that the activity of pure thinking, which is able to make *itself* the object of reflection, necessarily leads to abstract concepts. Thinking has to be free of sense impressions in order to become an instrument for gaining supersensible knowledge.

Steiner did not stop here, however. He wanted to achieve a transformation of the *soul forces* to make them a tool for direct spiritual observation. For Steiner, abstract thinking is not yet spiritual in itself; it is only *a form* of participation in the spiritual. It is the form of thinking activity of which we are capable in our normal, everyday consciousness. If the Cartesian horizon of cognition is taken as the absolute limit for any kind of knowledge, and our normal, waking consciousness is assumed to be the only one of which we are capable, there is a danger of becoming stuck in abstractions and reducing the living, all-encompassing spirit to its dry, intellectual residue. Steiner said, "Into our shadowy intellectual concepts the living wisdom that spiritual science is able to give must be received. The shadow images of the intellect must in this way be called to life."[1] Anthroposophy—spiritual science—is proof that Steiner responded to what he himself demanded.

This demand of Steiner's was not only his personal concern, but was a problem of the age, even though it presented itself to him in a special way. Since the sixteenth century, science, especially natural science and technology, had become an instrument that enabled human beings to understand, dominate, and change their world. "Science became the most effective weapon in the struggle with and against nature; it helped to transform it, to exploit it, and to rule over it. At least that is what our fathers believed. All this became possible through the application of mechanical laws to 'lifeless' nature, through what the European's thinking had gained when he became the master of the living space."[2] The counting, measuring, weighing way of thinking was well suited to controlling the outer world, as far as "lifeless nature" was concerned. But it was bound to fail in regard to living things and to the life of the soul. Contemporary philosophy and psychology reflect the inability to adequately solve the riddles of the human soul and spirit. The spirit was reduced to abstract concepts; the psyche was supposed to be limited to where this abstract spirit manifested itself, namely in ordinary, waking consciousness. In the view of this scientific thinking, soul and spirit lost their innate reality and legitimacy. The more the outer world was discovered and understood, the more religious truth as inner experience and as source of life's meaning became inaccessible. All that remained for the religious authorities was to defend their cause against the revolutionary natural sciences in a hopeless rear-guard action. A revival of spiritual life could not be expected from a religion that found itself increasingly in decline. Reliable knowledge about the human being, spirit, and soul could no longer appear clothed in prescientific disguise. It would have to be presented with the exactness and clarity that modern scientific thinking demanded. Consequently, what was needed was a science of the human being, a science of the soul, a science of the spirit. On the other hand, it was also necessary to overcome the narrowly confined thought patterns that modern science had developed over several centuries. For Steiner this meant that, in order to meet the requirements of the time, he had to present his "philosophy of freedom" as "the result of soul-observations, applying the natural-scientific method." He also had the task of conducting spiritual research that went beyond natural science, yet was true to its methods of exactitude.

He described the situation he was confronted with at the beginning of his path in A Theory of Knowledge Implicit in Goethe's World Conception (1886): "In this matter we must always keep before our minds the truth that the proper procedure is never that of creating a spiritual need artificially, but quite the contrary: that of discovering the need which exists and satisfying this need. The task of science is not that of propounding questions but that of giving careful attention to these when they are put forth by human nature and by the contemporary stage of evolution, and of answering them. Our modern philosophers set tasks for themselves that are not at all the outflow of that stage of culture whereon we now stand—questions for which no one is seeking answers. Those questions which must be propounded by our culture because of the position to which our great thinkers have elevated it are passed over by science. Thus we possess a philosophical knowledge which no one is seeking and suffer from a philosophic need which no one satisfies."[3]

With this Steiner, at the age of twenty-five, stated his life's goal: not to satisfy artificial, abstract quasi-needs, but to help answer burning human questions.

Jung's situation was similar. But since he was faced with an entirely different mission in life, and since a theory of knowledge was of no interest to him, the way of research diverged for the two men. As the young physician and psychiatrist was getting oriented in his new work, trying to make his own scientific contributions, he found the field to be largely uncharted terrain. Like Freud, he would not limit himself to mere descriptions of psychological phenomena; he began to experiment.

His psychiatric studies, contained in the first volume of his collected works, give a picture of these experiments. The manner and spirit in which they are conducted depend entirely on the epistemology and the prevailing scientific views at the end of the nineteenth century. This means they conform to the materialistic principle of causality characteristic of modern science. Jung finds this fixation also in Freud's work. In spite of the progressive thinking that psychoanalysis showed even in its earliest form, setting it apart from traditional psychology, it was clearly limited by the epistemological pessimism of the time. It was based on an image of the human being that does not know freedom. Freud's principle of the sex drive was based on the causality of the libido. Later, Freud overcomes this purely causative viewpoint in his ego psychology.

Freud, as well as Jung in his early psychoanalysis, saw the psyche as bound up entirely with biological drives. Although one must appreciate the importance and wholesomeness of this "dethroning" of the human being, it may have gone too far. After a phase of unrealistic and one-sided idealism in anthropology and psychology, there followed a view of the individual as motivated entirely by his or her drives, especially the sexual one. "Objective spirit" and the "spirit of science" had become practically identical.

When Jung, the young physician at the clinic in Burghölzli, joined up with Freud, the founder of psychoanalysis, the former had no idea that half a century of intense transformation lay ahead for him. (The work that marked the beginning of the break between Freud and Jung was characteristically titled *Transformations and Symbols of the Libido.*) This transformation can be traced in Jung's own psychology. To clearly mark the direction taken by Jung's concept of the soul and spirit, one could say that Jung's development took him from a psychology that was in the inexorable grip of biological functions to one that ended up with the notion of a transpsychological background. In a comparatively early essay, "The Contrast between Freud and Jung" (1929), Jung, anticipating later development, expressed what he saw as his future path: "We moderns are destined to see the spirit again, that is, to have archetypal experiences. This is the only possible way to break through the magic spell of the biological drives." And concerning the religious dimension: "Who does not see this aspect of the human soul is blind; and who wants to explain or rationalize it away has no sense of reality. The wheel of history cannot be turned back, but the step toward the spirit that was evident already in the primitive initiation rites shall not be obstructed. Science has to cut out certain partial sections of knowledge and apply to them limited hypotheses. But the psyche is a superior whole, she is mother and precondition of consciousness." Jung said that Freud foundered at Nicodemus's question: How can one know the spirit? But with this he only indicated that he himself made this question his own.

The Soul as the Anthropological Basis of the Spirit

What are we talking about when we say "spirit"? Can we find a common denominator for that which Jung calls "the reality of the soul" and Steiner calls "the spiritual world"? The difficulty in encountering and experiencing the spiritual begins with the fact that spirit does not manifest as an object among other objects of this world. Spirit is not available like a thing one can get hold of in any way one chooses. And yet it doesn't hide itself altogether like a *deus absconditus*, although it has that tendency sometimes. We are interested here mainly *in the way spirit manifests*. From this we seek to decipher some of its characteristics, while avoiding any theoretical definitions. There is the question of the relationship between human being and spirit. General experience shows that the spirit always reveals itself only in glimpses. Its whole dimension remains unknown, at least to the rational mind. What shows itself, again and again, are aspects of a larger whole, whose radius is the world of things and of persons, the world of the "it" and the "you." But this larger whole is at the same time permeated by the "open secret" (Goethe), the "depth of being," that "which absolutely concerns us" (Tillich), the transcendent in the immanent. Steiner once touched on this problem when he considered that it is not sufficient to see the "fabric of the world" only from one perspective. "There is not merely one conception of the world outlook that can be defended or

justified. There are twelve."[4] This points unmistakably to the need to
see each viewpoint relative to many others.

Which aspects of the spirit do we need to think about? We have
encountered one important aspect in Steiner's *Theosophy*, which also
sheds light on the relationship between soul and spirit. In this work, he
describes the "spirit nature of the human being" and explains how, by
freely adopting the laws of thinking, "we make ourselves members of a
higher order than the one we belong to through the body." Steiner calls
this "the spiritual order."[5] This does not imply a total identification of
thinking with spirit. We also have to consider that, according to
Steiner, this spiritual order is closely connected to the soul, anthropo-
logically speaking.

The spiritual, however, is of a different dimension from the soul
element, just as the soul element is different from the physical. This
soul element is the foundation of the spiritual, just as the physical element is the foundation of the soul.

The next task is to contemplate the self, the personal human being.
Such contemplation can bring to light one important aspect of spirit,
which also has to do with the *relationship of soul to spirit*. Let an example
illustrate what is meant here: someone who contemplates an object of
nature or of art will react with feelings of joy or admiration (or perhaps with the opposite). These feelings belong to the inner soul of the
beholder. They prove to be subjective, inasmuch as a different beholder
may develop very different feelings toward the object.

Thinking moves on a different plane, since its laws are not
restricted to individual preferences but relate to objective facts.
"Human beings look up to the starry sky; their feelings of delight
belong to their soul. But the eternal laws that we comprehend there do
not belong to us; they belong to the world of the stars." In this way the
individual soul is related to the spiritual as the subjective, inner world
is to the objective, which is superior to it. The "I," which is imbedded
in the soul (according to Steiner), has a double task to fulfill. On one
side, it contains the individual, unique soul; on the other side, it is also
capable of receiving the objective and the spiritual. We practice this
capacity in our waking consciousness by thinking. We know, however,

that thinking, even in its developed form of "pure thinking," is only one way of approaching the spiritual world. To enter more deeply into the supersensible world, the higher stages of consciousness, imagination, inspiration, and intuition, are necessary.

In this way the soul becomes the stage on which the spirit unfolds. Whatsoever has been fructified by the spirit takes root, grows, and ripens in the soul's ground. The spirit stamps its signature on the individual soul. As soul-beings, humans accept freely, through their thinking, willing, and feeling, what the spirit has to offer them. Spirit, as Steiner understands it, is not identical with Jung's unconscious; rather, the call of the spirit sounds from an initially unconscious sphere into our consciousness. In this way the spirit enters into communication with the conscious "I" that is embedded in the soul.[6] Once we have understood the relationship between spirit and soul as equal to the one between objective and subjective, we may add: The spirit is related to the soul as the content of a vessel is to the vessel itself. The intimate interconnection between spirit and soul is expressed in Steiner's terminology in the term *soul-spiritual*. Applied to developmental psychology and practical pedagogy, this means that the "soul-spiritual" of the growing human is being implanted into the physical body in successive developmental stages. It is a process of incarnation that has to be taken into account even in the school curriculum. In Waldorf education, developed by Rudolf Steiner, this has been done successfully for fifty years. Similarly impressive results have been shown in anthroposophical curative education.[7]

So far we have met the spiritual under the aspect of the *transindividual*. Two more aspects ought to be mentioned. One of them becomes evident from what was said above: the aspect of *order*. Order is based on laws. Spiritual facts can be considered as related to spiritual laws. We must not, however, understand this concept of order in too narrow a sense, since there are also paradoxes and apparent contradictions involved in the reality of the living, all-encompassing spirit. When we neglect to include the paradox in our understanding of reality, we lose sight of the innate polarity that is the basic element of life. When we can understand spirit as all-encompassing (*coincidentia oppositorum*), where "height" as well as "depth" point to the superior dimension, where individual soul concerns appear integrated into the "transpersonal," then *meaning* reveals itself as the additional aspect of the spirit. This is an aspect that can show us how much we have lost the spirit as a reality, as an active, sheltering force in our life. It has been lost, or at least it is inaccessible for many. Where egotism reigns, in what Luther called "the *in se curvatum*," the totally self-centered attitude, it ignores the transpersonal. This leads to spiritual blindness. When chaos destroys the spiritual order, meaning is replaced by absurdity, by a world without hope. With the loss of the spirit, the wholeness of the soul is destroyed. This problem has been recognized for thousands of years. It is simply the human problem.

As Jesus says in the Gospels: "What help would it be to man if he gained the whole world and yet was injured in his soul?" The actual symptoms of this condition are well known to anyone schooled in psychotherapy.[8] On the other hand, it is also well known how the search for deeper soul experiences, which is in reality a longing for spiritual knowledge, takes many forms and follows often unhealthy paths. These range from mystical ravings, often accompanied by pathological or hysterical symptoms, to drug abuse and black magic.

On the Way to Spiritual Experience

What will have to happen in order for us to experience and establish anew our spiritual roots? Pastoral admonishments and references to the absolute, to order and meaning, do not suffice because, as Karl Barth has written, "the Word is silenced by the words," and the Word's former binding authority no longer exists. The meaning of spirit does not allow itself to be rationally explained, defined, or taught. Spirit has to happen. Appeals, declamations, and manifestos must end if a true transformation of the human being is to begin. Mere information about spiritual facts has to be deepened by the possibility of personal, direct experience. "We have usually not sufficient regard for the Spiritual as a living reality; and a living reality must be grasped in the fullness of life."[9] "Today, when they speak of the spirit, most people mean something totally abstract and unfitted for this world, and not something that can make an impact on everyday life."[10]

Jung saw how vital it was to have experiences that relate to concrete life events while revealing the deeper layers of soul reality. This insight showed him the way for his work. His therapeutic mission presented itself to him in a great variety of clinical pictures and human life stories. It is comparatively easy to prove that his talk about spirit and soul is imprecise. No doubt in this respect he leaves something to be desired. Jung's critics should take into account, however, that the young psychologist began his work at a conventional psychiatric clinic, and not at a philosophical seminar, where epistemological studies would have been required. In addition, he met with the assumptions on which psychology as well as science was based at the end of the nineteenth century, of which we spoke earlier in this chapter. Jung himself called attention to this situation again and again. In his foreword to the second edition of his *Relations between the Ego and the Unconscious*, we read, as he points to twenty-eight years of psychological and psychiatric experience: "It is not concerned with a clever system of thought, but with the formulation of complex psychic experiences which have never yet been the subject of scientific study. Since the psyche is an irrational datum and cannot, in accordance with the old picture, be equated with a more or less divine Reason, it should not surprise us if in the course of psychological experience we come across, with extreme frequency, processes and happenings which run counter to our rational expectations and are therefore rejected by the rationalistic attitude of our conscious mind."[11] Here the context shows quite clearly what Jung was up against.

Jung saw himself as an empiricist, not as a philosopher. He was not so much after knowledge, but was motivated by the will and the professional need to help his patients as quickly as possible. Therefore he had to pay attention to the symptoms with which his patients presented him. He had to accept them with their inner voices and the fabrications of their unconscious. He needed to penetrate from the symptoms to the underlying causes, and he had to do this by groping, experimenting, led by a dim "sensing," not by a clearly defined "*a priori* knowledge."

Even when Jung did not arrive at his results in a way that he himself could clearly understand, one has to respect what he had to say about them: "My most fundamental views and ideas derive from these experiences. First I made the observations, and only then did I hammer out my views. And so it is with the hand that guides the crayon or brush, the foot that executes the dance step, with the eye and the ear, with the word and the thought. A dark impulse is the ultimate arbiter of the pattern; an unconscious *a priori* precipitates itself into plastic form."[12] A "dark impulse" has taken the initiative. Jung's autobiography is full of accounts of this kind of guidance.

Looking at this basic premise, it is understandable that Jung unashamedly confessed that he had no knowledge of what "spirit" really is, what "life" really is. One must not overlook, however, that his confessed ignorance relates only to the solving of life's problems by way of thinking. It cannot be denied that in Jung's confessed ignorance there hides a *docta ignorantia*, a wisdom of not knowing. "He strives beyond intellectually attainable knowledge to a state of soul in which knowledge ceases, and in which the soul meets its God in 'knowing ignorance,' *in docta ignorantia*," says Steiner of Nicholas of Cusa.[13] Something similar could be said about Jung's assessment of thinking. For "we do not need to *know* what truth is, but to *experience* it. We do not need an intellectual viewpoint, but what we need is to find the way to an inner, perhaps wordless, perhaps irrational experience. That is the great goal." This we read in the foreword to Jung's collection of essays *Modern Man in Search of the Soul*. At this point our comparison with Rudolf Steiner leads us to the following conclusions:

Jung and Steiner see eye to eye on the point that mere knowledge, mere rationality, does not lead to a genuine solution of inner problems. "When we are thinking is precisely when we 'are' not—for thoughts are only pictures of reality....We must become conscious of the reflective, mirror-image nature of mental activity, of our thought life."[14]

On the other hand, Steiner and Jung part ways in the evaluation of thinking for the purpose of penetrating into the realm of the unconscious or the supersensible. Jung takes the direct approach of investigating the fabrications of the unconscious, that is, the soul content his patients present to him in the form of dreams, fantasies, and associa-tions. Steiner deems it necessary to take the way *through* rationality, not to remain there, but in order to gain the clarity that is required for a reliable inquiry into the supersensible.

Jung's starting position explains thereby also his view of what he calls "spirit." He feels most closely connected to the soul, to the psyche, which all of humankind has in common. "Thus instead of 'life' I must first speak of the living body, and instead of 'spirit' of psychic factors. This does not meant that I want to evade the question as orig-inally put in order to indulge in reflections on body and mind. On the contrary, I hope the empirical approach will help us to find a real basis for spirit—and not at the expense of life."[15] Steiner, as we mentioned already, was concerned with spiritual knowledge right from the begin-ning of his scientific activity. He advanced in this effort to ever-higher levels, when he formulated his spiritual science, and also added a num-ber of concrete activities in the form of anthroposophical fields of practical work. Jung, struggling just as hard, had to do experimental pioneering work whereby he constantly had to expose himself to adjustments and revisions of his scientific views. This revision process is mirrored in his changing views of the psyche and of the transpsycho-logical. Jung speaks of the total dependence of our knowledge on our psychological reality. "All that we can ever know consists of psycholog-ical substance." He sees the psyche as "our only immediate, our most real being." This seems to point to a cognitive pessimism, especially since Jung leaves no doubt as to his belief in Kant's theory of knowl-edge that sets definite limits to what can be known. That is also why he is convinced "that in the last instance we do not really understand the essence of the psyche." Elsewhere he writes, "To inquire into the sub-stance of what has been observed is possible in natural science only where there is an *Archimedean point* outside. For the psyche no such out-side point exists—only the psyche can observe the psyche. Conse-quently, knowledge of the psychic substance is impossible for us." As if he had a hunch that he should qualify this statement, he added: "At least by the means presently available."[16] Theoretically, Jung adhered to this viewpoint well into his old age, but practically he could not sustain it. It did not remain his last word on the subject. If Jung talks about the fact that humankind is surrounded by psychic pictures, he implies at the same time that these pictures that arise in the psyche presuppose the existence and the effectiveness of an objective spiritual world. Jung himself never doubted the existence of such a world, even though he never theorized about it. The significance of images and symbols in Jungian psychotherapy is precisely that a symbol is not only nominally a sign, but represents and points to a reality. The archetype, initially unavailable and beyond the psyche as such, was only gradually included in his field of research and hypotheses. The acknowledgment of the transpersonal element was one of the results Jung arrived at toward the end of his creative life.

The concept of the archetype appears as a new element for the first time in 1919, as Liliane Frey-Rohn has proven. "Up to the year 1921 he called the archaic picture the 'original picture' (*urtümliches Bild*). After that time he also used the word 'archetype,' or 'archetypal picture.' These expressions gradually took root. In later years Jung distinguished between archetypal picture and archetype, understanding the latter in the generally accepted sense of the word, whereas he limited the former to symbolic manifestations and pictorial expressions of the archetype."[17] Jung's expanding horizon of psychological knowledge is reflected in this steadily increasing differentiation of the two concepts. This expansion can frankly be called an overstepping of formerly defined boundaries. A new dimension came into view. This new expansion of his field of vision is actually expressed already in the term "archetype." One can interpret the prefix *arche* as meaning "the beginning, the original, the basic ground"; and "type" as the imprint, or rather the result of an imprint. An imprint presupposes a printer, even if there are no clear definitions as yet about the nature of such a printer. In the early 1940s Jung began to express himself in this sense. Here he not only took issue with theology, which was ready to make statements about the omnipotence of God and about the validity of religious dogma, but he was skeptical about the idea of God manifesting in the soul. Jung also adds: "The religious view understands the imprint as the working of an imprinter; the scientific point of view understands it as the symbol of an unknown and incomprehensible content."[18] Obviously Jung at this time was already reckoning with the probability of an objective soul background (*Seelenhintergrund*). This presumption is confirmed when one turns toward his last great phase of work, in which he began to replace the concept of causality or determinism inherent in classical physics with a new principle of understanding. Surprisingly enough, he arrived at this new principle by entering into a dialogue with modern physics.

In view of the phenomena of synchronicity, which are characterized as an arrangement of similarly motivated, uncaused events or processes, Jung came to the conclusion that "the world inside and outside ourselves rests on a transcendental background."[19] The interrelationship, or rather the complementary relationship, of matter and spirit becomes demonstrable: "Since psyche and matter are contained in one and the same world, and moreover are in continuous contact with one another, and ultimately rest on irrepresentable, transcendental factors, it is not only possible, but fairly probable, even, that psyche and matter are two different aspects of one and the same thing.

"The synchronicity phenomena point, it seems to me, in this direction, for they show that the non-psychic can behave like the psychic, and vice versa, without there being any causal connection between them. Our present knowledge does not allow us to do much more than compare the relation of the psychic to the material world with two cones whose apices, meeting in a point without extension, a real zero-point, touch and do not touch."[20] With this the step has been taken, as Liliane Frey-Rohn summarizes it, from the subjective to the objective method of observation; in other words, the step from the mere idea of the archetype to the transpersonal character of the archetype has been taken. The background of the empirical world, which the alchemists of the Middle Ages called the *unus mundus*, can now be grasped by thinking. Such were the stages on the long path of development of psychology from Freud to Jung.

Jung's reserve as a scientist was not noticed by those who wanted to denounce him as an exponent of psychologism. Nor has his caution been appreciated by those who hastily assume that he has delivered proof of transcendence. Jung's reserve stems from his attitude. He could attest that he had researched the "knowable," the archetypal pictures, according to all the means of research available to him. The archetype itself, the superior, ordering principle, was not knowable to him. He therefore preferred to approach it with humble reverence. Indeed Jung's psychology is the kind of research that pays tribute to exact science by collecting data and recording and suggesting interpretations. At the same time, it is a science that appeals to our capacity for reverence and provokes feelings of reverence for what is above.

Steiner has called "the path of reverence, of devotion toward truth and knowledge" a prerequisite for the kind of schooling that would lead to experiences of a higher order. "Only a person who passed through the gate of humility can ascend to the heights of the spirit," he writes in the basic book about his path of schooling, *How to Know Higher Worlds.* "Every feeling of *true* devotion unfolded in the soul produces an inner strength or force that sooner or later leads to knowledge."[21]

It would amount to a severe violation of the law of humility if the psychological researcher pressed all the incorruptible, eternal, and creative content of the psyche into the templates of rational, abstract definitions. What is meant here can be clearly seen, for instance, in the dialogue between theology and psychology. Jung made a clear distinction between the image of God that is manifest in the human soul, on the one hand, and the unknowable God himself, the *deus absconditus*, on the other. Since Jung resolutely remained the psychiatrist and did not want to make theological statements or religious proclamations, he limited his research entirely to the material manifested in the psyches of his patients, which expressed themselves in pictures and symbols. This conscientious self-limitation has to be respected. His communications have nothing to do with proof of the existence or nonexistence of the transcendental. But one also has to point out that Jung never had any doubts about the existence of a reality beyond our consciousness. This is especially evident in his late work. This certainty enabled the depth psychologist to make certain confessionlike statements.

One must not, however, take these as scientific proofs and thereby transfer them to a completely different plane. Testimonies like these are based on intimate spiritual experiences and are not transferable to others. Everyone has to put himself into a properly receptive mood or prepare himself in some way to receive such experiences. Here to prepare means to be prepared. The time and hour when we might receive a gift from the "inaccessible" realm cannot be predetermined. In the language of religion, such a communication of higher wisdom that cannot be influenced is called *revelation*. The condition under which it happens is unconditional and is called *grace*. The content itself, the unavailable yet active reality, is called *spirit*. *The spirit bloweth where it listeth*. The spiritual scientist and the psychiatrist have this in common: their work begins and ends in the outer court of spiritual communication. Quoting Thomas Aquinas, Steiner has called his work a *praeambulum fidei*, a prologue of faith.[22] (See appendix: "Soul and Spirit Research as *Praeambulum Fidei*.")

The Necessity of Personal Experience

In Jung we find two different tendencies. The first is his insistence on remaining strictly empirical in his point of view as well as in his stated goal. As such, he has to forego any statements relating to the metaphysical. The second is that he constantly transcends the boundaries of professional competence that traditional science demands. Whoever holds it against him that he thus operated on two levels, and that he thereby almost disqualified himself professionally, only shows that he himself does not dare to look for a vision that may overcome the fragmented view of the scientific specialists. Even though Jung felt himself bound by respect for Kant's limits on cognition, as outlined in the *Critique of Pure Reason*, Jung the psychologist had to cross the borders constantly. It is easy to find testimonies from his pen that deny any certainty of a "view to the other side," or at least it seems so. For instance, in the introduction to D.T. Suzuki's book *The Great Liberation* we find the following pessimistic passage: "Of course we can never decide definitely whether a person is really 'enlightened' or 'released,' or whether he merely imagines it. We have no criteria to go on. Moreover, we know well enough that an imaginary pain is often more agonizing than a real one, since it is accompanied by a subtle moral suffering caused by a dull feeling of secret self-accusation. In this sense, therefore, it is not a question of 'actual fact' but of *'psychic reality,'* i.e. *the psychic process known as satori."*

It is hardly less surprising when Jung continues: "Every psychic process is an image and an 'imagining,' otherwise no consciousness could exist and the occurrence would lack phenomenality. Imagination itself is a psychic process for which reason is completely irrelevant whether the enlightenment be called 'real' or 'imaginary.' "[23]

This all sounds as if imagination based on delusion would have the same validity, or lack of validity, as the result of a genuine initiation process. Significantly, Jung adds: "The one who experiences enlightenment or pretends to have experienced it is convinced, in either case, that he is enlightened. What others think of it makes no difference to him as far as his experience is concerned." Obviously the emphasis lies here on the personal experience. It is removed from the doubts of others. It cannot be proven; it also doesn't need to be proven.

Here we are reminded of Steiner's answer to questions demanding proof for his spiritual-scientific communications. In the foreword to the first edition of his *Outline of Esoteric Science* (1910), he remarks that it is important not to take any of these communications about a spiritual world blindly at face value or to "believe" them. They must be judged by the individual's personal inner experiences. The soul activity required to receive spiritual-scientific facts furnishes its own "proof." Such proofs as outer natural science would require actually lead away from understanding the subject they are supposed to explain. They lead, one might say, to the "outer side of reality," while the facts that are meant for the soul to experience lie "within" the soul itself. Thereby they are not accessible to "outer" criteria. "Those who present spiritual-scientific facts must place this soul activity in the forefront, because their readers only arrive at the facts by making this activity their own in the right way. Unlike the facts of natural science, which—although not understood—are still available for human perception even without any soul activity, spiritual-scientific facts enter into our perception only through activity on the part of the soul. Thus those presenting spiritual science presume that the readers are accompanying them on the search for these facts....We learn to recognize that when natural science is explained, 'proof' is somehow brought toward it from the outside, so to speak. In spiritual-scientific thinking, however, the activity applied to proving something in natural-scientific thinking is already present in the search for the facts. We cannot find these facts if the path that leads to them does not constitute a proving process in itself. Anyone who really follows this path already experiences the element of proof, and nothing more can be accomplished by a proof applied from outside."[24]

Such statements obviously leave the door open to many misunderstandings concerning analytic psychology, understood as empirical science, as well as concerning Anthroposophy. It is also possible that Anthroposophists and psychologists can misunderstand each other on many points. And yet there is one thing that is crucial for both of them: personal experience. This cannot be replaced by even the most thorough head knowledge. Mere credulous acceptance, or critical rejection, of anthroposophical as well psychological teachings does not mean anything. A person must be willing and able to activate the impulse given by these theories in his or her own soul. That is why Steiner insisted relentlessly that "the student of spiritual science must gain an immediate and real relationship to the objective spiritual world." Steiner held this to be much more important than the student's relationship to the teacher, who should not be compared to an Eastern guru. The only thing that is crucial for spiritual schooling is what happens *within the soul* of the student. The analogous conviction has led analytic psychology since Freud to demand that part of a student's training must include a personal analysis. This cannot be replaced by any exam or academic diploma.

A number of questions remain about Jung's seemingly puzzling statements concerning the background and reality of spiritual experiences. It is significant that Jung emphasizes once more, just before the above-quoted remarks regarding Suzuki's "great liberation," his viewpoint regarding the Zen *satori* experience: "Since, out of scientific modesty, I do not presume to make a metaphysical statement, but am referring only to a change of consciousness that can be experienced, I treat *satori* first of all as a psychological problem."[25]

It will not do to accuse Jung of agnosticism because of certain passages in his written work. Rather, if we study his vast work carefully, we will become aware of the difficult task he had in trying to break through traditional epistemological limits and at the same time seeking acceptance as an exact scientist. Without doubt a risky undertaking!

It is known that Jung did not limit himself strictly to "intrapsychic" contents, mere soul-experiences, in spite of his self-confessed "scientific modesty." Willy-nilly he betrayed his own principles when he acknowledged that "spirit" was more than the subjective soul aspect. Jung the psychologist had always declared the latter as existent. But he also acknowledged the vaster, equally powerful "other spirit" when he explained the archetype as the creating principle behind the archetypal pictures, and finally every time he discovered an ordering principle in psychic manifestations, or when he became aware of wholeness and meaning. If all this has been admitted, then a foundation for truth and reality has been laid, and one can no longer speak of the "merely psychic." Because of its vastness, this reality cannot be grasped at all by the intellect. The *ratio*, rational thinking, is only capable of segmented insight. Its characteristic way of seeing things "in perspective" allows for a high degree of clarity, but only by sacrificing the totality.

Aspects of the Spirit

What does the above tell us about our initial question regarding the relationship between soul and spirit? Where does spirit enter into Jung's field of vision?

Starting from Steiner's distinction of soul and spirit, where soul is the subjective and spirit the all-embracing objective principle, we said that spirit could be approached from different aspects. Even though the differences between Jung and Steiner's viewpoints are great in principle as well as in detail, it may be fruitful to inquire about certain spiritual aspects in Jung's interpretation.

Jung devoted detailed studies to the phenomenology and symbolism of the spirit, starting with the dazzling semantics of the word "spirit," assembled from many linguistic terms that include rational as well as irrational factors. He studied the most varied historical descriptions, including the ones in fairy tales, in alchemy, which called spirit "the Spirit Mercurius," in Christian dogma, and in non-Christian religions. The results were accordingly diverse. To look for a common denominator and to try to define "spirit" would not only contradict Jung's method but also the "object" to be defined. (This does not mean that a philosophical attempt to define the spirit is unnecessary; it may be needed. But we must not expect such an undertaking from Jung.) Once more we have to fall back on Steiner's characterization.

Jung's hallmarks of spirit are: "first, it is the principle of spontaneous movement and activity; second, the spontaneous capacity to produce images independently of sense perception; and third, the autonomous and sovereign manipulation of these images."[26] There is also the differentiation between the "subjective spirit" that came to mean a purely endopsychic phenomenon, in contrast to the "objective spirit." It is important for the psychiatrist to state that "the psychic manifestations of the spirit indicate at once that they are of an archetypal nature—in other words, the phenomenon we call spirit depends on the existence of an autonomous primordial image which is universally present in the preconscious makeup of the human psyche." This archetype regularly appears in its characteristic form by "always spurring him on, giving him lucky ideas, staying power, 'enthusiasm' and 'inspiration.'"[27]

If one applies Steiner's precise differentiation of subjective for the soul, objective for the spirit, Jung's catalog does not completely satisfy, because he is not clear in this respect. More helpful are Jung's statements about the spirit as a transphysical and transpersonal reality, whereby he looks at these under the aspect of order. He recognized the existence of qualities and influences he called (beginning in 1946) "psychoid." He did this to express the view that the influencing factor that works in the human psyche is not identical with it, but certainly *works within it.* One of the most important features of this influencing factor is that it can overcome the law of causality. When he discovered this, Jung did not find a chaotic soul background, but rather a uniquely ordered structure, although an acausal one. One can speak, with Aniela Jaffé, of "ordering structural forms in the unconscious" that, on the one hand, explain the often identical motives of myths and symbols of people of all races and countries.[28] On the other hand, the archetype itself (which remains unseen, in contrast to the archetypal picture), presents itself as the creator of acausal events.

In so-called synchronistic phenomena, be they of a parapsychological, a psychological, or a physical nature, one can sometimes discover a meaningful relationship between something that happens within the human psyche and simultaneous, similarly motivated outer events that evade statistical analysis. Thanks to his vast, detailed knowledge of medieval, alchemically inspired nature philosophy, Jung discovered that the alchemists, thanks to their clairvoyant faculties, had come upon an important fact. This fact, which represents a unifying principle behind physical and psychic phenomena, was discovered, or rather rediscovered, by Jung in his depth psychology as well as by modern theoretical physicists. Jung named this unifying aspect that shows itself in the synchronistic events the *unus mundus*. This *unus mundus* is an aspect of the spirit insofar as it embraces both psyche and matter, unifying them.[29]

Jung acknowledges that psyche and matter can be seen as manifestations of one and the same reality, and that they point to the "background" of our empirical world, namely the *unus mundus*. He summarized his views in *On the Nature of the Psyche* (1946): "Since psyche and matter are contained in one and the same world, and moreover are in continuous contact with one another, and ultimately rest on irrepresentable, transcendental factors, it is not only possible, but fairly probable, even, that psyche and matter are two different aspects of one and the same thing. The synchronicity phenomena point, it seems to me, in this direction, for they show that the non-psychic can behave like the psychic, and vice versa, without there being any causal connection between them."[30]

A few decades earlier, in 1919, Steiner had declared such a view of the unity of all being as something that would have to flow into our present cultural development. It would not do merely to theorize in general about an abstract spiritual world. "For the future the essential thing is not to make an abstract distinction between the material and the spiritual, but to look for the spiritual itself in the material, so that one could describe it as spiritual and recognize in what is spiritual its transition into matter, and its way of working there."[31] Naturally, this viewpoint is also much older; it is evident in Goethe's view of nature and in Jacob Boehme's theosophy. Here we are approaching, historically speaking, the representatives of the *unus mundus* idea that Jung sought to verify scientifically.

If it is true that the spirit, the spiritual world, can be seen from different aspects (a view I would like to adhere to), then one aspect must not be forgotten. This played a significant role in Jung's life and work. It is the above-mentioned aspect of meaning. Aniela Jaffé, Jung's collaborator for many years, distinguished herself by assembling all the material for Jung's autobiography, *Memories, Dreams, Reflections*. She wrote a substantial monograph, *The Myth of Meaning in Jung's Work*. There are some statements, however, that give the superficial impression that Jung did not take the question of "meaning" very seriously. For instance, he wrote at the age of fifty-nine: "Life is foolish as well as meaningful. When we can't laugh about the former and don't speculate about the latter, then life is dull. Then everything has nothing but the most common dimension. There is only a little sense and a little nonsense." Even in the autobiography of the octogenarian Jung, we find sentences that seem to have been written down somewhat hastily: for instance, Jung calls it a matter of "temperament" whether one believes that life contains more sense or more nonsense. "If meaninglessness were absolutely preponderant, the meaningfulness of life would vanish to an increasing degree with each step in our development. But that is—or seems to me—not the case. Probably, as in all metaphysical questions, both are true: Life is—or has—meaning and meaninglessness. I cherish the anxious hope that meaning will preponderate and will win the battle."[32]

In spite of these rather vague formulations, Jung repeatedly discovered in his practical work that a patient could only be considered "healed" if she had found meaning in her life, in her destiny, and thereby in her suffering. For Jung, a life has only been truly lived and fulfilled if it has become "a criterion of the spirit." We enter the realm of the spirit at the moment when the door is opened to meaning. Whoever finds meaning does not find an additional item in the world of things; they also don't find a fragment, nor the long sought-after "missing link." To find meaning is to find wholeness. Basically, all human existence, living as it does in a climate of absurdity, tends toward wholeness. One finds this tendency already in the initiation rites of primitive humanity, even though it is hardly lifted into consciousness. Jung sums it up: "Every life is ultimately the realization of a whole, which means of a Self. That is why one can also call this realization individuation."

At this point, one should assemble all of Jung's rich materials and insights and consider them as a whole. Aniela Jaffé did this, making it clear that Jung, in dealing with the question of meaning, arrived at the reality of the spirit. However, he was not interested in clarifying the epistemological problem connected with his insight. Needless to say, a mere knowledge of the meaning of life is not sufficient. What alone is decisive is the inner realization of this meaning by the individual psyche as something transpersonal within the uniqueness of one's life.

Liliane Frey-Rohn was justified in pointing out the factor of uncertainty contained in all of Jung's statements about the reality of the transcendental. She holds that this uncertainty appears to cancel out any possible claim to real knowledge.[33] Even though he was personally convinced of the existence of the transcendental background of reality, Jung could not deny that it was difficult to have actual knowledge of this dimension of being: "The existence of a transcendental reality is indeed evident in itself, but it is uncommonly difficult for our consciousness to construct intellectual models which would give a graphic description of the reality we have perceived. Our hypotheses are uncertain and groping, and nothing offers us the assurance that they may ultimately prove correct."[34]

From Steiner's view one would have to say: One can appreciate such restraint in regard to the possibility of knowing the so-called transcendental background, but only as long as one deals with "hypotheses" and "intellectual models." This means that one works with ordinary, not yet transformed, consciousness. Therefore, one can agree with Jung conditionally when he speaks here of a *mysterium coniunctionis*, of the "dubious reality" of his direct awareness of an archetypal inner world. This declaration by the psychologist implies that he foregoes for the moment the possibility of consciousness-raising. He thereby denies himself the possibility of having a scientifically grounded certainty about the spiritual background of the world by acquiring the prerequisites for such knowledge through inner schooling.

Jung no doubt advanced beyond the reality of the psyche to the reality of the spirit; however, he does not offer a *knowledge* of soul and spirit.

1 0

INITIATION AND INDIVIDUATION

Beyond the Sphere of Impulses

"THE ONLY 'INITIATION PROCESS' that is still alive and practiced today in the West is the analysis of the unconscious as used by doctors for therapeutic purposes.... Originally, this therapy took the form of Freudian psychoanalysis." We find this statement in Jung's "Psychological Commentary to the *Tibetan Book of the Dead.*" The author supports his statement with the observation that psychoanalysis deals mainly with sexual fantasies, the same subject with which a certain part of the *Bardo Thödol,* or *Tibetan Book of the Dead,* concerns itself. He means here the state of being that individuals find themselves in either after death or in the process of preparing for rebirth. Jung reminds us here that the European, when trying to become aware of normally unconscious psychical contents, goes back into the world of infantile sexual fantasy (*usque ad uterum*). Thereby he or she goes in the opposite direction from the one that his or her life has taken so far, namely, back to the threshold of birth—or rather, prebirth. At the same time, this threshold is the limit of psychoanalytical searching. "One rather wishes that Freudian psychoanalysis could have happily pursued these so-called intra-uterine experiences still farther back; had it succeeded in this bold undertaking, it would surely have come out beyond the *Sidpa Bardo* and penetrated from behind into the lower reaches of the *Chönyid Bardo.* It is true that with the equipment of our existing biological ideas such a venture would not have been crowned with success: it would have needed a wholly different kind of philosophical penetration from that based on current scientific assumptions. But, had the journey back been consistently pursued, it would undoubtedly

183

have led to the postulate of a pre-uterine existence, a true *Bardo* life, if only it had been possible to find at least some trace of an experiencing subject. As it was, the psychoanalysts never got beyond purely conjectural traces of intra-uterine experiences, and even the famous 'birth trauma' has remained such an obvious truism that it can no longer explain anything."

This statement is important because it touches exactly the point where psychological research comes to an end. Even though it does acknowledge the reality of psychological experience, such research cannot begin to show the relationship between psyche and life. Traditional biological concepts present a formidable barrier to the understanding of a different reality. The reality that the Tibetan author of the *Bardo Thödol* has no reason to doubt because it is evident to him cannot be found with the tools of natural science. These tools are necessary to establish quantitative results that can be measured, weighed, and counted. Jung remarks show that Freud's concept of the unconscious is inadequate if one wants to penetrate to psychic experiences that are free of the body. For "anyone who penetrates into the unconscious with purely biological assumptions will become stuck in the instinctual sphere and be unable to advance beyond it, for he will be pulled back again and again into physical existence. It is therefore impossible for Freudian theory to reach anything except an essentially negative valuation of the unconscious."[1]

Here we may ask whether Jung, having given this evaluation of the limitation of Freud's psychoanalysis, could still uphold the verdict that Freud's kind of research is the only process of initiation that is alive in Western culture. This verdict has become questionable through Jung's astute assessment of Freud's psychoanalysis. It is emphasized even more by Jung's following characterization of the *Tibetan Book of the Dead*: "The *Bardo Thödol* began by being a 'closed' book, and so it has remained, no matter what kind of commentaries may be written upon it. For it is a book that will only open itself to spiritual understanding, and this is a capacity which no man is born with, but which he can only acquire through special training and special experience. It is good that such to all intents and purposes 'useless' books exist. They are meant for those 'queer folk' who no longer set much store by the uses, aims, and meaning of present-day 'civilization.'"[2]

One can only agree with Jung's observations, even without a pessimistic view of our civilization. He spoke of certain requirements without describing them in detail. If one has been able to obtain the requirements needed to break through the "instinctual sphere" to the spiritual, one can agree even more with Jung's words. The spiritual that is meant here is the sphere that is not limited by the rationalistic Western spirit that Jung repeatedly denounced.

Jung is absolutely correct: esoteric literature like the *Bardo Thödol* has been secret and still is, in spite of all the scientific and psychological commentary. The reason is that the content of such literature cannot be appreciated by *learning* the facts contained therein, but by *experiencing* them. At any rate, there is a great difference between a philological or historical explanation of a "secret writing," be it a passage from the New Testament or a philosophical essay, and a direct experience of it. The latter can work on the individual who contemplates it. This is what Jung means by the "special spiritual capacity" that we do not automatically possess but can often only acquire by laborious inner work. In view of such facts, demonstrated by Jung himself, it is questionable whether one could call psychoanalysis the only "initiation process" that is still alive and practiced today in the West. Obviously Jung is calling for a science of initiation that does not get stuck in the sphere of the instincts and shows a suitable way for Europeans to acquire the necessary "spiritual capacities."

On the one hand, it is puzzling that Jung, the creator of analytic psychology, who was not only very circumspect but also extremely open to the supersensible dimension, never once mentioned Steiner's spiritual science and its primary importance for a path to spiritual knowledge. Moreover, he declares Freud's psychoanalysis to be "the only initiation process in the Western world," although he himself had rejected it for good reasons. (Presumably Jung wanted to emphasize the methodological importance of psychoanalysis.) On the other hand, Jung's strange attitude may be understandable; had he tried Steiner's Anthroposophy as a way to obtain "knowledge of higher worlds," he presumably would have arrived at an altogether different evaluation of this way of research.

Nevertheless, there appears to be a way to compare Steiner's path of initiation and Jung's individuation process. Jolande Jacobi has called Jung's psychotherapy a "healing path that not only provides healing in the usual medical-therapeutic sense, but possesses the capacity to guide, educate, and strengthen the soul." It lies in the nature of things that only very few individuals attempt to follow the anthroposophical path of knowledge, and the same holds true for Jung's "healing path." Only a few are willing and feel destined to follow it. In *The Relations between the Ego and the Unconscious*, Jung alludes to a general human problem. Seen against the background of this problem, one can appreciate how significant it is to enter such a healing path. According to Jung, humankind is still in its infancy, psychologically speaking, as well as in regard to its soul-spiritual development. Only a few are capable of taking such decisive steps forward. "Even these few enter the path only out of great inner need, if not to say, out of desperation. For this path is narrow, like a knife's edge."

A similar qualification is in order in regard to Anthroposophy as a path of schooling. There are sufficient accounts of historical initiations to make it clear that a commitment of the whole person is required and that there is a definite possibility of failure. Steiner starts one of his basic books with the sentence: "The capacities by which we can gain insights into higher worlds lie dormant within each one of us."[3] This basic statement may certainly be correct, since it refers to the inherent human ability for inner development. But practical experience shows that only psychologically stable individuals should attempt this path. Occasionally, Steiner himself has hinted at this fact. (See appendix: "Mental Health through Spiritual Discipline.")

Two Kinds of Self-Realization

If we consider the problematic nature of the soul-spirit relationship, we can say with Steiner that it is of utmost importance that human beings develop their higher organs of perception in order to recognize the spiritual element that shines into the soul and can become conscious there. Drawing on Jung's point of view, we can say that self-realization intends to become conscious of heretofore unconscious soul contents and thereby to integrate both the conscious and the unconscious parts of the psyche into a greater whole: the Self.

Both Jung and Steiner have described the way to this realization, each in his own way. For Steiner, who sees his Anthroposophy as a modern initiation science, the path to "knowledge of higher worlds" is a path of initiation where knowing is of utmost importance. Jung speaks of individuation as a process, occasionally as a path, that leads to maturation and psychic wholeness. "Individuation means to become an individual being. If we see our individuality as our innermost, ultimate, incomparable uniqueness, we become our true Self. Therefore one could translate individuation also as 'becoming oneself,' or 'self realization.'"[4]

Both the anthroposophical path of initiation and the process of individuation in analytic psychology have characteristic features. Initiation, as Steiner understands it, must be prepared for by means of rigorous spiritual schooling, even though there are moments of spontaneity, since spirit is not accessible at will. By contrast, the path of individuation, as Jung understands it, is characterized by the naturalness and spontaneity of psychic processes that cause a confrontation between the ego and the unconscious. Both researchers emphasize the risk inherent in the process. In each case there are trials, crises, and dangers to endure. One attempting either initiation or individuation must be prepared for them.

In our comparative biographical sketches we have seen that Steiner considered Rosicrucianism to be the appropriate path to lead Western people into the process of soul-spiritual transformation. We have also seen how Jung undertook a detailed study of Rosicrucian and alchemical writings and symbols in order to use them as a key to his modern method of psychotherapy.

Steiner and Jung have both mastered their respective paths, each in his own way, experiencing it as leading to knowledge and healing. Moreover, each has described the individual stations of his path and has admonished his pupils to walk it. Both have described the individual processes objectively. Both have emphasized that it would not do to accept their teachings merely as information, since they cannot be treated as knowledge in the usual way. In the case of both teachings, concrete soul-spiritual experiences are required. Only these can be the basis for an evaluation of either Steiner's Anthroposophy or Jung's analytic psychology.

If one looks for relevant documentation of Steiner's intention when he began his life's mission, one comes upon a programmatic passage in a letter: "I will put my trust in the power that will make it possible for me to lead 'spirit-pupils' on the path of development. This will have to be my sole inaugural deed."[5]

These sentences, written even before the founding of the German section of the Theosophical Society, where Steiner was to become the general secretary, have to be seen in connection with *Anthroposophical Leading Thoughts*, written as his spiritual legacy one year before his death. "Anthroposophy is a path of knowledge to guide the Spiritual in the human being to the Spiritual in the universe."[6] The emphasis is on the word "path." Anthroposophy has too often been misunderstood as a complete, finished worldview. But in fact, the path is intended to show the individual soul a view of the spiritual world beyond sense impressions.

When Jung looked back to those years when he received overwhelming messages from the unconscious, it became clear to him that these messages pointed him in a direction far beyond his personal life. "There were things in the images which concerned not only myself but many others also. It was then that I ceased to belong to myself alone, ceased to have the right to do so. From then on, my life belonged to the generality....I myself had to undergo the original experiences, and, moreover, try to plant the results of my experience in the soil of reality; otherwise they would have remained subjective assumptions without validity. It was then that I dedicated myself to service of the psyche."[7]

Significantly, here we find side by side the "inaugural deed" of the spirit-seeker, and the physician's entrance into the "service of the psyche" after his prime experience. Each has its own significance and value. They do not cancel each other out. They support and complement each other, each in his own field. In each of them we find at the outset the same insight, formulated by Steiner in 1919: "New forces must be drawn up from the depths of human souls, and people will have to understand how they are linked in the depths of their souls with the roots of spiritual life."[8]

Old and New Principles of Initiation

A great misunderstanding has come about regarding the anthroposophical path of initiation. This has to do with the fact that Steiner initially referred to ancient methods of initiation. But these later turned out to have very little to do with the anthroposophical path. How did this misunderstanding come about?

In Steiner's early writings, which made Anthroposophy known within the framework of the Theosophical Society, the terminology of traditional mysticism, ancient occultism, and Eastern esotericism played a significant role. We have Steiner's 1901 lectures about mysticism, which he held even before his association with the Theosophical Society. The careful reader will recognize that the author is not really concerned with traditional mysticism but with "Mystics after Modernism," which is the title of these lectures. For Steiner, mysticism was characterized by subjectivity. Yet he was concerned with laying the foundation for a spiritual science, suitable for the modern age, that would be "as objective as scientific thinking," but would go beyond "merely registering the facts available to the senses" and advance "to comprehensive understanding."[9]

One year later, in 1902, *Christianity as Mystical Fact* was published. In later, expanded editions, the phrase "and the mysteries of antiquity" was added to the title. The title of *Theosophy* (1904) was bound to create further misunderstandings, as were articles alluding to a "secret apprenticeship" in the magazine *Luzifer-Gnosis* (1904). These were later consolidated in the book *How to Know Higher Worlds* (1909). In 1909, *An Outline of Esoteric Science* appeared—a title that again was bound to create misunderstandings. No wonder Steiner was constantly obliged to differentiate his intentions from those of (Anglo-Indian) Theosophy, as well as from those of the proponents of old initiation.

A comparison of Anthroposophy with Theosophy, ancient mystery cults, and Eastern esotericism shows that Steiner did not simply adopt ancient methods of initiation or carry on Eastern traditions. In *Christianity as Mystical Fact,* Steiner showed not only how old mystery practices still played a role in early Christianity, but also how Jesus of Nazareth distanced himself from these ancient practices as well as from the old Eastern path of enlightenment taught by the Buddha. The terms "occult schooling" and "occult science" are not in themselves contradictory, but modern science is not concerned with secrecy, and the arcane disciplines of antiquity had to be abandoned once and for all.

Steiner gave new meanings to the concepts "occult" and "esoteric." Unlike the proponents of the old esotericism, including his friend Friedrich Eckstein, Steiner broke with the tradition of secrecy and dedicated himself to opening up the mysteries to public knowledge. This intention was explicitly laid down in the statutes of the General Anthroposophical Society in 1923. Steiner was convinced that the emphasis on public knowledge of the contents of the mysteries was one means of overcoming the ever-threatening tendency toward sectarianism in the society. One example of this activity was that during the so-called "Christmas Conference" in 1923, he made public the lecture cycles that he had originally given exclusively to society members. This became necessary first of all because it was not possible to keep the contents of the lectures a strict secret anyway. Indiscretions had occurred. The second reason was that Steiner wanted to speak to people's consciousness. It was his declared intention to replace the "antiquated notion of secrecy" with a new understanding of the mysteries. Nonetheless, he decided to use a vocabulary that was rooted in older traditions. He did not want to disrupt the continuity between the spiritual schooling of yesterday and the inner needs of modern humanity. The anthroposophical path of schooling is also of an esoteric nature.

What is specifically esoteric here? It is the fact that the soul-spiritual substance of the human being is affected by the schooling, and that this is done in full freedom for the individual and in full clarity of mind. This esoteric process corresponds entirely with what Jung called "self-recognition." For Jung as well as for Steiner, it was essential that the process not only convey knowledge but bring about at the same time soul-observations and inner experiences that would lay a foundation for self-knowledge and world knowledge. To give an example of what Steiner meant by "esoteric": he called Fichte's theory of science or even any logarithmic table "esoteric" works, because a person would need to practice, study, and think about the contents before he or she could grasp their reality. The essential quality of the esoteric is that people take spiritual facts into their thinking, and these in turn change us and help us to develop.

Basically, the esoteric initiation process is an entering into an inner space of practice, of probation, and of experience. It is something extraordinary, intimate, and unique that cannot be protected by any outer rule of secrecy. It is inherently protected from unauthorized intruders. One can only enter the inner sanctum if he or she has mobilized the necessary soul-spiritual qualities. The uniqueness and intimacy of this experience is due to the fact that soul experiences happen to one particular person, even though the ways to achieve them are perfectly open to anyone. Esoteric experiences do not happen in the public domain.

Substitution is not possible, because the "I," the Self, which is the center and the goal of every initiation, cannot be replaced by that of another person, be it the most intimate friend. Karlfried Graf Dürckheim, who pursued a path different from both Jung's and Steiner's, wrote: "Initiation in this sense is a word that one should only use with great modesty and discretion. It means something so tremendous, goes so far beyond any normal human experience, that anything that happened and can happen in such an initiation will always be shrouded in deep secrecy. It has to be that way, it has to be protected from any intrusion by unqualified others. The word 'initiation' will always retain this quality. But the time is ripe that humankind should begin to move in the direction of this highest experience, should be on the way toward initiation."[10]

How is Jung's process of individuation connected to the initiation process? Jolande Jacobi has called the path of individuation the "keystone" of Jung's work, by which analytic psychology stands in marked contrast to all other schools of psychology. In her monograph on this subject she has shown that the individuation process, which represents a universal law of life, contains an "archetypal floor plan."[11] This "floor plan" shows some interesting parallels between modern psychological practice and the abundance of motifs in the history of religion and of the ancient mysteries. These materials were also the ones in which Jung found historical "prefigurations" for his depth-psychological observations.

Included in this material are, for instance, religious and mythical traditions about birth, life, death; the resurrection of a god; about the wanderings, trials, and battles of the hero with a monster. The tales of mystical and magical practices aimed at transformation and rebirth belong here. In the West as well as in the East, this mystery wisdom has been handed down in manifold ways. One can find traces of this knowledge in fairy tales and legends. Ethnology has a wealth of proof of secret cults and initiatory practices. In these practices, even though they stem from very different stages in the development of humankind, one can find the "archetypal" patterns for modern initiation techniques. Many of these traditions express projected hopes for the future. There can be no mere imitation or revival of ancient practices for the reasons indicated above, having to do with the evolution of human consciousness. Steiner made it abundantly clear that Anthroposophy is committed to the present stage of consciousness. This is shown by the fact that he refers to ancient symbolism only rarely, if at all.

Jung also aimed at freeing his patients from their entanglement by the unconscious pictures, even though references to symbolic, mythological, and spiritual history play a prominent role in his therapy. (The "hidden persuaders" of modern advertising, who know the power of images only too well, lead today's highly unconscious masses into a form of captivity by manipulating powerful symbols to induce desire in their minds.)

The individual archetypal pictures, however, make transparent a soul-spiritual reality that points beyond historical events of the ancient mysteries. This may be why Steiner's basic books use terms like "stages of initiation," "enlightenment," the "encounter with the Guardian of the Threshold," and so on. In his four mystery plays, from *The Portal of Initiation* to *The Soul's Awakening*,[12] the process of initiation unfolds in dramatic images. Steiner explicitly pointed out that these scenes depict mainly inner events, events of a soul-spiritual nature. The dramatic events do not serve to depict historical mystery cults. Steiner wanted his audience to receive them "with an open, unbiased inner being." In other words, they want to be experienced. "The meaning itself can be said to flow out of these pictures."[13] They induce an inner process in the soul, even though what is portrayed in the mystery dramas in picture form, and in the basic books more in the form of thoughts, is taken from the world of outer perceptions. "As the soul gives itself up to these images, it gains an understanding for the 'climate' of the spiritual world," said Steiner in the lectures (quoted above) that he gave during the Munich performances of the mystery plays in 1913.

Anthroposophical Meditation

Anthroposophy is distinguished from other cognitive methods in assigning an important role to thinking, yet does not limit itself to theoretical thinking alone. It works toward an altered consciousness. This altered consciousness is to be achieved by meditation.

Meditation, in Rudolf Steiner's sense, is a soul exercise in which the meditator remains in full control of his or her consciousness. This soul exercise, which can be freely varied according to a person's particular need, is designed to strengthen the individual's inner life. The functions of thinking, feeling, and willing are gradually freed from the realm of the senses and at last are transformed into organs of supersensible perception. One prerequisite is the totally free choice of what is to take place in the moments set aside for meditation; it begins with the free choice of meditative content. To promote attention and focus, anthroposophical meditation starts with clearly observable thoughts. "Living in one's thoughts...is an instance of the soul's getting away from itself, whereas living in feeling, sensation, emotion, and so forth are all instances of the soul's dwelling in itself." The soul is the stage where the world of thoughts comes to life. "A good preparation for understanding spiritual insights is to feel frequently what strength lies in the mood or attitude of soul when one meditates on the thought: *In thinking, I experience myself united with the stream of cosmic existence.* The value of meditating on this thought lies much less in the abstract understanding of it than in what is to be gained by repeatedly experiencing the strengthening effect it has on the soul if it flows powerfully through one's inner life. It expands in the soul like a deep spiritual breath of life."

Steiner points out in this connection that it is not so important to figure out what could be meant by such a thought; that could lead to abstractions that ought to be avoided. The emphasis is on experiencing the thought inwardly. This experience will have the desired strengthening effect on the soul life if it is repeated often.

For our comparison of the anthroposophical method of meditation with Jung's psychotherapy, a brief characterization must suffice. However, a few basic principles may be given here. The anthroposophical practice may begin as follows:

"First, you work your way through to grasping a thought that you can fully understand with the means provided by everyday life and ordinary thinking. Then you sink yourself repeatedly into that thought, become absorbed in it, and make yourself wholly one with it. By living with a thought known in this way, your soul gains strength."[14]

The word "sink" should be understood only in the sense of intense concentration on the object of meditation, not in the sense of "losing oneself" in the thought, which may lead to the loss of the light of consciousness. The goal is to build and strengthen the inner force that creates thoughts. It is also important that the relevant representations arise freely from within. Great emphasis is placed on this inner activity, which is guided by the "I." While sense perception may be fairly passive, meditation calls for a full measure of soul activity. To meditate means to "fill one's consciousness with ideas not derived from external Nature, but called up from within. In doing so we pay special attention to the inner activity involved."[15]

Steiner has taken thinking as the starting point for his path of knowledge. One has to be aware, however, that in meditation it is important to experience thinking in a different way than is usual. In our day-to-day life thinking is ordinarily guided by coincidence, or simply by "what comes to mind." One thought leads to another without any particular involvement by the conscious "I." Therefore, it is very important that during meditation one decides voluntarily, right from the start, to shut out all associations, memories, and sense impressions that seek to intrude into the process. Practical experience shows that this discipline of thought and will can pose some real difficulties for the beginner. But in the process of overcoming these difficulties, the soul life is strengthened. To this end, Steiner also recommended that one should not necessarily employ ready-made symbols, but should assemble a freely chosen image or symbol in one's mind. Thereby one avoids getting mired in rigid, dogmatic concepts and pictures.

Furthermore, it is important that immersion in the chosen object of meditation be done in complete selflessness. Selflessness is not identical with "egolessness." The object can be taken from the pure colors and forms of natural phenomena, for instance. Selflessness means here that one should be free of prejudice, of like or dislike. These can distort the process of meditation. It is not important *what I think* of the object of my meditation but *what the object has to say to me.*

A second step in meditative practice is to be able to erase all the pictures that present themselves before the inner eye and thereby to create an "empty consciousness." Thus one creates a "soul vacuum" that must not be filled with either concepts or images. This vacuum is like a *tabula rasa* that can receive inspirational imprints from the spiritual world.

The metamorphosis of soul forces can thus be characterized as a progression, starting from conceptual thinking. Meditation strengthens and schools this thinking until it is able to receive imaginative pictures (the level of imagination). Finally, the soul enters realms of spiritual experience that have been called *inspiration* and *intuition*. Each of the progressive stages of consciousness has to be prepared by appropriate exercises that complement the schooling of thinking with a schooling of the feelings and the will.

Jung's Active Imagination

If we juxtapose the anthroposophical path with Jung's process of individuation, we first have to remember that Steiner did not merely copy models from the ancient mysteries or Eastern spiritual practices. He devised a path that is suitable for modern Westerners. With careful study, one becomes aware that the continuity between the old and new mystery paths is fruitful. The terms used, for instance, in the book *How to Know Higher Worlds*, while reminiscent of traditional mystery language, refer to spiritual facts that can be experienced nowadays just as they were in the past. Our present language, suited as it is mainly to describe experiences of the sense world, is only able to hint at what is happening in the soul.

We find a similar use of the language in Jung's individuation. According to the nature of the process, Jung uses mythical pictures as well as mystical, Gnostic, and alchemical language to describe and amplify what is unfolding in the patient's soul. It is possible to detect phases and steps that indicate a forward movement. It is the task of the analyst to determine at what "station" the patient finds himself, and to recognize possible dangers and crises. The analyst does this by observing the psychic phenomena as they appear in the patient, and by consulting the relevant material from myth and mystery tradition. There is, for instance, the symbol of the *Nekyia* of Homeric tradition, which signifies the descent into "the land of the dead" that was the beginning of Jung's own self-analysis.[16] On the other hand, Jung employs the stages of the alchemical process as an expression for the psychotherapeutic *opus*, the process of individuation. In particular, Jung interpreted the alchemical process of preparing the *lapis philosophorum*, the "philosopher's stone," as projections of inner processes. This interpretation enabled him to gain a better understanding of maturation processes in the soul. (Jung did not, however, presume to pass judgment on alchemy itself.)

While the anthroposophical path is characterized by schooling and by a methodical meditative practice, these features are lacking in analytic psychology. The question of method can be clearly determined neither from Jung's writings nor from practical psychotherapy, at least not point by point. To be sure, one who is on the path to individuation is faced with many challenges. Dedication, cooperation, decisions are indispensable. The whole psychotherapeutic process demands full commitment, because only in the dramatic dialogue between analyst and analysand can the process begin to unfold. On the other hand, there is much emphasis on the spontaneity of the unconscious as it expresses itself in dreams, imagery, ideas, and even in outer "synchronicities." Therefore it is not possible to determine beforehand what needs to be done by the analysand, by the analyst, or by both of them in cooperation, or in what sequence.

The difference between the anthroposophical path and the one taken by depth psychology becomes especially clear when we compare the anthroposophical method of meditation with what Jung called "active imagination." Considering the great number of practices that pass for meditation in the Western world today, we could look at the practice developed by Jung as a form of meditation. This practice is predominantly used in the context of psychotherapy.

In 1957—at two important conferences of the Stuttgart group *Arzt und Seelsorger* ("medicine and pastoral care")—"active imagination" was introduced and discussed as a form of meditation.[17] Marie-Louise von Franz described it as "a special form of dialogue with the unconscious." Since we have already mentioned "imagination" in the context of higher stages of consciousness, it must be emphasized that Jung's "active imagination" is not identical with Steiner's "imaginative consciousness," even though both are active in that soul realm where pictures are seen as the expression of psychic realities. The main difference here is that Steiner's imagination comes about as a result of the special thought-exercises and thereby constitutes a form of enhanced consciousness above and beyond normal waking consciousness. In contrast, Jung's active imagination can be viewed as a hovering between waking and dreaming. It still takes place within ordinary consciousness.

In practice, active imagination works in such a way that images, concepts, and thoughts are produced that do not stem from "arbitrary, playful daydreams, but aim to reconstruct the inner logic of events that nature unfolds in the soul." Jung knew how to differentiate this *imaginatio,* this special power of imagination, from passive, vague, and arbitrary fantasizing. One can detect the analysand's degree of wakefulness by the character of the pictures that arise. Active imagination calls for the analysand to be awake and ready to make decisions in accordance with the events that unfold before the inner eye. He or she is never merely a spectator. "The therapeutic significance of active imagination lies in the possibility of influencing the unconscious, of working directly on affects, and of being able to accomplish a creative deed of liberation by effectively working with the symbols," wrote Marie-Louise von Franz.

There is no doubt that Jung's active imagination, although it differs from anthroposophical meditation, reaches deeply into the realm of psychic pictures. Therein lies its effectiveness, but also its danger, should the high ethical standards not be observed that Steiner called for in *How to Know Higher Worlds*: "Every insight that you seek only to enrich your own store of learning and accumulate treasure for yourself alone, leads you from your path, but every insight you seek in order to become more mature on the path of the ennoblement of humanity and world evolution brings you one step forward. This fundamental law must always be observed. Only if we make it the guiding principle of our lives can we call ourselves genuine seekers after higher knowledge. This truth of esoteric schooling may be summarized as follows: every idea that does not become an ideal for you kills a force in yourself, but every idea that becomes an ideal for you creates forces of life within you." And again, "for every single step that you take in seeking knowledge of hidden truths, you must take three steps in perfecting your character toward the good." Precisely because active imagination can be practiced in a dangerous manner, even to the point of black magic, Marie-Louise von Franz rightly demanded: "Ethical integrity of purpose is the absolute basic requirement for every attempt at active imagination." It follows that active imagination must be above all a tool in the hands of a psychotherapist.

When one sees the dedication with which Jung explored the creations of the unconscious, how he tried to decipher and transform them, one could say that analytic psychology gives full credit to those forces that emerge from the depth of the soul as thoughts and will impulses and need to be lifted into consciousness. Steiner calls these "the heart's language...asking from its unconscious life." In a lecture from the last stage of his active period, he confessed that he was not actually speaking out of himself, but that through him was articulated "what sounds forth in the hearts of human beings in our time." He said: "It is not I who have spoken these words. I have only formulated what human hearts are saying."[18] Nevertheless Steiner had no illusions about the fact that what was subconsciously desired in his age—to become conscious of the true nature of humanity and the world—was met with bitter resistance by his contemporaries.

Yet Anthroposophy was created to help answer those deeper questions that slumbered and still slumber in the depths of our souls. "The mighty task of Anthroposophy is given it by the voice of the human heart. It springs from nothing else but from human longing in our time." Such were Steiner's words. He added to these lofty claims: "The Anthroposophical Society will have to find a way to enable human hearts to speak out of their deepest, heartfelt inner longing. Then these human hearts will also feel a deep longing for the answers." Who will claim that one or the other of these lofty goals has been reached?

At this point in our study, we can see how close the intentions of Jung and Steiner actually were. Jung, the physician, is entirely focused on the emanations of the unconscious in the individual destiny as well as in that of the whole of humankind. In his writings, he pays close attention to outer events and diagnoses them as "psychopathic symptoms in the political arena." In his own way, Jung thereby practices what Steiner has demanded: "the symptomatology of contemporary events." The psychiatrist Jung is determined, with the tools available to him, to decipher the "language of the heart" as it becomes audible to him.

What is it that expresses itself thus? It is not easy to find a common denominator for all those symptoms and signs of the time that call for interpretation. The main factor may appear to vary significantly. depending on one's viewpoint. The terms "liberation," "coming of age," and "integration" come to mind. Then we have Jung's individuation, or Steiner's image of the "crossing of the threshold," which he used to describe the leap in consciousness, and modern humanity's crisis in its wake. Out of this insight he gave practical suggestions for a new orientation of spiritual, economic, and social life.

"I" and Self

In the description of the anthroposophical image of the human being, we pointed to the central importance of the "I." It was emphasized that this "I" constitutes a significant step in human development insofar as it gives us the ability to recognize ourselves as unique. However, it was also stated that the whole human individuality is not yet fully expressed by this "I." Steiner shows how, as a result of its inner schooling, the soul experiences the maturation of a spiritual core that is independent of the influences of normal conscious life. Picturelike but real, as if it wanted to manifest as a separate being, there arises out of the depths of the soul a second self, which appears to be superior to and independent of the "I" one has so far been conscious of. It appears to give inspiration to the "I." Finally, the individual merges the two and remains conscious of the higher, inspiring one.[19]

Steiner uses the expression "second, different, superior self," of which a person is not conscious in the normal waking state, even though the "I" receives inspiration from this second self from the depth of the soul. However, one should not conclude that elements of Steiner's concept of the human being and Jung's idea of the psyche could easily be seen as identical. Even so, Steiner's "second self" and Jung's "Self" certainly have one thing in common: in both cases something comes into view that is all-encompassing, includes the sphere of the unconscious, and is superior to normal waking consciousness. Steiner leaves no doubt that this "superior 'I'-being," as he has also called it, is not the result of theoretical speculation, but only after the discipline of inner schooling does it become possible to "experience…the living being of this 'I' in its reality as power in you, and to the sense that the ordinary 'I' is a creation of this superordinate 'I'. This feeling marks the true beginning of seeing the spiritual nature of the soul."[20]

Jung sees the Self, according to his terminology, as the center as well as the circumference that embraces conscious and unconscious. It is the center of this totality.[21]

Jung gives a very important hint when he calls the Self simply the "goal of life." As he wrote at the end of *The Relations between the Ego and the Unconscious*, "So too the Self is our life's goal, for it is the completest expression of that fateful combination we call 'individuality,' the full flowering not only of the single individual, but of the group, in which case each adds his portion to the whole."[22]

This remark is noteworthy because it is made in reference to the aim of individuation, and because Steiner also talks about his "second, superior self" in the context of the problem of human destiny. When he said that an inspiration is felt in the depth of the soul that flows from the "other self," he did not mean that the influence came in the form of thoughts or ideas, but that "deeds" were involved. According to Steiner's statements, a special dynamic is at work here. "It is this 'other self' that leads the soul to the details of its life destiny and evokes its capacities, tendencies, and talents. The 'other self' lives in the entire destiny of a human life. It accompanies the self that is conditioned by birth and death, and shapes human life with all its joys, exaltation, and pain."

Supersensible consciousness discovers a dynamic spiritual reality that causes—or rather creates—what the Hindus describe with the word *karma*. "The course of our life is inspired by our own permanent being, which continues from life to life. This inspiration works in such a way that the destiny of one earthly life is the consequence of previous lives. You learn to recognize yourself as another being, so to speak, different from who you are in sensory existence. This being manifests itself in sensory existence only through its effects."[23] If we are looking for a psychological term for what is meant here, the "unconscious" comes to mind. We would have to talk about a destiny-forming force of the unconscious, of a force that not only calls forth ideas and images, but also creates "synchronicities" that manifest at very specific moments as outer events, as illnesses, accidents, or significant meetings with other people. This force shapes our destiny and at the same time helps us to gain an understanding of our life. Steiner himself tried to focus on the psychological aspects of karmic relationships when he said on one occasion:

> With the help of the force that slumbers in our subconscious, we lay out our life's path from the moment of our birth, and even more so when we begin to say "I" to ourselves, in such a way that it crosses another person's path at a certain time.... This is not contradicted by the fact that often a person may find so little satisfaction with his life. If he could clearly see all the factors, he might well find that they could be satisfied. Just because waking consciousness is not as smart as the subconscious, it misjudges the events that are caused by the latter and says to itself: "Something unfortunate has happened to me." In reality, the wisdom of his subconscious had wished for this event to happen, even though in his waking judgment he considered it unfortunate. Knowledge of these deeper connections can lead to the realization that "someone wiser" has sought out those things that become one's destiny.[24]

Jung talks more about the *result* of karma or destiny having influenced the Self and manifested in a human individuality. Steiner, on the other hand, is more interested in the causal dynamics. With this, he already touched on the transpersonal realm, as we can see from Steiner's passages quoted here. They do not refer merely to a single incarnation, for the wisdom-filled force of karma that shapes our destiny works through many earthly lives. Jung was at least conscious of the fact that he had already stated "a transcendental postulate" by using the concept of "Self," a concept that could be justified psychologically, but could not be scientifically proven. He admits to having thereby overstepped the limits of empirical science. In the above-mentioned text he declares emphatically that overstepping these limits was for him an "absolute necessity. Without this postulate I would not be able to adequately describe the psychic processes that I observe empirically every day." This means, no doubt, that the psychologist has to leave the physical dimension when he wants to gain knowledge of the psyche, even if he has to resort to forming a hypothesis. Jung's postulate is limited here to the static aspect of the Self, as the "expression of the combined influences of destiny." One gets this impression when one compares Jung's postulate with the anthroposophical viewpoint, which contains the idea of karma. Of course, the value of Jung's therapy does not lose its significance in view of this statement.

In any event, Steiner is concerned with the dynamics of the Self as the "superior 'I'" that instills its inspirations into the life of the individual in the form of destiny patterns of which the "I" is unconscious. It is this dynamic aspect that allows Steiner to transcend the individual human life and see it as part of the ongoing movement of the "I" from incarnation to incarnation. Jung does not enter into this way of thinking. The idea of reincarnation plays no role in his depth psychology. The absence of the idea of repeated earthly lives constitutes an important difference between Jung and Steiner. In his lectures on psychoanalysis in 1917, but also before and after, Steiner pointed out that psychoanalysis, as he could see it at that time, "still worked out of insufficient understanding." This insufficiency was the result of the prejudices of natural science that stood in the way of recognizing the fact of reincarnation. It did not suffice to analyze the "primeval slime" of the soul (an expression that Steiner adopted from Freud). The important thing was to study the soul-germ that is embedded in this "primeval slime." Such an investigation presupposes the knowledge of repeated earthly lives as well as an understanding of a higher Self.[25]

It does not suffice to simply state here that Jung, for whatever reasons, did not consider the idea of reincarnation. One has to consider that in 1916–17 he had not yet discovered the symbol of the Self in its full significance. Only after 1928 did he describe the "Self" as an image of the total personality and as an entity superior to the conscious "I." He always based his psychological insights on empirically evaluated facts. Only these facts made it possible for him, on the one hand, to postulate a transcendental dimension and, on the other hand, to open up a way to true understanding of psychic processes. Nobody would claim that Jung thereby became a metaphysician or a spiritual researcher; Jung himself would have been the last to make such a claim.

He insisted on his empirical way of gathering knowledge. Considering what we know today, Steiner's words in his Zurich lectures of 1919, referring to the "Zurich professor Jung"—"psychoanalysis approaches the world of spiritual science, as it were, spiritually blindfolded"—are no longer relevant. These words were spoken at a time when Jung's analytic psychology was only in its infancy. There was no way of predicting then at which point this method of research would open up new horizons for our view of the world and of humanity. One such point was the psychological proof of the "Self," comprising not only the past development of the soul, but also that of the future, as decreed by destiny. At this point as well as at many others in his work, it becomes clear that Jung's psychology contains spiritual tendencies. This means that analytic psychology does not, to begin with, close off the empirical psychic field from the spiritual. Only by presupposing the spiritual is analytical psychology able to arrive at an understanding of psychical reality. It is this fact that makes a comparison of spiritual science and psychology necessary and meaningful.

Animus and Anima

Even though it is not our task here to describe Jung's path of individuation in detail, there is one important characteristic that belongs to this path, which is the path of becoming fully human. This is the aspect that presents the Self as a symbol uniting the polarities in the soul. Jung spoke of the "bipolarity of the archetype," which comprises not only conscious and unconscious, superior and inferior functions of the psyche, but also the male and the female principles. For these, Jung has coined the terms *anima* and *animus*.

In Steiner's work, we find passages that are analogous to, although they do not completely correspond with, Jung's terms. One of them is the statement that the etheric or life-body, which regulates all life functions, has the characteristics of the opposite gender. In other words, a man's etheric body is female, while the woman's is male. We find this remark in many of Steiner's lectures, but it is never elaborated, and he does not explain the significance of this fact or what its sociological implications might be. The pertinent remarks that were made in connection with male-female gods and goddesses, such as Isis and Osiris, Shiva and Shakti, can hardly be understood out of context. One will have to consider them together with Steiner's occult-physiological—"anthropogenetic"—concepts, but also with records from the evolution of consciousness. It certainly is interesting to see how Aniela Jaffé summarizes Jung's interpretation. She defines anima and animus as "personifications of the feminine nature of a man's unconscious and of the masculine nature of a woman's." Aniela Jaffé parallels this double gender in the psyche with the biological fact that the male as well as the female gender is determined by the larger number of either female or male genes.[26]

Even before we enter into a discussion of these connections, however, we will have to insert the following: Before one can deal with the anima-animus problem on the path of individuation, there is another factor to consider—the "shadow." This is what Jung calls the problem that the confronts the analysand when she discovers the heretofore unconscious negative or shadow side in her psyche. This has to be accepted and integrated into the whole person. Later on we will go into more detail about the shadow, which is reminiscent of the "Guardian of the Threshold" or the figure of the "double" encountered on the anthroposophical path (see appendix: "Evil as Shadow and Double"). Coming to terms with the shadow must occur before the process of individuation can proceed to the even more difficult problem of the anima-animus polarity. Jolande Jacobi explains why: Only the ego and the shadow together form the broader consciousness that is capable of confronting the archetypal powers, especially the anima-animus figures, and to enter into dialogue with them.

We have to forgo a detailed description of the confrontation with the Self here, but it ought to be said that it constitutes an extremely far-reaching process of cognition. Animus and anima point to the opposite gender aspect of one's own psyche, and they point to that region that must be thought of as lying "underneath" the shadow, which in turn lies in the personal unconscious. Animus and anima bear the imprint of the collective unconscious. Much as the unconscious shadow is often projected onto other persons, the anima projection of a man, for instance, occurs when he projects his own ideal anima, of which he is quite unconscious, onto a woman his destiny presents to him. He is then attracted to her.

The physical and psychical union of a man and a woman, the *communio*, decisive as it is for both of them, expresses the longing for the joining of the two "halves" of the human being. A further step in inner recognition, a goal that is logically reserved for the second half of one's life, is the inner *communio*, the recognition of animus and anima. One could also say it this way: In the first half of one's life one has to find the outer "you." This is a maturation process that may involve more than single contacts between two people. In the second half of life it becomes possible to discover the inner "you." This has to be understood as the interpenetration of two beings with the result of becoming one whole. This is to be understood in the sense of the Hebrew verb *yadah*: Adam "knew" his wife Eve. In no way is it just a mental recognition of rational facts or circumstances. This "knowing" implies that a psychic wholeness has been achieved that cannot be replaced by even the most harmonious outer partnership.

Psychologically speaking, this means retracting one's anima or animus projection. That which was sought exclusively between the two sexes can now also be found in one's inner soul. (The terms "exclusively" and "also" serve to make it clear that the retraction of the animus-anima projection does not mean a self-imposed isolation from others. One could rather speak of an enhancement of the existing interhuman relationships. A new dimension opens up.)

When we speak of a deep and far-reaching cognitive event, it is because at this stage of the individuation process a confrontation occurs with archetypes of numinous power, perhaps with the "Wise Old Man" or the "Great Mother." The descriptions by Jung, but also by Neumann, Seifert, and others, contain a wealth of documentation of many different encounters with the creative power of the unconscious. Symbols play an important role as well: wholeness in the form of a sphere, a circle, or a square. Then there are combinations of these, based on the number four as their structural element. One simply has to peruse Jung's most important works on alchemical connections or Far Eastern meditation practices to get an idea of what these images convey.

The encounter with the Self that is part of the path of individuation, mirrored as it is in archetypal images, has the ultimate aim of creating not only a new way of being in the world, but also a new consciousness. It can take many forms, depending on the individual. An image, *the image of the human being*, appears. More and more one experiences oneself as being at one with this human image. This experience can never be replaced by a "knowable" image of the human being that has been acquired by scientific study, be it ever so complex. As Goethe writes in *Faust, Part Two*, "The indescribable, here it is done."

One goal of humanity's development finds its realization under the aspect of the masculine and feminine poles being melded together, forming a new whole. Religious symbolism has expressed this countless times. Basically, the polarity between man and woman constitutes a deep mystery. In spite of many tendencies during the Hellenistic period to obscure their meaning, the words of St. Paul still remain relevant. He wrote of the union of man and woman: "This is a great mystery: but I speak concerning Christ and the church" (Eph. 5:32).

Anthroposophy seeks to regain the wisdom knowledge of the mystery of the human being. Steiner has again and again referred to traditions connected to this old wisdom. He sought to maintain continuity between ancient mystery traditions and his yet-to-be-founded initiation science. I am thinking here of all the communications and aphoristic representations he offered on the concept of androgyny (see appendix: "On the Problem of Androgyny").

The old myth of the androgynous human, male and female at once, is supplemented and developed in Anthroposophy. Referring to Steiner's model of the human being, one would have to say: What makes a person either male or female is to be found in the "garments" of their being, not in the core, the individual self. The gender differentiation is embedded in the physical, etheric, and soul bodies. In contrast, the "I," the center of the human being, is neither male nor female. What Steiner calls the "I" does incarnate in clearly defined male or female bodies, and in ethnic and racial groups. However, the spiritual sphere where the "I" is at home does not know such differentiation. Spiritually, man and woman are simply "human." Cultural or conventional prejudices appear only where the spiritual "archetype" of the human being is not understood or has not yet been realized. To achieve true humanity is precisely the task given to human beings. From here the words of St. Paul receive new light: "There is neither Jew, nor Greek, there is neither bond nor free, there is neither male nor female: for ye are all one in Christ Jesus" (Gal. 3:28). This means that the communion with Christ as the representative of the "I" (or of the Self, in Jung's terminology) bridges the chasm of ethnic, national, societal, and gender differences. Total integration replaces these differences, as long as Christianity is not taken merely as a conversion to a certain religious group. Looked at in this way, gender and species can only have temporary significance. *The androgynous archetype appears as a prophecy of humanity's future total humanness.*

In his early work *Intuitive Thinking as a Spiritual Path*, Steiner anticipated the insight of the androgynous nature of the human being when he included the chapter "Individuality and Genus," writing:

> What is generic about us serves only as a medium through which we can express our own distinct being....Those who judge beings according to generic characteristics stop before the boundary beyond which people begin to be beings whose activity is based on free self-determination....Just as a free individuality frees itself from the characteristics of the genus, cognition must free itself from the approach appropriate to understanding what is generic.[27]

The anthroposophical image of the human being has evolved from its early roots as an illustration of what Steiner postulated in his *Intuitive Thinking as a Spiritual Path*. The concept of "free individuality" poses a challenge to which the individual, as well as the whole of humankind, will have to rise.

11

CONTRASTS AND SIMILARITIES
IN EAST AND WEST

JUNG AND STEINER BOTH had a far-reaching worldview that embraced all of humankind. This is demonstrated by the fact that both men addressed the East-West problem. By this we mean the tension between the Western mentality and Asian spirituality, especially the religious and spiritual traditions of the East.

Both Steiner and Jung approached the East-West problem at a time when there still was very little public awareness of the importance of a dialogue between Orient and Occident, and before a certain snobbery had become fashionable. Both Steiner and Jung, independently of one another, contributed much to acquaint the West with the spirituality of India and the Far East. Thus they belong within the ranks of those thinkers who, from the early nineteenth century on, provided important impulses for expanding the horizons of Westerners. But one has to become clear about the specific contributions of Jung and Steiner and how they differ from those who harped on Goethe's line from "West-East Divan": "Admit it, the poets of the Orient are greater than those of the Occident."

Two fundamental misconceptions should be avoided from the outset. One is that to take an interest in Eastern spirituality or in movements that view Eastern traditions positively is a sign of decadence and should be rejected outright. The notion exists that such interest blossomed especially after the World Wars. This shortsighted view was taken toward Anthroposophy, for instance. We forget that the anthroposophical movement was outlawed in Nazi Germany, and that it existed well before the First World War. Many of Steiner's important statements about Eastern traditions were made before that war. In the other misconception, both Jung and Steiner are criticized out of fear that occupation with Eastern spirituality could serve to introduce a certain relativistic synchronism that would intermingle Christianity with Eastern religious ideas or, even worse, replace Christianity with an "alternative religion."

The charge of being a "modern alternative religion" has been leveled at Anthroposophy as well as at Jung's analytic psychology. In addition, Jung has been accused of "psychologizing esoteric teachings."[1] The well-known theologian Willem Visser't Hooft writes: "The most powerful force...that contributes to a syncretistic mood is the school that was founded by C.G. Jung...in any case Jung's psychology contributes, directly or indirectly, to create a religious eclecticism in which all kinds of religious concepts are collected together without serious spiritual discernment."[2]

Yet utterances like these, made sometimes by renowned religious scientists like Georg Vicedom or Gerhard Rosenkranz, lack precisely the serious spiritual discernment that is needed to appreciate Steiner's as well as Jung's relationship to Eastern spiritual life. Such discernment is also needed for the understanding of Asian religions. It is understandable that those researchers who, as a result of their special farsightedness, tend to step out of the narrow confines of a specialty are attacked by the experts. But it is only right that the experts should go to the trouble of finding out what was intended by the assumed illegitimate overstepping of these confines. Such an attitude would be useful, especially when it comes to the question of the "East-West polarity." We must also consider here the question of East-West *unity*. Furthermore, clarification is needed to see whether East and West are indeed opposites, and whether one can speak of a possible bridge between the two.

Steiner's Relationship to Eastern Spirituality

Steiner gave no complete description of his relationship to the East and its spiritual life. If we want to inform ourselves about this subject, we are obliged once more to try to assemble his most important remarks from widely scattered sources. First of all we have to look at the lecture cycles.

If one is acquainted with the composition of Steiner's lectures as well as with his approach, one will not expect to find even a remotely systematic treatment of a certain theme. He always endeavored to satisfy the needs of his particular audience at the time; therefore he often approached his original theme in a spiral fashion, drawing wider and wider circles around it. Often the original title seems to be forgotten in the course of the lecture. This is true for the lecture cycles on the *Bhagavad-Gita* as well as for *The East in the Light of the West* and *West and East: Contrasting Worlds*. Aside from a short study by the Indologist Hermann Beckh, there exists, as far as I know, no single work that, taking into account Steiner's findings, deals with this problem in a detailed fashion.[3]

If Jung's affiliation with the psychoanalytic movement became a problem for him, Steiner's joining the Theosophical Society put him in a similar situation. This becomes especially evident when we deal with the question of his relationship to Eastern wisdom teachings. From very early on, in his Goethe studies as well as in his own thought, Steiner continued the European tradition of German idealism and modern natural-scientific thought. In contrast, the writings of H.P. Blavatsky, Annie Besant, and the other leading Theosophical writers of the turn of the century can be characterized by a strong leaning toward Eastern traditions, especially Hinduism and Buddhism. This is evident, for instance, in the way that Western thought and Christianity are judged in the main Theosophical works. They postulate the basic equality of all religions and extol a certain syncretism of all religions and faiths. One cannot say that the leading Theosophists fully recognized Christianity's unique spiritual message. To prove this to yourself, you only have to open Blavatsky's main work, the two-volume *Secret Doctrine*, or Besant's *Esoteric Christianity*. The latter is based on the construction of a pre-Christian Jesus.

There is no doubt that Steiner was in a precarious situation. Being affiliated with the Theosophical Society as the general secretary of its

German section, he used its vocabulary and took advantage of its social platform. On the other hand, he promoted views substantially different from those of the society whose name he used up until 1912. This difference in opinion finally led to his separation—or rather, his expulsion—from the Theosophical Society. Without compromises and without mutual concessions, it was simply impossible to continue their coexistence. That is why in Steiner's writings from the "Theosophical period" we find certain careful wordings like the one in an essay titled "The Relationship of the Buddha to Theosophy" (January 1905). We read: "Under certain conditions it may actually be un-Theosophical [he means un-anthroposophical] to teach the Buddhist and Hindu doctrines in the Occident. The Theosophist should not force foreign doctrines upon people, but should let everyone find the truth by his own path. Why should one teach a Christian Buddhist doctrine when one's own religion has its own kernel of truth? Theosophy must not be Buddhist propaganda but must try to help anyone who wishes it, to find true understanding of his own inner world."[4]

Steiner still carefully writes here: "under certain circumstances"; he still uses the typical Theosophical expression "kernel of truth." Yet he does not hide his own conviction that there must be no propaganda for either Buddhism or Hinduism in Europe. With this he unmistakably distances himself from Anglo-Indian Theosophy. The reality of the spirit cannot be found in a particular geographical location or in a certain cultural connection. It can only be found in one's own "inner space." One can hardly accuse Steiner of hiding his true conviction while he was general secretary of the Theosophical Society. When Annie Besant began to proclaim her protégé, the young Hindu boy Jiddu Krishnamurti, as the reincarnated Christ, Steiner objected immediately and strongly and distanced himself from such machinations. His lectures from that time, as well as his emphasis on the historic uniqueness of the Christ event (not to be confused with the Second Coming), must be seen as further reactions to the orientalizing tendencies of the old Theosophical movement.

The problem of hermeneutics, meaning the question of whether and to what extent Eastern spirituality and Western thought can be mutually understood, has been debated for a long time. It cannot be denied that since the nineteenth century, historical-critical philology has made inroads into the world of Eastern religions. However, this refers mainly to the deciphering of the old texts and traditions. The actual spiritual essence of these writings presented—and still presents—profound riddles to Western thinking.

The special task of the Theosophical movement was to open up a mystical path to Eastern spirituality grounded in faith, removed from critical analysis of the texts. The Theosophists had realized correctly that spiritual traditions require adequate interpretation. Critique as such—historical and philological awareness—played a subordinate role in these interpretations. So it is not surprising that no collaboration came about between Indian Sanskrit philology and science of religion on the one hand and the Theosophists on the other. "The nasty abyss" between modern scientific thinking and spiritual striving, which was certainly justified, could not be bridged. Steiner, too, was interested in the spiritual dimensions of the Eastern religious texts, just as much as he was in those of the Bible. At the same time, he did not neglect the conscientious efforts of philological and historical research.

The Indologist Hermann Beckh, who has made a name for himself as a scholar of Buddhism,[5] came to the following conclusion:

> Between the merely historical, critical, neophilological research of scientists and the unhistorical, uncritical, unphilological efforts of the Theosophical, neo-Buddhist, and related movements, we find the spiritual science of Rudolf Steiner. It shares the viewpoints of historical critical research with modern science; indeed, it follows them even more exactly. In addition, spiritual science is in agreement with philology and linguistics without falling into the trap of philological exclusiveness in areas where it does not suffice. Spiritual science is in accord with the Theosophists in its goal to reach beyond the limits of the sense world. However, it is not willing to be bound by dogmas that originate in foreign geographical regions and have been created according to preconditions and values of foreign cultures.[6]

Just as anthroposophical research can shed light on the biblical tradition, it is able to apply its ideas about the evolution of consciousness to Eastern teachings. Based on an understanding that human consciousness is changing over the course of time, it necessarily differentiates between the specially structured consciousness of ancient oriental humankind and that of modern Westerners. We have detailed descriptions by Steiner that characterize past human cultures exactly, such as the ancient Indian, ancient Persian, and Egyptian-Babylonian cultural epochs, up to our present time. Here the general statement must suffice that Indian people at the time of the *Bhagavad-Gita*, at the time of Buddha, of the *Upanishads*, and, even further back, at the time of the *Vedas*, possessed, to a greater or lesser degree, the gift of clairvoyance. This state of mind found its expression, in gradually changing nuances, in the different types of Eastern religious literature.

Hermann Beckh, who proved the value of the anthroposophical view for his specialty, has shown, for instance, how helpful this approach is to the understanding of the deities of the ancient Indian *Rig-Veda*:

> The songs of the *Rig-Veda*, as they have been handed down to us, are the mere echo of an ancient, living clairvoyance. These songs tell us quite clearly how the old clairvoyance was fading even then, and how intellectual doubts about the reality of the divine began to press in.... Even more do we see in the later products of Indian spirituality (for instance, in the *Upanishads* and the Samkhya philosophy) how the ancient clairvoyant consciousness seeks to find a transition to a consciousness more based on reason, and on thinking. It is Steiner's achievement to have pointed out that consciousness based on reason, which for modern humanity is the *starting point* for all further development, was for the ancient Indians *a distant goal*. They had to grow out of the old clairvoyant state and gradually achieve logical thinking. Even now we do not find logical thinking as highly developed in India as it was in ancient Greece.[7]

If we want to form a concept of Steiner's views on Eastern spirituality we find two aspects that seem contradictory at first. However, we find that fundamentally they complement each other. Steiner initially emphasized the big difference between the soul configuration of the oriental and the Westerner as far as their view of the outer world and of their own "I" is concerned, and in the value each places on spiritual and material reality. Steiner's remark about the contrasting worlds of East and West is the result of these considerations. However, Steiner would not have been happy with Rudyard Kipling's verse: "Oh, East is East, and West is West, and never the twain shall meet," written in 1889. Steiner saw Eastern spirituality and Western thinking as interrelated. Sarvepalli Radhakrishnan's programmatic work, *Eastern Religion and Western Thought*, and his *Community of the Spirit*, based on Hindu concepts, should by no means be confused with Steiner's views.

First of all, Steiner does not embrace the idea of the equality of all religions. He considers the unique event of the appearance of the Christ to be the central turning point in the history of the development of human consciousness. Steiner made this clear for the first time when, around Christmas 1912, in Cologne, he held the first official meeting of those Theosophists who refused to follow Annie Besant's path, which strongly emphasized the oriental teachings. At this meeting the Anthroposophical Society was founded. At that time Steiner gave a lecture cycle titled *The Bhagavad-Gita and the Epistles of Saint Paul*. These lectures are noteworthy insofar as Steiner, while juxtaposing two important documents of the history of religion, emphasizes an important point about the East-West problem. For our specific inquiry here, the following is important: From the anthroposophical viewpoint, the Eastern religious traditions are seen as documents that show the clairvoyant capabilities of ancient epochs. These capabilities were truly a treasure, but they diminished over the centuries to the extent that "I"-consciousness began to emerge. The yoga path was taken by those who wished to stay connected with the old, gradually dimming clairvoyance or wanted to restore it. "Man was originally endowed with a primal wisdom, and in the course of successive incarnations this wisdom was gradually lost. The appearance of the great Buddha marks the end of an old epoch of evolution; it provides the strongest historical evidence that men had lost the old wisdom, the old knowledge, and this explains the turning away from life. The Christ is the starting-point of a new evolution, which sees the sources of life eternal in this earthly life."[8]

The appearance of the Christ, who has not only created a "mystical fact" by his life on earth but also constitutes a historical fact, becomes the decisive factor in Steiner's discussion of the East-West problem. (Eastern religiosity is marked by an absence of historical facts.) In the East, the "I" lacked the decisive strength it had developed in the West thanks to the Christ impulse. While in the East, the deeds and destinies of the old gods and heroes pass before the souls of the masses just as in times of old, something entirely new begins to stir in Palestine. Geographically speaking, Palestine constitutes the threshold between Orient and Occident. The Mystery of Golgotha, interpreted and described by Steiner again and again from many different viewpoints (always as of central significance), is experienced by St. Paul. He possesses a mental attitude distinctly different from that of the oriental mind. In Paul we meet a strong individual personality, while the East presents us with superhuman, larger-than-life figures. In contrast to the serene yoga- or Krishna-wisdom of the *Bhagavad-Gita*, Paul's letters show the vital temperament of a strong personality. One only has to read these letters to realize that here we have to do not with a remote lawgiver from above, nor with a teacher of ancient wisdom, but with a man whose "I" has become the vessel for the Christ. "I live, yet not I, but Christ within me" (Gal. 2:20). The evaluation that Steiner gave of Paul in his lectures about the *Bhagavad-Gita* and on other occasions prompted Emil Bock to call Paul "one of [humanity's] greatest creative catalysts and innovators."[9] Earlier, Albert Schweitzer had called Paul "the guardian angel of thinking within Christianity." Both of these theologians saw that the apostle gave Christians the right forever to think for themselves, a right that Western humanity had to acquire painfully, step by step, and that is still lacking in the East in the same form.

The picture that Steiner evokes in the comparison of the *Bhagavad-Gita* and the letters of St. Paul is this:

In the *Gita* is the fully ripened fruit, a wonderfully beautiful outgrowth of human evolution throughout thousands of years, which finally comes to a ripe, wise, and artistic expression in the sublime *Gita*.

In the Epistles is the seed of something entirely new, which grows and must continue to grow. Only when one sees it as germinal, as prophetic of what could come of it after thousands and thousands of years of development into the future, can one sense the full significance of this steadily ripening seed laid into human soil by the Pauline Epistles. For a true comparison, this has to be considered.[10]

According to this interpretation, the song of the sublime, the *Gita*, is the ripe result of a long development, whereas Paul's letters have the quality of something new and still imperfect. If Steiner, in spite of all his admiration for Eastern spirituality, prefers the seemingly imperfect, which is only in the beginning of its development, it is for one reason: he is convinced that only with the incarnation, the death, and the resurrection of Christ Jesus has humankind been given the possibility to develop its own "I" in freedom. Christ's wholehearted affirmation of life, his "yes" to his painful death, his subsequent resurrection, were necessary. (In contrast, Buddha's advice was to flee life as well as death.) The spiritual Christ impulse needs to be accepted, and with it the ongoing maturation of the human "I," in order to further the development of humankind. "The elements necessary for understanding [that a God could unite himself with human nature] were present in the stream of thought that came over from the East; they needed only to be raised to a higher level. It was in the West that souls were ripe to grasp and accept this impulse.... So we see how that external understanding for the divinity of Christ Jesus was born in the East, and the emergence of conscience came to meet it from the West."[11] At this point we begin to see how East and West could and should complement and help each other. The Christ-Sun rose in the East; yet it was, and still is, understood only in the West. Putting aside the differences in consciousness, it is interesting to note a significant phenomenon in the course of historical events: Buddhism has conquered vast parts of

Asia, while the triumphant march of Christianity proceeded from East to West! And even where today "young churches" have sprung up in Asia, they have been initiated by Western missionaries. (An altogether different question is whether the gospel that is thus being introduced into Islamic, Hindu, and Buddhist environments has found the proper expression and can live in the souls of these people.)

Steiner considered it important that the scientific idea of evolution, having its roots in Christianity, should be used to arrive at an intimate understanding of the truth of what the Christ represents. Spiritual science sees this task as its very own. As is known, Teilhard de Chardin arrived at the same insight, even though he came from a somewhat different spiritual background than Steiner.[12]

What did Steiner think about the "inflow of Buddhist sentiments into the Occident"? He observed that this phenomenon began with Schopenhauer's philosophy. Basically, Steiner saw in European leanings toward Buddhist religiosity and way of life an anachronism, a regression that he attributed to a lack of understanding for the "purest form of the Christian impulse." This is why he felt it would be shortsighted if any spiritual-scientific movement transplanted Buddhism into Europe.[13] Steiner had this opinion about all oriental missionary efforts in the West. Yet this conviction, repeatedly emphasized in no uncertain terms, did not at all stem from any antipathy toward the East. Even less did he intend to give moral assistance to various Christian missionary institutions. These statements were made out of the need for clear knowledge. In the final analysis they were meant to serve true East-West understanding.

The fact that the idea of repeated earth lives (reincarnation and karma) is an integral part of the anthroposophical image of the human being has given rise to criticism of Anthroposophy. According to Steiner, the human individuality, incarnating in the body-soul element, forms together with it a body-soul-spirit entity and goes through many incarnations. The superficial observer concludes from this that the idea of reincarnation has been borrowed from Eastern thinking. However, this is to overlook the fact that Eastern humanity does not acknowledge the concept of a lasting individuality, based on a strong

"I"-consciousness. This the West has developed during its long spiritual history. Eastern humanity strives to escape the painful suffering of life on earth imposed by the law of karma. The Buddhist saying: "It is good not to live on earth" is not only a negation of life on earth. The very essence of the Buddhist view of the self and of the world is the belief that life is suffering, and that the cause of this suffering is the "thirst" to live, which leads again and again to incarnation and suffering. It is the aim of the Buddhist to overcome this "thirst," because earthly life is *maya*, illusion and unreality. Siddhartha Gautama's encounters with old age, illness, and death inspired him to seek buddhahood. Whoever claims, as is still the case, that Steiner embraces a Buddhist worldview, will soon discover himself embroiled in contradictions. Steiner's concept of reincarnation cannot be reconciled with the Buddhist aim of escaping the dreaded repetitions of life on earth, if the two are rightly understood.

In the course of his discussions of Buddhism, or rather in his comparison of Buddha and Christ, Steiner has repeatedly shown that his idea of reincarnation, based as it is in the Central European mentality, cannot be compared with Eastern spirituality. It only shows once more that East and West walk different paths. In any case, his concepts of reincarnation and karma are developed, like his whole spiritual science, from the standpoint of modern natural science.

"If our way of thinking comes to grips with life's phenomena and does not hesitate to follow thoughts from living, vital observation through to their final ramifications, we can indeed arrive at the idea of repeated earthly lives and destiny through mere logic." This is written at the end of the chapter about the reincarnation of the human spirit in his basic book *Theosophy.*[14]

Steiner sees the "the mighty impulse of the Buddha impulse as it flamed in a last gleam across the evening skies of Indian spiritual life" and of the whole of humankind up to that time. The pioneer of the Eightfold Noble Path shares with all orientals an entirely unhistorical worldview in which the concept of evolution, and a thinking that is focused on the goal of self-development, is entirely absent. While the Buddhist's aim was to stop the wheel of incarnation, the Christian, according to Steiner's view, strives to find the "higher self," the Christ self, within. The Christian strives to awaken this within herself, or to allow it to be awakened. To shape the world with the help of Christ is the task. "Yet [man] need not alienate himself from this world in order to enter into blessedness. Rather he must overcome the forces that make him see the world of illusion, and thereby be led back to his true original nature. There is a higher man who, if he could look upon the world, would see it in its reality."[15]

Since Judeo-Christians have become aware of their sinful state and are willing to atone for their sins, a way of redemption is open to them. This cannot simply be found in "personal achievement," for the ordinary "I" is not capable of this. "Atonement is only possible, however, when the will arises in [man] to press forward with his present ego consciousness to that higher state described in Paul's words, 'Not I, but Christ in me.'"[16]

At this point it will be necessary to juxtapose what Steiner calls the "inner nerve" of Buddhism and of Christianity. This juxtaposition leads to the realization that the Christian must not fear the possibility of repeated earthly lives, but should welcome them as opportunities to serve the Christ again and again. For Steiner, the historical event of the life of Christ on earth is unique and will not be repeated. It has its permanent place in the history of humankind. However, one lifetime does not suffice to exhaust the wealth of what the Christ impulse has brought to humankind. In addition, Christian thinking is, unlike its Buddhist equivalent, entirely historical. In the Christian concept of time, there is a beginning and an end, not an "endlessly repetitive cycle of the same." This makes progress over the course of time possible. In this vast framework, individual incarnation occupies a comparably short time. Reincarnation is not a repetition of the same, over and over again, but the continuation of what has been started in a former life. Here is how Rudolf Steiner sums it up, casting further light on the East-West situation:

Thus Christianity gives reality to the doctrine of repeated earthly lives. Now we say that man passes through repeated lives on earth in order that the true meaning of human life may repeatedly be implanted in him, each time as fresh experience. Not only the isolated individual strives upward. A yet deeper meaning lies in the striving of humanity as a whole, and we are bound up with it. No longer feeling himself united with a Buddha who urges liberation from the world, man, gazing at the central spiritual sun, at the Christ impulse, grows conscious of his union with the one whose deed has balanced the event symbolized in the Fall.[17]

The Buddha's achievement lay in reminding humankind of its connection to the "ancient wisdom" of the beginning. The Christ impulse points powerfully toward the future. And it is up to humanity's active engagement with Christ to wrest meaning from earthly existence.

Furthermore, Steiner put great emphasis on the fact that Western spirituality is not only equal to that of the East, but truly contains everything that the East has inherited from the past. Eastern wisdom can be compared to the wisdom of old age, Western thinking to the creative vitality of youth. "There is no wisdom of the East that has not streamed into Western occultism. In the Rosicrucian teachings and investigations of the Rosicrucians [which Steiner acknowledged as his favorites] indeed, you will find everything that has been preserved by the great sages from the East. Nothing, absolutely nothing, known through Eastern wisdom is missing in the wisdom of the West." This statement is also true for depth psychology, as becomes clear when we learn how Jung, in the course of his inquiries, discovered numerous correspondences between the results of his own research with patients and certain esoteric traditions of the East, especially the Far East. In the lecture just quoted, Steiner continues: "There is only this difference. The wisdom of the West had to illuminate this whole body of Eastern teaching with the light kindled in humanity by the Christ impulse, but without losing any of it."[18]

With this we have found, as it were, the key to Steiner's relationship to the East. The founder of Anthroposophy is no emissary of Eastern teachings in disguise. On the contrary, he saw it as the task of Western humanity to interpret the "East in the light of the West." This was the title of a lecture he gave in 1909. This view, inspired by the Christ event, made both possible: to clearly see the contrast between East and West (the theme of the great East-West Congress in Vienna in 1922) and also to find the common ground between East and West. The latter is an unavoidable task for modern humanity; ignoring it has already brought a bitter harvest whose further extent and consequences cannot yet be foreseen.

Only a person who has no illusion about the soul-spiritual individuality of each, and about the very real difference in consciousness, can speak of an East-West community. Steiner and Jung must not be castigated as trendsetters, initiating a fashionable Asia fad in the West. This allegation has been widely accepted through a misunderstanding of the true circumstances. Both men contributed much to the understanding of both the Orient and the Occident. Anthroposophy is definitely a science founded on Western thinking, and tries to bring to Western humanity an understanding of Eastern humanity and its truly different consciousness.

Jung's Relationship to Eastern Spirituality

Like Anthroposophy, Jung's analytic psychology can claim the distinction of being a thoroughly Western science. And yet this fact has always been doubted. Jung's commentaries on Eastern texts, for example, *The Secret of the Golden Flower*, were certainly not written with the intention of accompanying Western humanity on this path, but to aid in understanding such a document of Eastern spiritual training, which cannot be utilized by just anybody in the Western world. Jung pursued such studies in order to understand his own—as well as the differently structured Eastern—psyche. To attempt to understand something and to proselytize on its behalf are two different things.

Jung's evaluation of Eastern spiritual traditions resembles Steiner's in two respects: Jung acknowledged the incomplete character of the Western mentality, which is overly dominated by the intellect. He also knew that Orient and Occident make two halves of one spiritual universe, and that "the two standpoints, however contradictory, each have their psychological justification. Both are one-sided in that they fail to see and take account of those factors which do not fit in with their typical attitude. The one underrates the world of consciousness, the other the world of the One Mind. The result is that, in their extremism, both lose one half of the universe; their life is shut off from total reality, and is apt to become artificial and inhuman."[19] Moreover, Jung does not deny his own deep roots in the Western Christian tradition. These make it impossible for him to suggest that Western humanity should adopt or imitate creations of an Eastern spiritual tradition untested, even though Jung admired them. Here we also find the clear understanding of East-West contrasts that Steiner so eloquently expressed. We find recognition of these contrasts, as well as a wish for conciliation, in Jung as well.

Before dealing with Jung's numerous comments on general as well as specific problems of Eastern spiritual life, one should ask: how much weight did Jung himself give to his discussions of these questions? In Jung's collected works we find relevant passages in volume 11, *Psychology and Religion: West and East*. Clarification is especially desirable here, because it seems that the above-mentioned warnings against Jung's syncretistic leanings can be traced to similar misunderstandings as in Steiner's case. In the foreword to the second edition of his commentary on a Chinese text, *The Secret of the Golden Flower*, published by Richard Wilhelm, Jung takes the opportunity to point to "certain misunderstandings to which even well-informed readers of this book have succumbed: not infrequently people thought that my purpose in publishing it was to put into the hands of the public a recipe for achieving happiness. In total misapprehension of all that I say in my commentary, these readers tried to imitate the 'method' described in the Chinese text. Let us hope that these representatives of spiritual profundity were few in number!"[20]

Jung saw a second misunderstanding in the fact that people wrongly assumed his commentary to represent his special psychotherapeutic method "which, it was said, consisted in my instilling Eastern ideas into my patients for therapeutic purposes. I do not believe there is anything in my commentary that lends itself to such superstition. In any case, such an opinion is altogether erroneous, and is based on the widespread view that psychology was invented for a specific purpose, and is not an empirical science. To this category belongs the superficial as well as unintelligent opinion that the idea of the collective unconscious is 'metaphysical.'"[21]

In other connections Jung has also tried to dispel such misunderstandings. Characteristic of his attitude toward Eastern spirituality is a commemorative address he gave on May 10, 1930, at a memorial for his friend and collaborator, Richard Wilhelm. These words—which have been incorporated into the foreword to *The Secret of the Golden Flower*—give testimony to the deep appreciation that Jung had for the great Sinologist, who had, in his words, "the rare charisma of spiritual motherliness." Here Jung again demands the overcoming of prejudices that stand in the way of an understanding of the East. Yet when he calls for openness toward Eastern traditions he does not mean to give the green light to uncritical "India tourists." He means instead "appreciation beyond all Christian resentments, all European arrogance." This appeal stems from a time when a dialogue between Christianity and non-Christian religions hardly existed. At the same time, Jung predicts that "all mediocre spirits will lose themselves either in blind self-elimination or in ignorant criticism."

Jung speaks of Richard Wilhelm's cultural achievements when he says that Wilhelm brought new light from the East. In particular, Wilhelm recognized "how much the East could give us to help us heal our spiritual agony." But again one has to see these remarks in their special context. Jung says further: "The spiritual beggars of our time are inclined, unfortunately, to accept the alms of the East, and to blindly imitate its methods. That is the danger of which one cannot warn enough, and of which Wilhelm was keenly aware. The spirit of Europe is not served with a mere sensation and with a new thrill. Rather we have to learn to earn what we want to possess. What the East has to give us can be of help for the work that we ourselves have to do. What can we gain from the wisdom of the *Upanishads*, what from the insights of Chinese Yoga, when we abandon our own roots as if they were useless errors, and settle like shiftless pirates and thieves on foreign shores?"

This certainly is clear. The figure of speech "spiritual beggars" is turned to the positive by Steiner in a different context, when he interprets Jesus' words in the Sermon on the Mount "blessed are the poor in spirit" as meaning "blessed are those that beg for the spirit." Here he means those who are aware of their spiritual neediness and long for spirit as a beggar longs for alms on which his further existence depends. One must not confuse this spiritual hunger of the "poor in spirit" of the Sermon on the Mount with that of the "spiritual beggars" whom Jung condemns, because they seek to steal a foreign spiritual inheritance "like pirates on foreign shores."

Jung is just as clear when he points to the need for the expansion of European scientific thinking. He continues: "We need a truly three-dimensional life if we want to experience Chinese wisdom in a living way. That's why we need first of all a European wisdom about ourselves. Our path begins with European wisdom, and not with yoga exercises that deceive us about our own reality." Writing in 1930, Jung already foresees: "The spirit of the East is indeed *ante portas!*" And he already sees two possible results of the anticipated encounter between East and West: it could either bring a healing force or a dangerous infection. After having made this diagnosis, he leaves it to the "patient" what he will do with these new possibilities. The patient is every contemporary human being.

Five years later, Jung wrote an article in English in the journal *Prabuddha Bharata*, published in Calcutta. It was called "Yoga and the West." While thus far his collaboration with Richard Wilhelm had inspired him to penetrate into the Eastern Asian traditions, in this article he shows how he judges the spiritual-physical system of schooling from his standpoint as a Western psychologist. First of all, Jung sees the development that has led Western humanity to the conflict between faith and knowledge, between religious revelation and logical thinking. Jung diagnoses this condition as "a lack of direction that borders on psychic anarchy." He says further: "Through his historical development the European has become so far from his roots that his mind has finally split into faith and knowledge, in the same way that every psychological exaggeration breaks up into its inherent opposites."[22]

With this the psychologist expressed the fact that humankind had entered into a critical phase. Steiner also saw this low point and had sketched it as a necessary phase in the development of humankind. He saw it as his mission to overcome this crisis. When making the above-mentioned statement, Jung did not overlook the fact that certain aspects could be gleaned from the crisis that would throw light on the history of consciousness. In his book *The Origins and History of Consciousness*, Jung's pupil Erich Neumann has thoroughly scrutinized these connections. Steiner, from his viewpoint, spoke of "the spiritual guidance of the individual and of humanity."

Jung's conclusion—published, remarkably enough, in an Indian journal—reads: "The split in the European psyche prevents from the outset an adequate realization of the intentions of Yoga.... The Indian not only knows his nature, he also knows to what extent he can identify with it. The European, on the other hand, knows of nature through science, but of his own nature, the nature within him, he knows remarkably little."[23] The call for a comprehensive image of the human being, encompassing the whole of reality, resounds here again. Above all, Jung sees a "psychological disposition" that is different in Eastern and Western humanity. His advice is not to ignore Eastern spiritual life, but rather: "I say to whomever I can: Study Yoga; you will learn an infinite amount from it—but do not try to apply it, for we Europeans are not so constituted in a way that we apply these methods correctly, just like that. An Indian Guru can explain everything, and you can imitate everything. But do you know *who* is applying the yoga? In other words: Do you know who you are and how you are constituted?"[24]

Obviously, Jung is not against yoga as such. On the contrary, like Steiner, he seems to think of it as one of the greatest creative achievements of the human spirit. Jung is decidedly critical, however, of the practice of yoga by Westerners. "The spiritual development in the West has taken a totally different turn from that of the East, and thereby it has created extremely unfavorable conditions for the practice of yoga."

Jung's thoughts culminate here in prophetic, even provocative, words when he says: "In the course of the centuries, the West will produce its own Yoga, and it will be on the basis laid down by Christianity."[25] This statement, too, will have to be weighed carefully so as not to confuse it with what has come to us as "yoga for Christians" or "yoga for Westerners." Jung is thinking of something more than just the practical application of Eastern practices by Western people. Although it would be tempting to simply take the author of "Yoga and the West" at his word, here we can only ask: "What might a yoga look like that would be suited specifically to Westerners, to their unique mission, their psychological disposition—and would be based on Christianity? Maybe some rudiments of such a path already exist?"

It may suffice here to say that Steiner, aside from the descriptions of a path of schooling published in his basic books, has compared the Eastern path of yoga with the Christian or Rosicrucian path of initiation in many of his lectures.

This means that what Jung demanded, a Christian path of schooling, Steiner had inaugurated decades before; he had compared it with historical examples and differentiated it from Eastern practices.

We have from Jung's pen psychological commentaries on texts from the sphere of Eastern religions, like the aforementioned *Secret of the Golden Flower*, the *Tibetan Book of the Great Liberation*, and the *Bardo Thödol, The Tibetan Book of the Dead*. He has taken a position in his 1943 article "The Psychology of Eastern Meditation," and has written numerous extensive forewords, for instance to books by D.T. Suzuki and Heinrich Zimmer and to the *I Ching*. In contrast, he mentioned Western religious teachings (except medieval alchemy) in a scarcely differentiated manner that was often confusing for nonprofessional readers. He often mentioned these teachings in one breath, and called them "mass imports of exotic religious systems," such as the religion of Abdul Baha, the Sufi sects, the Ramakrishna mission, Western Buddhism, Christian Science, the Anglo-Indian Theosophy of H.P. Blavatsky, and Rudolf Steiner's Anthroposophy, even though the latter was expressly connected with the Central European spiritual heritage.

In 1938, Jung accepted the invitation of the British government of India to participate in the festivities of the twenty-fifth anniversary of the founding of the University of Calcutta. In addition to essays that appeared in the New York magazine *Asia* in 1939, we find records of this event in *Memories, Dreams, Reflections.*

"India gave me my first direct experience of an alien, highly differentiated culture. Altogether different elements had ruled my Central African journey; culture had not predominated.... In India, however, I had the chance to speak with representatives of the Indian mentality and to compare it with the European."[26] He made the acquaintance of S. Subramanya Iyer, the guru of the Maharajah of Mysore. Strikingly, Jung emphasizes the fact that he was introduced to numerous representatives of India's cultural life, but at the same time had consciously avoided any contact with "all so-called saints," esotericists, and spiritual leaders of India.

The Indologist Heinrich Zimmer, the friend to whom Jung owed important insights into the Indian mentality, asked him whether he had at least visited Sri Ramana Maharshi. Jung had to admit that he had not. In 1944, when Jung wrote the introduction to Zimmer's last work, *The Path to the Self*, entitled "About the Indian Holy Man," which centered around the life and work of Ramana Maharshi, he remarked: "Perhaps I should have visited Shri Ramana. Yet I fear that if I journeyed to India a second time to make up for my omission, it would fare with me just the same: I simply could not, despite the uniqueness of the occasion, bring myself to visit this undoubtedly distinguished man personally."[27] Why? Suddenly Jung had his doubts about the uniqueness of this man. He believed that he could only see the typical, something that was manifest in many forms in everyday Indian life. Only from the European standpoint could it claim to be unique. "That's why I didn't have to meet him. I have seen him everywhere in India, in Ramakrishna's portrait, in his disciples, in Buddhist monks, and in countless other figures of Indian daily life. His words of wisdom are the *sous-entendu* of the Indian soul." So it says in this particular passage.

Jung has many good things to say about Ramana, and about the Indians and their advanced spiritual maturity. He emphasizes that he does not underestimate the significance of the Indian holy man. Yet he, the psychologist, would never presume to judge him correctly as an isolated phenomenon. The ultimate reason for such reserve is given as the deeply rooted, different condition of the Western psyche.

It is certainly revealing to read what Jung once said in his memoirs: "I would have felt it as a theft had I attempted to learn from the holy men and to accept their truth for myself. Neither in Europe can I make any borrowings from the East, but must shape my life out of my self."[28]

For Jung, the need "to shape his life out of his self" and out of Western spirituality meant that he continued his studies in alchemy while he was on his trip through India. The compendium *Theatrum Chemicum*, an important alchemical work written in 1602, was his traveling companion. According to his own report, he studied this work from cover to cover. "Thus it was that this material belonging to the fundamental strata of European thought was constantly counterpointed by my impressions of a foreign mentality and culture. Both had emerged from original psychic experiences of the unconscious, and therefore had produced the same, similar, or at least comparable insights."

Something is expressed here that reminds one of Steiner's double aspect of differences and similarities. Steiner states that nothing that can be learned from the East is missing in Western wisdom. Jung speaks of "archetypal experiences of the soul," Steiner of "the human being's partaking of archetypal wisdom." These views certainly invite synoptic interpretation. The specifically Christian aspect is especially striking in Steiner's view, even though Jung considers it as well. Steiner felt it was necessary not only to unearth the common archetypal sources of wisdom in Eastern and Western thinking, but also to experience the wisdom of the East in a new way, inspired by the "fountain of youth, the Christ impulse." There can hardly be a doubt that Steiner and Jung would have agreed on this important point had it been possible for these two men to have a conversation bridging all possible misunderstandings and prejudices.

When one considers what weight the creations of his own unconscious had for Jung, one may finally be reminded of one dream he related. The dream occurred toward the end of his visit to India, which had been extremely rich in impressions. It appears as a summation of all that India and Eastern spiritual life meant for him. The dream imagery itself had nothing to do with the traditions of India, even though he had just experienced them firsthand. The content of the dream was the very core of Christian esoteric tradition, the Holy Grail. "Imperiously, the dream wiped away all the intense impressions of India, and swept me back to the too-long-neglected concerns of the Occident, which had formerly been expressed in the quest for the Holy Grail as well as in the search for the philosopher's stone. I was taken out of the world of India and reminded that India was not my concern, but only a part of the way—admittedly a significant one—which should carry me closer to my goal. It was as though the dream were asking me, 'What are you doing in India? Rather seek for yourself and your fellows the healing vessel, the *servator mundi*, which you urgently need. For your state is perilous; you are all in imminent danger of destroying all that centuries have built up."[29]

It is hard to escape the impact of these words, even though they may have a whiff of the confession of the octogenarian. What does it mean to walk the path of Parzival? Rudolf Steiner has said much that sheds light on this question. What he says is enlightening because it clarifies much about the individual path as well as that of humankind as a whole.

Jung stated: "No one should be deluded by the oft-heard cry: 'Rebirth out of Asia.' While 'orienting' yourself, you should also 'occident' yourself." No one today can underestimate the urgency of Jung's questioning, as we are faced with an acute East-West problem and with a drug-seduced youth that tends toward an illusionary Far Eastern mysticism. "What are you doing in India?" Jung asked himself. Steiner answered a similar question: "In honoring the Orient for its spirituality, there is something we still need to be clear about: we must build up our own spirituality from the first step we have taken in the West. We must so shape it, however, that we can achieve an understanding with any view that may exist on earth, especially old and venerable ones. This will be possible if, as Central and Western men, we come to understand that, although our philosophy of life has faults, they are the faults of youth."[30]

1 2

ALLEGATIONS OF GNOSTICISM

BOTH STEINER'S ANTHROPOSOPHY and Jung's psychology have been suspected of being "modern forms of gnosis." Those who have a solid knowledge of either Anthroposophy or analytic psychology understand why people who are only slightly acquainted with them, or their superficial critics, could arrive at such a judgment.

An accusation like this can arise from observations of the outer development of either one of the two movements. Nevertheless those who make such a claim can find themselves in an awkward situation. How can one compare a relatively unknown entity in the history of the mind with another—equally unknown and often ill-defined? Gnosis (or Gnosticism—a differentiation will be necessary) poses several problems. Whoever tries to learn about even the most important aspects of this movement will soon find that there is no clear, commonly known definition of gnosis. Interpretations of its pre- and early Christian, as well as its later, forms do not have a common denominator. Even the origins of this spiritual movement have not been clearly defined. Church historians and scholars of gnosis have called it a "world religion" (Quispel), a "Gnostic religion" (Jonas), as well as a legitimate or heretical form of cognitive Christianity. It is supposed to have received its most important impulses either from Hellenistic thought or Persian dualism. Within the Christian churches, it was mostly considered heretical, which is interesting to us, since this is the basis for some of the criticism. Church history states that the Christian church was victorious and was declared the state religion in imperial Rome, and that it succeeded in pushing gnosis aside and in having it declared a dangerous heresy. The church itself claimed—and still claims—to possess the only right faith and the only truth.[1]

Considering this, we must conclude from the outset that it is impossible to have an objective discussion about whether either Anthroposophy or analytic psychology contains Gnostic elements. This verdict seems to fall back on the very same critics who condemned the Gnostics in the first place.

Rudolf Steiner

Where are the historical references to the Gnostics in Steiner's work? Among Steiner's very first publications when he was general secretary of the Theosophical Society were two lecture series, entitled *Mystics after Modernism* and *Christianity as Mystical Fact*. In these lectures, published as books, great significance is accorded to the Gnostics as well as to mysticism. Steiner goes so far as to say: "The term Gnostics is applied to all those writers from the first centuries of Christianity who sought for a deeper, spiritual meaning in its teachings. They are to be understood as thinkers steeped in the mysteriosophy and striving to understand Christianity from the viewpoint of the mysteries."[2] Steiner gives very few literary references, in contrast to Jung, but he refers again and again to G.R.S. Mead, the English scholar who, in Steiner's opinion, "gave a brilliant account of the development of the gnosis." Jung also refers repeatedly to Mead.[3]

While Steiner's later written work does not deal much with gnosis, in the shorthand lecture notes we find numerous, mostly brief, remarks on the gnosis problem. From these remarks one can gather that Steiner assumed the existence of a pre-Christian gnosis. In his lectures on the Gospel of Mark, he says: "Greek philosophy was prepared in such a way that it thirsted for the Mystery of Golgotha. Consider the Gnosis, and how it longed in its philosophy for the Mystery of Golgotha."[4] Steiner was not interested in the history of gnosis; he looked at it from the viewpoint of spiritual development. This becomes clear in the chapter "Gnosis and Anthroposophy," and in numbers 159-161 of his *Anthroposophical Leading Thoughts*. There he says: "Gnosis was the way of Knowledge—preserved from ancient time—which, at the time when the Mystery of Golgotha took place, was best able to bring home this

Mystery to human understanding." However, humankind has developed since then; we have gone from the "sentient soul" to the "consciousness soul." It is no longer appropriate for a modern spiritual movement like Anthroposophy to go back to gnosis, which was suitable to an older form of consciousness. "Anthroposophy cannot be a revival of the Gnosis, for the latter depended on the development of the *sentient soul*; while Anthroposophy must evolve out of the spiritual soul...a new understanding of Christ and world."[5]

As we can see from leading thought number 258, Steiner maintained to the very end of his life that in the past, gnosis was of the greatest importance for understanding the Christ event. He respected its "wonderful treasures of wisdom," its "unique mode of comprehension," and its underlying spiritual openness, as "something grand." This sheds a certain light on those theologians who condemned gnosis as mere heresy. Steiner's positive attitude toward the Gnostics is, however, considerably qualified when it comes to their complete failure to grasp the significance of the *incarnatus est*, the incarnation into the flesh-and-blood person of Jesus of Nazareth. They understood the *mystical* aspect of the Christ, but not the historical one. In no way must we overlook the fact that Steiner was just as deeply interested in the historical fact of Christ's appearance as in the mystical one. After all, it was his greatest concern to open a path to a modern understanding of the Christ that would take seriously the cosmic importance of Christ's life, death, and resurrection. If this was understood, he thought, the world would become aware of a great impulse that was in the process of changing our whole cosmic reality. For this reason he demanded (in 1920) that natural science also embrace the Christ event. "Christianity will not be understood until it has penetrated into all our knowledge, right down into the realm of physics."[6] In this connection, Steiner even spoke of a "new substance" that has been incorporated into the world by the Christ event. One would have to reckon with this just as with material, physical, and chemical facts. Where such thoughts come into play the cognitive base of second-century gnosis has been abandoned entirely. Before one could maintain the accusation of a strong Gnostic influence on Anthroposophy, one would have to analyze anthroposophical thought more closely.

For instance, Catholics claim that Anthroposophy supports a false gnosis by confusing the difference between knowledge and faith and does not sufficiently differentiate human cognition and religious revelation.[7] Yet this was exactly Steiner's concern (see appendix: "Soul and Spirit Research as *Praeambulum Fidei*"). Catholic critics refer to Martin Buber's dialogical thinking. Martin Buber rejected Anthroposophy, although he hardly studied its intellectual content; however, he studied Gnostic thinking extensively. Buber makes a clear distinction between the (personal) "I-thou" relationship and the (objective) "I-it" relationship. When gnosis claims to be able to extend knowledge into the realm of the divine-spiritual by pretending to possess "higher sense organs," there is a confusion of the "I-thou" relationship, where the human being finds himself in a personal relationship with God, and the "I-it" stance, where the human being makes whatever he encounters into a freely available object. In his essay "Christ, Hasidism, Gnosis," Buber characterizes gnosis as having "a knowing relationship to the divine, knowing because of a seemingly unshakable conviction that the self is sufficiently divine."[8] According to Buber, our time projects mysteries into the psyche. This results in a tendency toward gnosis. This tendency belies the reality of faith, according to Buber. This "claim to know" betrays the need for introspection, and ultimately, for God's transcendence.

Here we are reminded of the argument between Buber and his friend, the German-Israeli philosopher Hugo Bergmann. Bergmann, who was a student of Steiner, tried to persuade Buber to abandon his skeptical stance toward mysticism and gnosis.[9] Buber's answer is of interest: "I am against gnosis because it pretends to know and describe events and processes within the divine realm. I am against it, because it makes God into an object with whose reality and history one can be familiar. I am against it because it replaces the personal relationship of man to his God with an excursion into a higher world, rich in communication, and full of more or less divine spheres." In response to one of Steiner's demands he said: "I certainly respect a man's high regard for truth, and the absolute faith he has in knowledge, but they have nothing to do with what I call direct, devotional communion with God, unless they are an outcome of it and are directed by it."[10] Naturally the question presents itself: Is it really necessary to split up the important and helpful distinction between the "I-thou" and "I-it" in such a way that it precludes the possibility of knowing?

The difference between Steiner's and Jung's thought structures on the one hand, and Buber's on the other, becomes very clear in Buber's work *The Eclipse of God*. Here the dialogical thinker distances himself from Jung. Buber sees the "spontaneity of the mystery" violated as soon as one aims to "experience the experience": "Only he reaches the meaning who stands firm, without holding back or reservations, before the whole might of reality and answers it in a living way. He is ready to confirm with his life the meaning which he has attained."[11]

C. G. Jung

From his memoirs, we know how important it was for Jung to study the history of religion and of the human spirit in order to make comparisons with certain phenomena in the modern psyche. He saw in the old mentality certain "prefigurations" of these phenomena. According to his own accounts, he studied the Gnostics intensively from 1918 to 1926. He maintained an interest in the subject all his life, even though the study of alchemy and its symbols yielded far more material for him than the "fragments of a faith forgotten," as Mead called the gnosis of the second century. "As far as I could see, the tradition that might have connected Gnosis with the present seemed to have been severed, and for a long time it proved impossible to find any bridge that led from Gnosticism—or Neoplatonism—to the contemporary world. But when I began to understand alchemy I realized that it represented the historical link with Gnosticism, and that a continuity therefore existed between past and present. Grounded in the natural philosophy of the Middle Ages, alchemy formed the bridge on the one hand into the past, to Gnosticism, and on the other into the future, to the modern psychology of the unconscious."[12]

When Jung turned to alchemy, he did not discount gnosis as such. Rather one could say that Jung discovered in alchemy a more accessible, better-documented version of gnosis. In addition, there were times when he felt there was an affinity to the gnosis in modern souls. In his 1928 essay "The Spiritual Problem of Modern Man," he diagnosed certain dark, almost morbid phenomena in the background of the soul that reminded him of the gnosis of the first centuries A.D.[13] As usual, Jung here does not bother to differentiate among Theosophy, Anthroposophy (which he called pure gnosis, but Indianized) and the Indian kundalini yoga, all of which he mentioned in one breath. He sees it as a positive sign, not as an attempt to deceive, that "this modern gnosis" claims to be scientific. For in contrast to the traditional forms of religion that prevailed in Europe at that time, modern people do not want to "believe" by uncritically accepting church dogma. They want knowledge instead; by which Jung means the need for "archetypal experience," not just the usual thirst for knowledge. Jung wants to show the way to such archetypal experiences, to a conscious partaking of the treasure trove of experiences in one's own soul.

Gilles Quispel, the Dutch scholar of Gnosticism, states, quite rightly, it seems: "The most important gnosis in our century is C.G. Jung's complex psychology. It presents scientific discoveries and observations whose value and truth no one can deny. It is an open secret that behind this psychology there is a type of gnosis. This proves beyond any doubt that gnosis belongs to the Occidental tradition."[14]

Most recently, Hedda J. Herwig has accused Jung of being a Gnostic. She supports this claim by declaring that he took the "occult step from a hypothetical *mundus intelligibilis* into the substantialization of a world of 'principles' into a world of spirits."[15] These few accounts, especially Jung's own testimony, could create the impression that there can be no doubt about Jung's gnostic tendencies, either hidden or openly confessed. Must we therefore place Steiner as well as Jung alongside those Gnostics or pseudo-Gnostics whom the church has dragged along throughout its history—along with all the other heretics—as embarrassing ballast? The church has always tried to rid itself of them, according to the mood of the times, either by eliminating, ignoring, or denouncing them—without success.

Basically, we can only answer this question if we try to differentiate carefully. It is a fact that, even after 150 years of intensive gnostic research, the necessary differentiation is missing. Even in a leading theological handbook we read about the "strange spiritual movement of antiquity called 'gnosis' or 'Gnosticism.'"[16] We can ask what is meant here. Gnosis, in the sense of spiritual knowledge that even the New Testament recognizes as legitimate? A knowledge that reaches down into the "deep things of God" (I Cor. 2:10) and is "life eternal" itself (John 17:3)? Or is it an ism, an ideology? The "gnostics" Paul and John in the New Testament, as well as the later "gnostic," Clement of Alexandria, had to defend themselves early on against the danger of a "pseudo-gnosis." There is no doubt a legitimate "gnosis of Christianity," which the Catholic Koepgen acknowledged in his work of the same title.[17] He understood it to be a way of knowledge superior to the logical as well as the dialectical views because it is capable of penetrating into religious reality.

The English Dominican Victor White no doubt made some helpful contributions to the gnosis question when he distinguished "gnosis" and "gnostics" on the one hand, and "Gnosticism" and "Gnostics" on the other: "The distinction is important for the reason that the erroneous opinion can easily arise that the rejection of Gnosticism by the mainstream Christian churches includes also gnosis and the gnostics. This is definitely not the case, and it would not be necessary. The revelation that the early church accepted, and that gave it its *raison d'être* in the first place, was in itself a gnosis."[18] No doubt "gnosis" is a fundamental New Testament term that relates to faith, hope, and love. In the Latin Vulgate Bible, Jerome translates the well-known verse of St. Paul as *scientia inflat* ("Knowledge puffeth up"). Knowledge divorced from faith, hope, and love leads to self-inflation. Jung has used the word "inflation" to describe the danger that befalls those who are overwhelmed by the flood of their unconscious, when they overestimate themselves and end up in unlimited egotism. Such people then lose their social sense, and sense for reality.

If we juxtapose the inflated type described above with the picture of the Gnostic, we see a broken sense of reality; this is demonstrated by a dualistic view where creation consists of the good, light-filled, divine spiritual world that is radically separated from an antidivine, evil, earthly-material, dark world. There is the "two gods" theory, which claims that the world was not created by a benevolent god but by an evil, menacing demiurge (Marcion). There is also a social dualism in Gnosticism. The individual who claims to possess gnosis feels superior to those who merely believe. Early Christianity accepted both gnosis and *pistis* (faith) as parts of a unity.

Later, the two movements—Gnosticism and "Pisticism"—denied this unity. Therefore, there is a need to point to the "cognitive function of faith" (Alfred Dedo Müller).[19] The Gnostic is in danger of confusing gnosis with salvation in the sense of an already achieved, permanent condition.

The ridge between gnosis and Gnosticism is narrow. And just along this unavoidable ridge runs the "hidden, sacred path, called gnosis" ("Naassene Hymn"). It is due to the human condition that gnosis is in constant danger of Gnostic inflation. The Christian's life plays out among the tension between liberty and grace.

Two Gnostics after All?

Whoever calls Jung and Steiner Gnostics must acknowledge that both men belong to the long tradition of those who did not resign themselves to the limitations of human knowing but dared to penetrate into regions that remain closed to mere rational thinking and empirical science. Both Jung and Steiner paid close attention to all the old paths of cognition. Yet gnosis, alchemy, Rosicrucianism, and others were to them nothing more than historical points of reference. Thinking of gnosis in particular, it is clear that Steiner as a spiritual scientist, and Jung as a psychologist, had long since left behind the premises of the old Gnostics when they published their own work, comparing and interpreting gnosis and seeking to integrate it into the spiritual movements of the Middle Ages. They never accepted either gnosis or Gnosticism uncritically. Steiner was never in danger of accepting or restoring Gnostic ideas, since his method was to study the history of consciousness.[20]

On the other hand, it cannot be denied that the attitudes of both Steiner and Jung toward cognition, even though they differed in many

ways, set themselves apart from the personal-dialogical thinking of
Martin Buber and from certain theological schools. There the emphasis is on the I-Thou relationship and on the I-it experience, and the
human responsibility to understand, is taken seriously. *In this sense* one
may call both our scientists gnostics.

The gnosis of Steiner and Jung are "safe" in two respects: the high
value Steiner gives to thinking, and his commitment to scientific
exactness, which he shares with Jung, protect their methods of
research from sliding back into subjective mysticism. By consistently
avoiding any religious activity, and by distinguishing their spiritual-
scientific research from religious revelation, both Anthroposophy and
analytic psychology are free of that personal inflation that is characteristic of Gnosticism.

APPENDICES

1

Mental Health through Spiritual Discipline

Paths of spiritual schooling have an important practical side insofar as they bring into focus the value of daily soul-spiritual hygiene for mental health in general. There may be some justification for occasional misgivings about the detrimental effect of such practices on a person's well-being. Such misgivings are in order, because the method chosen is not without importance. A person may have psychological imbalances to begin with; she may plunge indiscriminately into practices, immerse herself too deeply, or practice seemingly "harmless" breathing exercises whose purpose and effects she does not know.

Indeed there are right and wrong ways into the spiritual world. Aside from the fact that Steiner's instructions can be followed incorrectly, it has to be emphasized that any path of schooling has to be entered with the greatest sobriety as well as modesty. Every illusion, every gesture of sentimental exuberance when clear thinking is in order, every form of self-aggrandizement and arrogance when personal modesty is required, leads to delusion instead of the desired "higher worlds." Steiner's terse statement from *How to Know Higher Worlds* lends special weight to this truth: "Spiritual heights can only be attained when one enters through the gate of humility." Steiner not only warned of the dangers of going astray, but from the outset he laid out his path of schooling in such a way that no harm is done, as long as the instructions are followed correctly. Steiner's insistence on devotion—which means dedication to truth and knowledge, not to be confused with a personality cult—does not at all exclude critical distance. Nor does it ask for uncritical "faith" in the results of spiritual research, which would mean an unwholesome dependency on the person of the researcher.

Experience shows that there are many individuals who must be considered spiritually immature, fixated on a certain teacher, or incapable of critical discernment. Such people are frequently found in religious and ideological communities that make grandiose claims. The anthroposophical neurologist Rudolf Treichler has pointed out that persons who tend toward hysteria are frequently found in such circles. For them a path of spiritual schooling can have devastating consequences. Treichler has extensively studied the symptoms and therapy of schizophrenic patients, concluding that proper spiritual schooling can prevent mental illness.[1] Indeed he sees in the initiatic path a remedy for the psychological ailments of civilization, as long as this path is followed correctly and with attention to the individual structure of the psyche. In the sphere of the will, the training harmonizes the material that arises chaotically into consciousness from the depth of the soul. Thus psychic energy is not repressed but transformed. Similar results ensue for thinking. Thinking is not eliminated, nor is it one-sidedly fixated in the intellect. Rather it is transformed, and can serve as an organ for spiritual perception. Even if it does not result in the formation of spiritual organs as described in the literature, and if the stages of consciousness, imagination, inspiration, and intuition are not reached, the exercises still have a positive effect. Psychopathological patients, however, should not attempt to enter the anthroposophical path of schooling.

All in all, one should not underestimate the beneficial, harmonizing effects of the anthroposophical path of schooling on the healthy psyche.

2

Evil as Shadow and Double

One insight gained by spiritual research as well as by psychology is the observation that human beings are accompanied throughout life by a negative factor, their shadow side. Jung points out emphatically that what he calls the "shadow" does not consist "of small weaknesses and blemishes, but of a truly demonic dynamic.... The living form needs

deep shadow if it is to appear plastic. Without shadow it would remain
a two dimensional phantom, a more or less well brought-up child."[1]

We are acquainted with the shadow from ethnology, myth, literature, and religious and spiritual history. It is called the "other I," "the
dark brother," the antagonist, the tempter, and so on. Jung sees in the
shadow an archetypal figure that can appear in either a personal or collective form, depending on whether it appears within the personal or
the collective unconscious. It always corresponds to the inferior part of
the personality, to what is hidden, repressed, rejected, or considered
unworthy or sinful. Since the shadow compensates for what is conscious, it does not necessarily have to be negative. It can also have a
positive effect. "The shadow personifies everything that the subject
refuses to acknowledge about himself and yet is always thrusting itself
upon him directly or indirectly. For instance, inferior traits of character
and other incompatible tendencies."[2] According to this description,
the unconscious manifests itself as the shadow of the conscious self
and therefore as its counterpart. Jung has further shown that the
shadow often manifests as a projection quite unknown to the subject
herself. This means that a person looks for and finds in another person
certain negative traits, like a fault, an offense, a misdeed, that in reality
belong to her own shadow. The person does not see the projection as
what it really is—her own shortcoming. To recognize this, and thereby
to dissolve the power of the projection, belongs to the process of self-
realization that Jung advocates.

Jung makes it very clear that the shadow is a moral problem that
challenges the ego-personality in its entirety. "No one can become conscious of the shadow without considerable moral effort. To become
conscious of it involves recognizing the dark aspects of the personality
as present and real. This act is the essential condition for any kind of
self-knowledge, and it therefore, as a rule, meets with considerable
resistance."[3]

The statement above outlines a process that analytic therapy calls
the acceptance or the realization of the shadow. It is a problem whose
solution requires a great deal of courage. What does Anthroposophy
have to contribute in this respect?

At first, it seems as if the problem of the shadow receives very little, if any, attention in Anthroposophy. Often this impression is the result of observations made of so-called "Anthroposophists" (note the quotation marks!). For these people, their worldview, their ethos is the quintessence of truth, perfection, and unique knowledge. Steiner himself is seen as an absolutely "shadow-free" individual. There seems to be no room for error on his part. Critique of any kind is taboo. Steiner's own admonition, "Test, examine, again and again!" seems to have been forgotten. No depth psychologist will have any respect for such pseudo-taboos. However, one cannot draw serious conclusions from such impressions. Some believable statements by Steiner have been recorded in which he not only spoke very humbly about his own spiritual experiences ("well, this is grace..."), but also admitted freely: "When you look into your own inner self, you find things that you would rather not talk about."

No doubt Steiner here is touching on the point that Jung has called the "unavoidable basis for self-knowledge." It is as if Steiner is answering the depth psychologist directly when he says in his *Outline of Esoteric Science*: "The important thing, therefore, is that we must first have a true and thorough knowledge of ourselves so that we can perceive the surrounding world of soul and spirit in a pure way." He then describes how "the 'I' now acts as a center of attraction for everything that belongs to the human individual. All our inclinations, sympathies, antipathies, passions, opinions, and so on gather around this 'I,' as it were, which is also the point of attraction for everything we call an individual's karma." For this we find no parallels in Jung, at least not where karma reaches beyond the individual existence and includes the idea of reincarnation. However, there are numerous possible deceptions that stand in the way of serious self-knowledge. Steiner finds "a type of hidden shame in the hidden depths of the soul, a shame that we do not become conscious of in our physical, sensory life. However, this hidden feeling works in a way that is similar to the way the ordinary feeling of shame works in everyday life— it prevents a person's innermost being from appearing to that person as a perceptible image.... This feeling conceals us from ourselves and at the same time it conceals the entire world of soul and spirit."[4]

This means that the only person who obtains insight into the spiritual world is one who has perceived the depth and darkness of his own soul and has been able to withstand the terrifying realities therein. Obviously the spiritual scientist as well as the psychiatrist are here describing one and the same inner experience, even though they do so from different standpoints and using different methods of research.

What is this inferiority, this shadow, in Steiner's view? In his meditations about self-knowledge he has described the experiences that have to be endured at the entrance to the spiritual world. "You learn...to consider yourself from a standpoint that is possible only when you are outside the sensory body": he means the activity of the imaginative consciousness, in which sense perceptions and memory are not engaged. "The crushing feeling that follows on this becomes the beginning of true self-knowledge. Experiencing the erroneousness of your relationship to the outer world helps to reveal your soul's true being as it really is."[5] Before all else, it becomes clear that the mere wish, the decision, to conquer the negative element that is seen in the soul for the first time, is not enough. This negative appears like a "force of nature," much more powerful than what one could have imagined. Even the "I" is inadequate. "To enter the suprasensory world, you must look back at your whole soul, your 'I,' as something to be cast aside."[6]

What this really means can only be fathomed when one considers that human beings consider their empirical "I" to be their natural, real one. The experience at this stage shows, however, that on the path of spiritual-scientific development a certain reevaluation is required of those values that have served so far, and have seemed sufficient for everyday consciousness. In Jung's process of individuation, the conscious "I" has to be transformed into the Self that integrates the conscious as well as the unconscious. In Steiner's path of schooling the everyday "I" has to be transformed into the "true I." Steiner sometimes calls it the "other self." Steiner emphasizes that this "true I," the "other self," does not have to be created. "Spiritual vision does not create the true 'I,' for the 'I' is present in the depths of every human soul. Suprasensory consciousness merely experiences knowingly something previously unknown to the human soul, something which, none-theless, belongs to its nature."[7]

Without doubt, Jung's concept of the "Self" corresponds with Steiner's "true I" and his "other self," as long as we do not overlook the fact that both concepts are used in different contexts. The same applies to the anthroposophical analogy to Jung's concept of the shadow. Steiner actually introduced two terms for this concept. He calls the experience of one's own self before the gates of the spiritual world the "Doppelgänger," the double. The other name is the "guardian of the threshold." Steiner uses this term in order to point out a certain function of the double. "It stands like a guardian in front of that world, refusing entry to anyone not yet suitable for entering. The double can therefore be called 'the guardian of the threshold to the world of soul and spirit.'"[8]

One of the guardian's tasks is to warn of self-deception that can arise on the path. To assure a clear, objective look at the spiritual worlds, it is essential to meet the guardian. For he stands exactly where the "true 'I,'" which had hitherto been hidden from consciousness, begins to show itself. "There on the threshold our true ["I"] is able to clothe itself in all our weaknesses, all our failings, everything that induces us to cling with our whole being…to the physical sense world."[9] In the framework of his instructions for spiritual schooling, Steiner gave certain precautions that will be effective in eliminating such illusory moments. For instance, pupils must learn to withstand the encounter with the guardian of the threshold without becoming discouraged by the negative attributes in the depth of their own soul that are being shown them. To achieve this, there are some preparatory exercises that will strengthen the soul's positive, active side. Steiner counts among these courage, a strong feeling of personal freedom, of love, and energetic thinking.[10] What is meant here in particular will only be fully understood when one considers the Alpha and the Omega of the spiritual-scientific path of schooling.

Since Jung thinks of the shadow as having an inferior quality, it is important to note that Steiner, too, often describes the "double" as "evil." Evil, a transpersonal entity that manifests in the soul, is seen in

Anthroposophy as having a dual character, reminiscent of the Persian polarity of light and darkness. Evil appears on the one hand as the dark, abysmal, material figure of "Ahriman," on the other hand as his polar opposite, "Lucifer." Consequently, those soul forces that favor harden- ing of the body are called "ahrimanic": materialism in the soul, dry intellect, pedantry, and philistinism. "Luciferic" means the opposite: in the soul it manifests as phantasms, tending to ecstasy and mysticism. Steiner is concerned with overcoming this dualism. Overcoming does not mean, however, the destruction of either Ahriman or Lucifer, but creating a balance between these extreme tendencies. The one pulls us "down," the other "up." In the striving for balance, we have the working of the Christ principle. Steiner made this struggle—which each person must carry on individually—visible in a monumental wooden sculpture. This sculpture, known as the *Group*, which stands in the Goetheanum in Dornach, Switzerland, is composed of the figures of Lucifer and Ahri- man, with the "Representative of the Human Being" standing between the two. In a lecture Steiner gave to the construction workers at the Goetheanum in 1923, he said: "To be Christian is indeed to look for the balance between the ahrimanic and luciferic elements."[11]

In Steiner's view as in Jung's, "evil" in its shadowy existence is not simply to be eliminated. According to Jung, it has an important role and function on the path to self-realization. Certainly the shadow has to be made conscious. Jung carried out this demand consistently in his analyti- cal practice. But this is not all. On the way to individuation, the shadow must be accepted and integrated. This is more than acknowledgment of the shadow aspects. "A content can only be integrated when its double aspect has become conscious and when it is grasped not merely intellec- tually but understood according to its feeling value."[12]

There can be no question of the mere elimination of an inferior trait that the intellect may find undesirable. This also applies to Lucifer and Ahriman. They do not allow themselves to be simply eliminated or ignored as machinations of religious fantasies. These two principles— who are ever-present in the soul—must be reckoned with as realities. "Clearly, it is quite wrong to think that to avoid falling victim to the luciferic and ahrimanic elements, one should eradicate them in oneself

...you can bring yourself into a proper relationship to these elements only by creating a proper counterbalance to each with the other."[13]

Thus the "shadow," which for Jung is the unconscious counterpart of the conscious "I," finds an interesting equivalent in Steiner's image of the encounter with the "double," or the "guardian of the threshold." In both instances, it is of decisive importance whether individuals find the strength to withstand the reality of their own unconscious soul content. In both cases, this marks a critical point on the path to individuation as well as initiation.

3

Androgyny

Individuation, which is of central importance for Jung, and humankind's evolution toward self-identity and wholeness, have been in human awareness since long before the discovery of the unconscious anima in man and the animus in woman. To the extent that humankind still had direct access to soul-spiritual realities, it was in a position to say something about the human mystery, which is the polarity as well as unity of male and female. One cannot speak of "knowledge" in the modern sense; these abilities had to be learned step by step. The stories and messages came in the form of pictorial language, depending on the state of consciousness at a certain time. We are talking here about the archetypal image of the androgyne or hermaphrodite, a mythological figure that must not be confused with sexual abnormalities, "intermediate stages," and such. Sexual pathology knows about these.

In spiritual history, the androgynous being can be traced back to very ancient mythical traditions. In those times, the human being was not yet divided into two separate sexes but was asexual, or suprasexual. The memory of such a condition can be found in the Asian religions, in Greek mythology (see Plato's *Symposium*), in Egypt, and in the Germanic cultures, among other places. The biblical creation story touches on this mystery (Gen. 1:27), even though this is fiercely denied by theology, especially by theological anthropology. However, it is a fact that

the passage in question ("male and female created he them") was interpreted as meaning "androgynous" in prerabbinical Judaism by the rab-
bis themselves; by Philo of Alexandria; in the Talmud; in the Kabbalah;
and of course in the Gnostic tradition.[1]

The idea of the androgynous human has also found many adherents
and interpreters in Christian circles, in spite of vigorous "official repression," as Ernst Benz has called it. One of the most important is the eminent Protestant mystic Jacob Boehme. He developed a whole
"anthroposophia," a wisdom of the human being.[2] His followers, the
"Boehmeans" or "Behmenists" of the seventeenth century, exerted influence all over the European continent. They included the great Swabian
theosophists Friedrich Christoph Oetinger and Johann Michael Hahn
(the latter of whom became the spiritual leader of a sect named after
him). Through the eighteenth-century French mystic Louis-Claude de
Saint Martin, Boehme was rediscovered by the German Romantics, and
the idea of the androgyne aroused renewed interest. Franz von Baader
was one of many who took an interest in it. The Russian thinkers
Vladimir Solovyov and Nikolai Berdyaev carried this ancient knowledge
into the present time.[3] Nor should Rosicrucian and alchemical thought
be forgotten. One cannot understand these currents without considering the underlying idea of the whole, androgynous human being. Jung
has kept this ancient wisdom alive in our own time. But he did not simply continue old traditions. He used the idea as a means of helping people understand his own ideas. Jung's concern is best expressed in the
words of the physician Gerhard Dorn, a pupil of Paracelsus, whom Jung
often quoted: *"Transmutemini in vivos lapides philosophicos"* ("Let yourselves
be changed into living philosopher's stones"). For *"ex alio numquam unum
facies quod quaeris, nisi prius ex te ipso fias unum"* (you will never make the one
you seek, unless you have first *become* one.")

In Rudolf Steiner's Anthroposophy, the idea of the androgyne is
integrated into the process of anthropogenesis. Steiner has commented
many times on the androgyne idea, but nowhere has he done so systematically or completely.[4] A brief sketch of Steiner's views on the subject
produces the following picture: Again, it is the development of humankind that forms the framework within which the gradual changes take

place. At one specific stage—Steiner even speaks of planetary incarnations—humankind, having been androgynous, was separated into the duality of two genders. What in the past had been contained in one person was now divided into two. This "individualization" occurred in the service of the awakening light of consciousness and of the development of the human "I." Since Steiner thinks in very large contexts, the division of the sexes takes on an episodic character. His gaze is directed not only toward the ancient mythical archetype of humankind, but also toward the most distant future. In fact the appearance of the "I" marks the beginning of a suprasexual wholeness. It shows the beginning of "humanness." The further development of the "I"-consciousness will lead to an androgynous future humankind—a development takes place over a very long period of time. Steiner describes the result of this development as follows: "Both the male soul in the female body and the female soul in the male body again become double-sexed through fructification by the spirit. Thus man and woman are different in their external form; internally their spiritual one-sidedness is rounded out to a harmonious whole."[5]

There is no doubt that, as with other relevant remarks from Steiner's lectures, we have here some extremely difficult material that leaves many questions open for the interpreter. It may suffice to say that we are looking here at a soul-spiritual process of self-realization, much as in Jung's work. For Steiner, this is not only meant in the narrower sense of a person's individuation in one lifetime. Rather he directs his gaze at the farthest horizons of humankind, so that one is tempted to bring his view into connection with apocalyptic statements in the Bible.

4

Soul and Spirit Research as PRAEAMBULUM FIDEI

When we were dealing with the problem of soul and spirit in Jung's as well as in Steiner's work, we mentioned Thomas Aquinas's term *praeambulum fidei* ("preamble of faith") and applied it to soul and spiritual research. We did this in order to counter the often-voiced accusation that those who occupy themselves with spiritual research are not only confusing "spirit" with "Holy Spirit" or with the divine and the transcendental. They also make Anthroposophy or psychotherapy into a surrogate religion. The rumor of alleged tendencies of "self-redemption" seems never to die, even though Steiner and Jung both emphatically fought such accusations. We have already discussed Jung's clear distinction between the hypothetical archetype of the transpersonal and the image of the divine, which can only be approached with psychological methods. Steiner, too, has drawn clear lines of division, for instance, when it became important to differentiate between his spiritual science and the Christian Community, a movement for religious renewal that received its orientation from him.[1]

What is the relationship between spiritual vision and religious revelation? Anthroposophy *does* employ the concept of revelation. Hans Erhard Lauer, in an excellent study concerning this problem, has clarified to what extent Rudolf Steiner's spiritual science does contain communications of revealed spiritual truths.[2]

Steiner himself addressed the question of the relation of religious revelation to spiritual research. Informative in this respect is a lecture he gave in Switzerland in 1916: "Human Life from the Viewpoint of Spiritual Science." The fact that he had the lecture printed soon afterward shows how important its content was for him.[3] In this lecture Steiner refutes the accusation that the study of Anthroposophy undermines religious faith. Under attack by Catholic theologians, he points to Aquinas for clarification of his own position. Aquinas differentiated between two modes of cognition. First were insights gained by divine revelation that are reflected in church dogma, like Christ's Incarnation, the doctrine of the Trinity, and the sacraments. Besides these doctrines of faith, Thomas recognized a second kind of insight, namely those one can gain through his or her own cognition. Steiner summarizes: "Such truths are for Thomas *praeambula fidei*. Among those he counts everything that is knowable about the existence of the divine in the world. The existence of a divine spirit that creates, rules, supports, and judges the world is not purely a matter of faith. It can be known through the effort of human reasoning. All that can be known about the spiritual nature of human thinking belongs as well in the realm of the *praeambula fidei*."[4]

To which one of Thomas's two modes of cognition does Anthroposophy belong? Steiner has made some amazing statements as a result of his spiritual research, statements that pose great difficulties even for his best-informed readers. Lauer has pointed out that one would expect to have to take Steiner's communications as revelations in Thomas Aquinas's sense. Many of them are not based on traditional scriptures, as for instance *From the Akasha Chronicle* or *The Fifth Gospel*. Surprisingly enough, this is not the case. Steiner stated that the distinction made by the Scholastic thinker applies to Anthroposophy. Steiner wrote in this connection: "The standpoint of Thomas Aquinas in regard to the *praeambula fidei* is absolutely compatible with spiritual science. For everything that is accessible to independent human powers of cognition has to be considered as *praeambula fidei*."

In what realm does the spiritual researcher travel? Steiner's answer is unequivocal: "Anthroposophy does achieve an expansion of consciousness; it is in a position to make statements about dimensions of reality that go far beyond the reach of ordinary, untrained consciousness. Yet the whole of Anthroposophy is limited to the Thomistic realm of *praeambula fidei*." It is very important to keep in mind Steiner's view in this matter, because there are certain statements in some of the lecture transcripts that may make one think otherwise.[5] Steiner adds: "When spiritual science, by expanding cognition, also adds insights about the soul that cannot be gained by mere intellectual thinking, it only widens the knowledge that is contained in the field of *praeambula fidei*. It never steps outside this field. It gains a knowledge that supports the revealed truths even more than those insights that can be had merely through the intellect."[6] With that the higher forms of consciousness—imagination, inspiration, and intuition, as they are called in anthroposophical terminology—are also clearly delimited from sovereign divine acts of revelation, because they are the result of human effort. Or, if applied to the anthroposophical method of spiritual knowledge: To enter the path of spiritual research is an entirely free human decision. It is up to the individual to devote himself wholly to this work. Yet to attain "knowledge of higher worlds" is in the end not achievable through human means alone. Steiner himself has called it "grace."

Contrary to Steiner, Jung does not have access to Thomas Aquinas. Yet in important parts of his work he expresses his high regard for Christian dogma. He approaches dogma merely from an empirical standpoint, "essentially as a physician," as he once confessed to Martin Buber. He is not interested in divine revelation. This shows clearly how he wanted his work to be interpreted. Dogma itself, which interested him mainly psychologically, "represents the soul more completely than a scientific theory, for the latter expresses and formulates the conscious mind alone."[7]

For this reason, Jung valued dogma far more than products of the rational mind. He never looked for the spiritual sources of dogmatic formulas—at any rate, not in his role as psychologist. He felt that such questioning would overstep his competence, and that religious revelations were beyond the reach of human cognition. By Thomistic definition, revelation lies outside the *praeambula fidei*. After all this we may be justified in declaring that neither Jung's psychological research nor Steiner's spiritual science claims to make religious statements like those we expect of the founders of great religions, of preachers, or of religious reformers. This was not their intention. Yet we cannot deny that their work has created new impulses that have enriched and fructified religious life, and still do.

5

Unus Mundus *and the* Cosmic Christ

The alchemist's concept of the *unus mundus* plays an important role in Jung's late work. The alchemical scientists understood it to be the eternal, all-encompassing foundation of being, the one world called *sapientia Dei* ("the wisdom of God") or *anima Christi* (the spirit of Christ"). This was thought to be the ground of all creativity, where psyche and matter are united as one. Jung, with Richard Wilhelm, explored the phenomena of synchronicity in Chinese esoteric writings, and, with the physicist Wolfgang Pauli, in the field of physics. These studies convinced Jung of the existence of a wholeness that embraces psyche and matter. He supported his findings with the help of parapsychological observations.

Jung has created a foundation from which the separate but complementary fields of matter and psyche can be seen as a whole. He has done this through his concept of the principle of synchronicity. In the synchronistic occurrence, the same meaning is revealed within the psyche as well as in the arrangement of a simultaneous outer event. Often there is "*a priori* intuition of a fact" that could not have been known at the time. This is something like a picture without a subject. Thus the phenomenon of synchronicity points to a unifying aspect of being that transcends consciousness. This is what Jung has called *unus mundus*.[1]

Steiner encountered the same phenomenon at the beginning of the twentieth century in the course of his spiritual research. Obviously the time was not yet ripe when he presented this "eminently important discovery" to those attending one of his lectures to a more intimate circle. In the Munich lectures of 1909, *The East in the Light of the West* (a title characteristic of his intentions), Steiner developed his conception of two ways into the spiritual world that play a prominent role in the development of humankind.[2] He pointed out how the sense-perceptible outer world works like an illusion (*maya*) that hides any view of the spiritual world. He saw it as our task to penetrate this veil in order to gain glimpses into supersensible regions. However, this he saw as only one of two possibilities. On the other side, he explained, our thoughts, our feelings, our sentiments, as well as the more complicated phenomena of our soul life, such as conscience, form another kind of veil that hides the spiritual world from us. When the awakened consciousness penetrates this veil, it once again arrives in a spiritual world.

These are the two ways that Steiner characterized in other connections as the "chymical path"—the one directed toward the outer world—and the "mystical path." The "chymical path" was that of the Rosicrucian alchemists, and the method used by Goethe in his scientific studies. Steiner himself was deeply committed to this path in his theory of knowledge and in his work in Goethean natural science. Steiner also spoke of the "mystical path" that is concerned with turning the gaze inward. The respective goals of the two paths have been called the "chymical wedding" and the "mystical wedding" (*unia mystica, hieros gamos*). Here it is not hard to recognize the two psychological types, the "extravert" and the "introvert," that Jung discussed in his work.

Once more we have here some interesting material for comparison that can serve to show how Jung, the psychologist, represented exclusively the inner soul aspect. Even so, he always paid attention not only to the individual psyche but to the collective one, encompassing all of humankind. Steiner, on the other hand, is concerned with knowledge and with the description of cosmic facts. He expresses this in such a way that he speaks in the above-mentioned lectures of the workings of "upper" and "lower" deities. The former are presented as Sun-Beings, the latter as Moon-Beings that, seen from this aspect, are the more powerful of the two. Steiner emphasized that it is not the task of modern humanity to exclusively pursue *either* natural science *or* the mystical path. Whoever takes the one path and disregards the other entirely will not find a satisfactory picture of reality. "But where the two faculties of penetrating through the external sense world and through the veil of the soul life are united, man makes the very significant discovery that what is to be found behind the veil of the soul life is exactly the same, in essence, as that behind the veil of the outer sense world. A uniform spiritual world is revealed from without and from within. If a man should get to know the spiritual world by both paths, he realizes their unity. Whoever reaches the spiritual world on the path of inner contemplation finds it behind the veil of his soul life. When he then also has the possibility, by developing his supersensible forces, to penetrate beyond the veil of the outer sense world, he then knows that what he has found in his innermost being is the same as what he has found in his outer search."[3] No doubt this is the same truth that Jung called, connecting himself to medieval nature philosophy, the *unus mundus*. We may mention here that Anthroposophy is committed to bringing together these two paths to the spirit. When one confuses Anthroposophy with either Gnosticism or mysticism, one misunderstands

Steiner's intentions. It is no coincidence that Jung was and still is subject to similar misunderstandings.

Here we need to point to an important Christological connection
that Steiner communicated in his lectures about the Gospels, especially
those about Matthew and Luke. According to Steiner, the two great
spiritual streams that we have called the chymical and the mystical
streams were united in the historical moment of Christ's appearance on
earth. This discovery constitutes an essential core of anthroposophical
esoteric teaching. Adding to this interpretation of the historical Christ
event, which can be understood as both a chymical *and* a mystical fact,
Steiner announced another important fact: the second appearance of
the Christ in the realm of the life forces (the etheric realm).[4] After
1910, Steiner worked hard to make this fact known to his audiences in
many lectures in many cities. It even plays a role in his mystery dramas.
Anthroposophy is to prepare humankind for this second coming,
which constitutes the Christ event of the twentieth century. What
Jung, in his work on the level of the individual psyche, called introversion and extraversion, has found a further broadening and deepening in
Steiner's Christology.

Considering this selection of themes, it is certainly a sign of the
times that a search has begun from many different directions—a questioning after the reality of the spiritual, after the descent of the spirit,
and after the evolution and renewal of humankind—that calls for a
synoptic evaluation. For years, there has been communication between
the universalistic system of Teilhard de Chardin and the vision of the
Indian sage Sri Aurobindo. Hans Hasso von Veltheim-Ostrau, in his
conversations with Indian initiates, has pursued whether Eastern esotericism could offer Western esoteric seekers anything to add to or
confirm the notion of an imminent reappearance of the Christ. The
author of the *Asian Diaries* was given a surprising answer from Sri
Ramana Maharshi in Tiruvannamalai: "Yes, you are correct, we mean
the same thing; the event you are referring to occurred in 1909. In this
form, and in that it takes place in the atmosphere of the earth, it is
something completely new that has never happened before. It will last
for many generations, will change everything, and then will disappear

again, having been something unique."[5] Von Veltheim asserts that he himself had expected such a special event, taking place in the supersensible realm, to occur in the late 1870s or around 1930. Maharshi's announcement agrees exactly with the one Steiner made when he gave that same year as the beginning of the above-mentioned new Christ activity. In his Berlin lectures of 1917, Steiner said: "Even though it seems as if in its present deeds on the physical plane humankind is far from being filled with the Christ-spirit, the coming Christ is very near to the souls now, if only they would open themselves to him. The occultist can indeed show how since the year 1909, approximately, that which is to come is being prepared in an unmistakable way, and that we live since the year 1909 in very special times."

Steiner's statements about this second coming are remarkable insofar as awareness of this event is not supposed to be dependent on any special clairvoyant faculties, like those required for the anthroposophical path of schooling. It can manifest spontaneously. It is significant that the new Christ revelation occurs in the "etheric world," the lowest spiritual sphere, closest to the physical. Von Veltheim comments: "We have to do here with a glimpse into the imponderable world of life-giving forces where impulses arise and take on creative force that will then manifest in the sense sphere. This is sometimes felt, and it is perhaps called 'providence,' 'Zeitgeist,' the 'mental attitude' of a time, a race, or a nation."[6]

This sphere can refer to nothing else than what is described from the psychological viewpoint as the collective unconscious, where the original, archetypal images are found as if in a mirror. How do the above communications strike a depth psychologist of Jung's caliber? Is he at all in a position to make statements, rooted as he seemed to be in the mentality of modern natural science? There is no doubt that Jung sensed that he was confronted with a mystery that could only be alluded to and described in a tentative way. It is understandable that he hesitated to prove metaphysical matters with psychological observations, a procedure he considered illegitimate. Yet he did not shy away from admitting certain personal convictions in intimate conversations with his friends. Here are two examples. In a letter of January 13,

1948, he wrote: "I thank God every day that I was allowed to experience the reality of the *Imago Dei* in myself...thanks to this *actus gratiae* my life has meaning." Five years later, Jung revealed the immediate relationship of his depth psychology to the Christ: "Just as Origen understands the Holy Scripture as the body of the *Logos*, so must the psychology of the unconscious be understood as a 'manifestation of receptivity.' The *a priori* image of Christ has not been created by human beings, however. The transcendental (total) Christ has created for himself a new, more specific body."[7]

One can hardly overestimate the broad significance of these words. It is as if Jung had forgotten for a moment that he wanted to be exclusively a physician and a psychologist. Here he leaves far behind those philosophical principles that were the reason for his skepticism toward spiritual knowledge. Here, as well as in several other passages in his work, vistas are opening toward a further development of his psychology. The Austrian Alice Morawitz-Cadio, a pupil of Steiner as well as of Jung, developed a "spiritual psychology" in which analysis and therapy are in principle geared toward the spiritual. In this way one can draw, from the above-mentioned passage in Jung's letter, comparisons to early theological ideas of an *incarnatio continua*, a continuous incarnation of the Christ-Logos. But not only that. We have to agree with Wilhelm Bitter when he writes: "In reference to the tradition of Christ's *incarnatio continua*, where he creates a new body for himself again and again, suited to the historical situation and at the same time transforming it, Jung interprets the psychology of the unconscious as the manifestation of receptivity that is appropriate to the unique incarnation of the *Logos* in our time."[8] Bitter brings Jung's research about synchronicity and the *unus mundus* as the eternal origin of the empirical world into close connection with the event that the New Testament calls the "effusion of the Holy Spirit." (It remains puzzling that Jung, unlike Steiner, did not make a connection to the Gospel of John, in which the Christ, taking leave from his disciples, emphatically prophesies to them the coming Paraclete that will "guide them to the perfect truth.") Nevertheless Jung's statement alluding to the permeation of the world with the spiritual ("pneumatic") Christ seems to parallel

Steiner's announcement of the Christ event of the twentieth century. Besides, we have a wealth of references that reckon with the reality of the spiritual, the descent of the spirit, and the working of the cosmic Christ amidst a rampant God-is-dead theology.

Final Remarks

Having arrived at the end of this inquiry, the question arises of the result. I had set myself the task of holding the life and work of Rudolf Steiner and C.G. Jung side by side and exploring the possibility of a synopsis.

On the one hand, I came to the conclusion that these two great men cannot be compared, since neither of them can be put into any kind of category. Each followed his own law, his own inescapable destiny. Each had to fulfill his unique, demanding task to its fullest consequence. That excluded any attention to or consideration of the other, even though they were contemporaries for half a century and lived in close proximity. They never had a common path, nor could they have had, not so much because of outer circumstances, but because of their different goals and dissimilar views of how knowledge could be achieved.

Despite these differences in principle and method, I encountered a wealth of converging ideas that invited synopsis. Steiner and Jung have both significantly contributed to a new image of the human being and to a wider understanding of reality. It is not a question of a quantitative addition to our knowledge of the world and of humanity, but of a genuine breakthrough to new horizons.

Jung's contribution is the discovery of the collective unconscious. This affords us not only glimpses into the human psyche and being, but also into the mystery of the *unus mundus*, the unity of soul and matter. Steiner's decisive achievement was the creation of a new science of the spirit, a modern initiation method. Building on natural science, he created a way to achieve true spirit knowledge.

In view of the range and importance of each of these achievements, one cannot do justice to either of them by mere lip service. Nor is it adequate to simply borrow some of the results of their serious work, an occasional remark or insight, and to quote them on occasion when one feels so moved. What Steiner and Jung have given us is not merely a new knowledge that can be used at will like some technical formula. They require us to work on ourselves, to enter a path of individual experience with the help of their advice and guidance.

For this reason, *only those who have created within themselves* the necessary conditions for the experiences Jung and Steiner describe are entitled to judge either Anthroposophy or depth psychology. Acquiring data in the usual rationalistic manner is not sufficient. Consequently, psychoanalysts themselves insist that those who want to practice depth psychology must first undergo analysis themselves. All communications of the anthroposophical scientist relate to the path of knowledge that must be entered in the form of meditative work. Neither initiation nor individuation can be achieved by the mere accumulation of factual knowledge.

New standards are set by the attempt to experience new dimensions individually. Both Steiner and Jung encouraged their pupils to go beyond the personality of the teacher and freely find their own methods of schooling and self-realization. Nowhere is it as inappropriate as here to constantly swear by the words of a "master." The whole idea is to arrive at *our own insights,* however modest they may be. Nowhere else is the saying more apt: "You give little credit to your teacher by always merely remaining his or her pupil, by always repeating his or her words, and believing them to be the ultimate wisdom." What is needed is to embark yourself on the arduous way that leads to higher or deeper knowledge.

Finally, the experiences one gains in this way must not be used merely for individual self-improvement. Individuation and initiation each have a social component. Insight must never be a goal in itself; it must be used as the basis for action. Self-realization must become fruitful in the social realm. If there is a question of whether this is happening, one can well ask whether the attempted "self-realization" has indeed been achieved.

Here I will quote Martin Buber: "The experience of the self, the spiritual experience, the meeting with the 'higher I' is not given us so that we can speculate on it just as we would speculate on other phenomena of this world, but in order to give meaning to *our life in the world*." All revelation, including this one, presents a calling and a mission.

One final personal remark: the reader may have noticed that in the course of this study I have sometimes addressed those who have gained decisive teachings from Rudolf Steiner, and sometimes those who have received their inspiration from Jung. They all have a claim to the following statement of St. Augustine. In his *Contra Epistulam Manichaei*, he writes to his former brethren, who had been accused of heresy by the church: "I not only find it impossible to be angry at you, I also implore you that we, on each side, lay aside all arrogance and presumption. Let no one assume that they have already found the truth. Let us seek it together as something that none of us knows. Because we can seek for it in love and peace only if we forego the bold assumption that we alone have found it and possess it. If, however, I cannot expect that much from you, at least allow me to listen to you and to talk with you, as with people that I do not presume to know."

THE

RIDDLES

OF THE SOUL

Depth Psychology and
Anthroposophy

HANS ERHARD LAUER

Preface

In response to numerous requests, these lectures—originally given in various versions and locations—are being published. The text of the first two lectures was taken from a tape recording, with very little editing. This allows the fluid style of the spoken word to be retained. I have summarized the contents of the third lecture in condensed form from my notes.

The survey of the different types of depth psychology given in the first lecture is intended to be no more than a sketchy indicator. The literature in this field—by both its proponents and itsadversaries—has become so vast that there is no need to cover it here. I touch on it solely because depth psychology has brought into clear focus the problems I wish to discuss in these lectures: the riddles that arise when one makes a distinction between the conscious and unconscious realms of the soul.

Of course, I am aware that there are individuals who consider a comparison between Anthroposophy and depth psychology impossible. There may be good reasons for this objection; nevertheless, in the third lecture I have give compelling reasons for attempting such a comparison. After all, it is no coincidence that both of these important methods of research arose at the same time. Both of them spring from the same deep impulses of our times, even though they differ in their levels of awareness and often take different directions.

Hans Erhard Lauer
Basel, Spring 1959

1

THE RIDDLES OF THE HUMAN SOUL IN THE LIGHT OF DEPTH PSYCHOLOGY

THE FOLLOWING WORDS have come down to us from Greek antiquity, spoken by the philosopher Heraclitus, who was called "the obscure one": "You can never uncover the depth of the human soul, even if you would explore all the paths of the world; so all-encompassing is the soul-being." This points to the impossibility of knowing the human soul, but there is also another saying that was written over the entrance to the temple at Delphi, according to legend: "Know thyself." The latter admonishes us to try to penetrate into the mysteries of our soul as best we can, at different times in our life, even though we know that we can never *fully* comprehend it. This is a responsibility given us by our human nature. Indeed, throughout history there has been no other enigma as important to human striving and thought as the riddle of the soul. Over the course of time people have found many ways, have explored many paths, in search of the solution to this riddle. Again and again they made many new discoveries in the boundless realm of the soul.

My aim in these lectures is to speak about some of the achievements made in the realm of "soul realization" (*Seelenerkenntnis*) in the twentieth century. On the one hand, the "science of the soul" (psychology) has made a mighty leap forward and gained significant depth in this century, compared with the past three or four centuries. This has come about largely through *depth psychology*, which was founded at the beginning of the twentieth century and has found wide acceptance in scientific circles. It has influenced the intellectual life of the present to a significant degree. On the other hand, during the same period, Rudolf Steiner's Anthroposophy also had its beginning.

Anthroposophy has, albeit in a different way and along different paths than depth psychology, given extraordinary depth to soul recognition. The depth it has brought goes even beyond that which we owe to depth psychology.

This evening I wish to start with an overview of the most important results achieved by depth-psychological research. Tomorrow I shall introduce the picture of the soul offered by Rudolf Steiner's Anthroposophy. Since both of these portrayals here can only be quite sketchy, I shall compare the two concepts in some of their finer points in my third and final lecture.

Depth psychology was founded, as is well known, by Sigmund Freud under the name *psychoanalysis*. It was augmented by Alfred Adler, and further by Carl Gustav Jung with his "psychology of the complexes." The starting point for the development of this whole field of inquiry was the discovery of the unconscious in the human soul. This discovery must not be understood to mean that the unconscious had previously been altogether unknown. This was not at all the case. I need only remind you of the book by Eduard von Hartmann, *The Philosophy of the Unconscious*, which appeared in the 1870s. It was only that the leading psychologists of the last century did not consider the unconscious to be a very important part of the human soul. Therefore they did not develop any methods to explore it further. The so-called "discovery of the unconscious" merely meant that at some point the immense importance of the unconscious for the whole human soul was recognized. This recognition made it imperative to develop specific methods for its exploration. Both the discovery of the unconscious and the need for its further exploration stemmed from the way depth psychology came about.

Depth psychology owes its conception to the needs of practical psychiatry. It did not arise out of an interest in pure knowledge. All its founders and its practitioners were—and still are—psychiatrists, and to this day most research in this field serves the needs of psychiatry and psychotherapy. Nevertheless, the fundamental psychological principles have gained wide recognition and have influenced the thinking of contemporary society to a high degree. Initially the object of investigation was not the sane but the sick human psyche. The question posed was: "How do mental illnesses come about, and what can be done to heal them?" The so-called discovery of the unconscious occurred at the moment when the study of mental illnesses like neuroses, hysteria, and others revealed no physical conditions that may have been related to the symptoms. This meant that, in contrast to the beliefs of the nineteenth century, the causes for these illnesses could no longer be found in disturbances in the physical body, especially the nervous system, but must be sought in the psyche itself. In even earlier times—the Middle Ages and into the eighteenth century—it was believed that mentally ill persons were possessed by demonic entities. This was, in a way, a "spiritual explanation." Therefore one tried to drive the demons out by exorcism—or otherwise merely to lock up those afflicted or put them in chains.

In the twentieth century, physical causes were discounted. The only way to get at the mystery of mental illness was to seek the causes in the psyche itself, especially in the unconscious. For it was obvious that not only did the patient have no conscious knowledge of the cause of his or her illness, but for the observing physician the symptoms—such as depression, hallucinations, or compulsive, irrational actions—seemed to arise out of mysterious depths of the psyche, overwhelming the patient.

The Enigma of the Unconscious

Now the question arose: "How can one acquire knowledge of the unconscious, which by its very nature is removed from conscious recognition?" This would only be possible if one could find within normal consciousness phenomena that would have a special relationship to the unconscious.

Once found, these phenomena would allow conclusions to be drawn regarding the nature of the unconscious realm of the psyche. They certainly occurred in mental patients, but they were not sufficient proof for a link to the unconscious. The task at hand was to find other phenomena in the consciousness of "normal" persons that, in contrast, could give greater certainty to conclusions about the unconscious. Freud's fundamental scientific accomplishment was the discovery of a number of relevant phenomena in normal consciousness. The first of these are the unintentional "Freudian slips" that occur in everyday life: forgetting, misspeaking, mishearing, wrongly acting. If I want to say of a person: "he is my best friend" and instead I say: "he is my best enemy," or when I arrange to meet someone at a certain time and place and then forget the appointment, something from my unconscious seems to be playing a trick on me. This is nothing that could be called an illness; it happens to us in everyday life. Even so, it can have unfortunate consequences.

A second kind of phenomena consists of dream experiences. These do not arise out of our normal, waking consciousness but out of a dimmer one. On the one hand, one can rightfully say that many of our dreams merely reflect and help to "digest" the experiences of the day. On the other hand, there are those dream images that, often interspersed with "ordinary" images, seem to have symbolic meaning for us. They cannot be explained simply by events of the last few days; rather they seem to be symbolic expressions of processes going on in the depths of the psyche.

A third kind of phenomenon consists of those that can be artificially produced when the therapist asks the patient certain leading questions. These can produce answers that usually would not arise from the unconscious on their own.

A fourth group includes the phenomena that Jung used extensively in the treatment of his patients: so-called free associations. These arise when the patient is encouraged by the physician to tell, write down, draw, or sculpt things that he or she feels the need to convey out of inner necessity.

The different schools of depth psychology arrived at their manifold interpretations of the unconscious through a synoptic comparison of all these different phenomena in the healthy as well as the unhealthy psyche. The methods they used to uncover the unconscious were essentially the same as those applied by modern natural scientists to explain the phenomena of the sensory world and their relationship to human consciousness. I will clarify this with a simple sketch (figure I).

EXTERNAL WORLD   SOUL

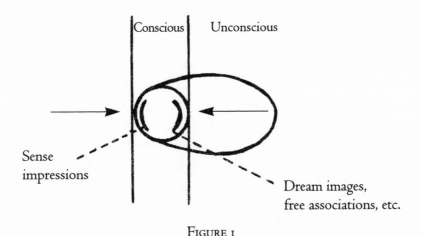

FIGURE I

The little circle above represents the field of our consciousness. On one side, this directly touches the external sensory world. Where it touches this external world, we experience sense impressions—the colors we see, the tones we hear, the smells, and so on. Without a doubt these experiences arise because something in the sensory world influences our organs of perception in some way. Modern natural science is of the opinion that the qualities of warmth, tone, color, and so on that arise in our consciousness are not to be found in the outer world. According to this view, the external world consists merely of "matter" that, owing to its innate forces, is moving and vibrating in different ways. When these manifold vibrations of matter come into contact with our senses, they call forth seeing, hearing, and so on. The task of scientific research is to find out which of these vibrations and movements will cause one or the other sense impression. The findings of this research form the content of scientific theories about the character of the physical world and its relationship to human consciousness.

These theories have by necessity the character of mere hypotheses, of speculation, since in the view of modern science we have no immediate access to the material world. We are locked within the limits of our consciousness and cannot get beyond these limits.

Depth psychology looks in exactly the same way at the unconscious in our psyche, even though it is not as removed from ordinary consciousness as the material world may be, since, together with consciousness, it apparently forms the whole of the human psyche. Nevertheless the *inner side* of normal consciousness, at the point where it comes into contact with the unconscious, is obviously the point where we experience all the phenomena that I have mentioned: the missteps, dream images, and free associations that occur in normal life, along with the phenomena of mental illness. Depth psychology holds that all of these phenomena are caused by a certain stimulus that the unconscious imparts to the realm of consciousness. But depth psychology believes that the phenomena themselves, as they appear in our consciousness, cannot be found in the unconscious, precisely *because* it is unconscious, whereas the phenomena themselves have become conscious.

The task of depth-psychological research is to discover the occurrences in the unconscious that cause in one case a dream picture, in another a misstep, in yet another a hallucination. The results of this research then form the theories about the unconscious. These theories have the same hypothetical character as do the theories of natural science in regard to the material world and its relationship to human consciousness.

When the theories of the unconscious were first published, they shocked the public as well as the scientific community. They entirely contradicted the concepts people had held up until then. Only gradually, after the greatest initial resistance, were the theories accepted by scientists.

Psychoanalysis and Individual Psychology

We will now characterize the different types of depth psychology, concentrating initially on Freud's psychoanalysis. Due to the brief time available I will only address the first form of psychoanalysis developed by Freud; in later years he modified and enlarged it somewhat. As you probably know, Freud was led to believe that all experiences and activities of the psyche of which we become conscious can be traced to one common root that represents an archetypal and basic impelling force. Freud believed this to be desire or lust, in particular the sexual urge. Consequently, Freud believed this urge to be present to a very high degree, even in the young child. He thought that this urge expressed itself in the child in the form of unconscious wishes characterized by the Greek myth of Oedipus: that he killed his father and married his mother. In the male child these wishes were supposed to exist in this form; in the female child the same was true in the corresponding form, according to its gender.

Now, as we know, the human psyche does not really develop in such a way that it is occupied exclusively with the wish to satisfy sexual urges. The reason for this is that in the course of our development into adulthood—and here we can speak of the individual as well as of humankind as a whole—we rise from our unconscious state into a more conscious one. Hand in hand with this increased light of consciousness goes a refinement, a spiritual growth—or, as Freud would call it, a sublimation of basic urges. In the course of this development, there arise in our consciousness certain ideals, certain moral value judgments that consider the gratification of the raw sexual urge to be something gross, low, or even sinful.

An exception is granted when the sexual act is legitimized by serving the need to propagate the human race. Now it happens in some cases that this process of sublimation has not been sufficiently accomplished by the psyche, but there is no possibility of gratifying these strong sexual urges because of outer circumstances like the taboos of society or even the individual's own moral convictions.

Consequently, an individual meets a certain person toward whom he has a strong sexual attraction, but because of the above-mentioned taboos, he doesn't dare admit these feelings. Instead, they are shoved into the unconscious—repressed, as Freud would say. In this way a "congestion" develops in the unconscious, and when this congestion becomes excessive, it can express itself in the conscious psyche as an illness. Fixed ideas, obsessions, or compulsive behavior may serve to give the patient gratification of his or her hidden urges in a perverse manner.

Freud's one-time pupil Alfred Adler arrived at a different interpretation of the essence of the human psyche. He felt compelled to focus his attention on the fact that the most important outcome of the development of the human soul, even though its roots seem to lie in the unconscious, is to achieve consciousness. Furthermore, he had to look at the fact that the essential characteristic of human consciousness, the one that differentiates it from that of the animal, is the ego, the "I." Everything that we experience and do we relate to the "I." We say: "I think, I perceive, I feel, I remember," and so on. Adler said: "If indeed the development of the human soul has as its final result the achievement of 'I'-consciousness, it must be that this is its original aim. I see how a plant produces first the sprout, then the stem, the leaves, and finally blossom and fruit, and I must assume that all this is preprogrammed, as it were, from the outset to achieve this ultimate result. I must conclude that the same must be true for the human psyche. From this it follows that the essential compelling force in the human soul is not the sexual urge but the urge to assert the 'I,' the ego." Furthermore, Adler thought that it was not enough to develop the "I," but also to find ways in which the "I" should be recognized in the world as something important that would give power and influence to the individual. Adler then concluded that the compelling force in the psyche was egotism—what Nietzsche called "the will to power."

Adler was strengthened in this belief when he compared the development of the animal with that of human beings. In contrast to the animal, which is born almost ready to cope with life and in a very short time acquires all the necessary skills for its survival, human beings are born helpless and without any skills. They require a long and careful upbringing by their parents. And all the specific human attributes, like walking upright, speaking, and thinking, must be acquired through a long period of time by one's own effort. Adler believed that the circumstances of this long and tedious process create in human beings a feeling of inferiority toward their surroundings. They compensate for this feeling of inferiority by developing a strong egotism that allows them to win respect and recognition from others. Adler also observed that in the course of normal development this strong egotism is somewhat ameliorated and dampened, so that feelings of idealism and community with others arise in the soul, making communal life possible. All through history, communal life has existed in many different forms. If this weren't the case, life would be a constant war of all against all.

It happens now and again that the amelioration, the taming of the strong egotism, is not sufficiently accomplished in certain individuals. According to Adler, this may be due to a faulty upbringing that encouraged ambition, careerism, and narcissism in the child; or it could stem from an abnormal, mostly inherited weakness in a physical organ. This weakness could cause an enhanced feeling of inferiority in the young person that is then overcompensated by an especially strong need to dominate.

As a rule, such a person feels too weak to live out his or her wishes to dominate others, or may have his or her own thoughts about the inappropriateness of such behavior. Such a person represses the urges, and they become unconscious. Again a "congestion" occurs in the unconscious, and when the pressure becomes too great, the urges break through in the form of neurosis or hysteria. Indeed anyone who has lived with a neurotic person has had the experience that such a person is able to dominate his or her surroundings. Everyone is obliged to pamper the person, give in to her and her whims, and worry about her constantly. In this way the patient pathologically carries out her secret wish to tyrannize others.

As you can see from these two brief descriptions, Freud and Adler explained the origins of mental illness in a fairly similar way, at least in the way they formulated it. However, since they each assumed a very different compelling force to be at the root of the illness, their approach was not by any means the same.

Freud, who saw the driving force of the psyche in the sexual urge, considered mental illness to be almost a force of nature and explored it in the way of the natural scientist, describing it as mainly caused by the repression of the sex drive. Consequently, the curative method he developed was mainly concerned with eliminating the cause of the illness.

Adler, on the other hand, who saw the cause of the illness in the frus-
trated need of the ego to assert itself, looked at the aims the psyche
might have. Since in his view the ego is always at work to accomplish
certain goals in life, Adler tried to act more as an educator. He tried to
influence his patients by helping them to recognize the illusions and
contradictions contained in their wishes and to reconcile them with the
necessities of real life.

Jung's Psychology

Jung was led to yet another basic understanding of the human
psyche. Of course he was familiar with both Freud's psychoanalysis
and Adler's "individual psychology." He had no doubt that each of
these theories—both of which attempted to explain the causes of
mental illness—contained a measure of truth. Certain psychoses call
for Freud's interpretation, and others seem to fit Adler's—and there
are even those that could be explained by both theories. But precisely
because each of these theories contains a certain measure of truth,
they turn out to be not exactly half-true, but only partially true. They
each look at certain aspects of the psyche, and at best, therefore, can
explain those particular aspects of mental illness. Jung had the ambition to develop a theory that would be so broad and all-encompassing
that it could take into account the totality of the human psyche. This
would also enable him to understand all forms of mental illness. To
accomplish this, it would be necessary to answer two questions: What
is the common denominator in Freud's and Adler's theories and what
is the deeper reason that they differ? As I have pointed out, what these
theories have in common is that both find as the cause for the illness a
crisis brought about by the repression of certain strong impulses in
the unconscious. They do, however, understand the nature of these
impulses quite differently. What exactly is the reason for their differences, their contradictions?

Let's look once again at Adler's theory. As I have mentioned, it
evolved out of his observation that the development of the human psyche
leads to individual consciousness, which in turn is centered around the

ego. Jung concluded from the above facts (which certainly cannot be denied) that the forces in the human psyche that bring about consciousness are identical with those that create in us the feeling of individuality, of being unique and different from everyone else. He left it open whether these consciousness-creating forces were the only ones active in the psyche, or whether there might be others that needed to be discovered. Adler had called his theory "individual psychology" because he felt that developing the individual was the foremost trait of the psyche.

Now let's have another look at Freud's theory. He declared the sexual drive to be the main driving force in the development of the psyche. He did not speculate about whether there might be other forces at work as well. This means that Freud saw the human being mainly in the context of the species, for the sex drive serves essentially to propagate the species. Whenever we follow the sex drive, we act as members of our species, not as individuals. Now let us consider that while those forces that are at work to develop our consciousness are identical to those that bring about individuality, conversely, those forces that make us merely a part of the species by their very nature have no relationship to consciousness. There is wisdom in using the term "sleeping together" to describe the sexual act. It points to the fact that the processes having to do with life, particularly with procreation, are in themselves related to the unconscious rather than to consciousness. They resemble sleeping, not waking.

Jung concluded from the above that the polarity between consciousness and the unconscious could also be characterized as follows: We are dealing here with two different streams, one that brings about consciousness and another that makes us members of the species.

While Freud and Adler both believed that all mental illness was caused by an overwhelming discrepancy between the conscious and the unconscious, Jung concluded that illness manifests when a person becomes overwhelmed by the conflict between what makes us a member of the species and what makes us individuals.

Jung wondered what could happen in the life of a person that could cause this conflict, this discrepancy in the soul that triggers mental illness. He often used his method of "free association" as a research tool.

He thereby tried to gain an understanding of the unconscious, and he discovered that we are members of the species not only through the physical body we possess, but also in our soul life, in the drive to become an individual. It became clear to Jung that the human psyche is not the simple entity Freud and Adler had thought it to be. To Jung, the psyche was a complex structure containing a multitude of impulses. Thus he named his theory "complex psychology." What does this actually mean?

It means that there are processes and experiences in the human psyche that occur simply because it is a *human psyche* independent of any claim to individuality. These happen in a similar way in all human beings. Jung calls these our collective experiences, and they are, typically, completely unconscious. But it always happens that some of these unconscious experiences that are common to the whole species seep into consciousness. This happens to healthy as well as unhealthy individuals. It happens in a form that is so characteristic that it clearly indicates that here we have to do with "intimations" from the unconscious—the experiences are clothed in the form of symbols. As soon as the symbol appears in our consciousness, it takes on an individual character; this is because in the conscious realm we are indeed individuals. But the manifold individual expressions are different only in the same way as variations on a musical theme are different. The composer, said Jung, has the same theme in mind when he writes the variations, even when he writes twenty or thirty of them. Where do we find these symbols, these "archetypes," as Jung called them, that are common to all human beings?

They are to be found in the essential contents of the great world religions, in the mystery teachings, the secret teachings that are woven into the history of humankind. Let's say there is the symbol of the Father in heaven. We find this in the Greek Zeus, in Yahweh of the Hebrews, and in the Indian Brahma. Another such symbol is that of the *Magna Mater*, the great earth goddess that appears in the figure of Demeter in Greek mythology, in the Egyptian Isis, in the Christian Mother Mary, as well as in the Chinese Kwan Yin. Or take the idea of the Holy Trinity. We have it not only in Christianity, but also in the

Indian *Trimurti*, and similarly in Greek and Egyptian mythology. Or the symbol of the God-Man; it appears in many religions. Finally we have Satan, the devil who appears in every religion in the most varied ways. These symbols, as Jung pointed out, do not originate with individuals; they have an anonymous origin, and they have the power to attract millions of people who make them their own.

This is the sphere of the unconscious. How do we contrast it with the sphere of consciousness? Consciousness is characterized by the fact that it produces not symbolic images but abstract concepts. These are the concepts that we find in philosophy and natural science. Unlike symbols, they are formulated by individuals who had these thoughts for the first time. Therefore they are always connected to the individual originator, even when they have been universally recognized. In this sense we talk about Plato's, Descartes's, Kant's, Leibniz's, or Hegel's philosophy, and of Darwin's theory of the origin of the species, Einstein's relativity theory, or Planck's quantum theory. These two worlds, one of the unconscious and one of the conscious, stand opposite each other in our psyche.

Now comes the question: How does mental illness come about? As part of his answer, Jung pointed to the fact that, even though mental illness has always existed to an extent, there has been a tremendous increase in such illnesses in the twentieth century. Freud and Adler had also recognized this, but Jung was especially adamant about it. He considered mental illness to be typical and symptomatic for our time.

While these kinds of illnesses certainly existed in former times, they have now assumed avalanchelike proportions, so that no matter how many mental institutions we build we cannot accommodate all the patients. In fact depth psychology would not have been created had it not been for the tremendous need to help such a great number of sufferers. Neuroses and psychoses occur nowadays not only in particular individuals, but as massive epidemics and mass psychoses, as we have seen in full measure in our century. Indeed they create the impression of mass madness.

What is the reason for all this? The spheres of the unconscious and the conscious existed in a reasonably harmonious balance all through history, up to the modern age. But since then the tension between the two spheres has increased, and can be characterized as the conflict between belief and knowledge or between religion and science. I need not describe this conflict in detail, for everybody who acquires even a modest amount of modern education grows up with this conflict and has to deal with it one way or another. I have to point out, however, the way in which modern society from the middle of the nineteenth century on has tried to solve the problem. It is common knowledge that in the last hundred years the findings of individual philosophers and scientists have become accepted truth. Meanwhile the collective symbolic images—which are of an anonymous nature and are the essence of religion and mythology—were branded as superstitions or old wives' tales. Anyone who wished to be recognized as modern and enlightened was inclined to throw out the "old superstitions." When Nietzsche declared in the 1870s "God is dead," would anyone have still believed in the devil?

Religious and symbolic images were repressed more and more by modern society until they almost disappeared from the consciousness of the age. Consequently, something happened on a large scale: the content of the unconscious—which has the desire to be part of the conscious and normally "seeps through" into the healthy psyche—was no longer able to do this in a normal way. The danger existed that human soul life would be split apart so that there would be no connection anymore between the conscious and the unconscious.

In the end there was no other way to escape this danger without the repressed collective unconscious breaking through with great force. This happened in the form of individual mental illness where a person experienced hallucinations, often of a religious nature. But it also happened in the form of collective psychoses, where we see perverse religious experiences or pseudoreligious manias. In these collective manias, millions of people rally around a certain powerful symbol. One of those was the swastika, an ancient religious-cosmic symbol that was used by the National Socialists; others are the fasces of the Italian Fascists and the Soviet star. The Marian movement within Catholicism, which gained large masses of followers in our century, has as its symbol the physically resurrected Mary. All these movements are based on collective experiences that are strong enough to sweep away modern philosophical and scientific concepts and rob the affected persons of their independence and self-directedness. Mass consciousness takes over, and every member of the mass has identical experiences that are expressed in the beloved symbol.

This represents Jung's view of the situation. He asked himself: "How can I find a means to heal not only the individual illness, but also what can rightly be called the great cultural illness of our time?" Jung believed that healing can only be achieved by a thorough understanding of the true nature of the psyche, as he described it in his psychology of the complexes. This psychology says that in the psyche we have two streams that, even though they originate in the same root, will develop in different directions. As the soul matures, these two streams become more and more diametrically opposite, so that one can speak of the two sides of the soul as the day and the night sides. It lies in the nature of the human soul that these two poles must develop. They are the individual consciousness and the collective unconscious. The process can perhaps be compared to the way that in puberty the male and female sides of the human being become clearly defined. The development of the two poles carries in it the seed of mental illness. This is not something that is imposed on the soul from outside; it is inherent in the soul and can become dangerous when the two poles become so far removed from each other that excessive pressure is created. What creates this unhealthy pressure?

It happens when the individualized daytime consciousness is allowed to become ever brighter and more awake while the night side, the collective unconscious, sinks down from a state of half-awareness into greater and greater darkness. The consequence is that we finally come to believe that our daytime consciousness—in which we feel ourselves to be individuals—is the only consciousness we have. The unconscious is condemned to oblivion or even believed to be nonexistent. This is what has actually happened in our recent history. Since Descartes, the father of modern philosophy and psychology, the soul has been declared identical with consciousness, and well into the nineteenth century, nobody paid particular attention to the unconscious. Descartes' famous statement, "*Cogito ergo sum*," sought to prove the existence of the human psyche in the ability to form individual, abstract thoughts. Thus the other, collective side of the psyche was abandoned and the way paved for the development of the strong individualism that has dominated and shaped our Western culture. The backlash that has taken place has already been alluded to in this lecture.

Jung was convinced that today a new, all-encompassing psychology must be created. This psychology will show the way to an understanding of the "two souls in the human breast," as Goethe says in *Faust*. It is not entirely correct to put it this way. There are not two souls, but one that has two aspects to it, two sides. On one side is the consciousness, where we experience our individuality while we formulate abstract thoughts and try to understand the world with our thinking. We are unconscious of our other side, through which we are connected to all other human beings and to universal wisdom. When this other side rises into consciousness, it appears in symbolic images. Human beings must come to admit that as far as the soul is concerned, we are more than just thinking, reasoning individuals. We also belong to all humankind and carry ancient wisdom within us. We must learn to understand that the whole truth cannot be found in abstract thinking and philosophizing, but must be sought in the ancient symbols as well. If this is understood, we can arrive not only at a synthesis of faith and knowledge, of religion and science, but we will also be able to reconcile our individualism with our common humanity.

When we apply these insights in the way we conduct our lives, we will experience a reconciliation of the two poles in our psyche. What has been torn apart will reunite, or, as Jung puts it, what was differentiated will be reintegrated and become whole again. An important consequence of this reintegration will be the formation of a new center in our psyche. In our present state of consciousness we are aware only of the ego.

But if we bring together the two halves of our psyche in a harmonious way we will become aware of the Self. Only with the birth of the Self can one be a complete human being. Jung calls the process of finding the Self *individuation*. He considers individuation the highest goal humankind can achieve in the development of the soul. The great spiritual leaders of humankind have pointed to this goal in many different formulations and pictures. Jung calls the Self the center of a new equilibrium that will give human beings a secure foundation on which to stand. He says: "I will admit that such visualizations are only an attempt of the clumsy intellect to formulate inexpressible and hard-to-describe psychological facts. I could perhaps express the same concept with the words of St. Paul: Now not I live, but the Christ lives in me. Or I could quote Lao Tsu and make his Tao my own, the way of the middle and center of all things. In every case the meaning is the same."

We see that Jung's depth psychology is meant to be more than simply a diagnosis and therapy for individual mental illnesses. He diagnoses the present historical and cultural dilemma of the Western world as a whole, and he wants to show the way out of this dangerous situation.

This is what I wanted to bring you today about the different streams of depth psychology. When I speak tomorrow about the anthroposophical approach to knowledge of the human soul, you will see that it fully accepts the important truths contained in depth psychology. In addition, Anthroposophy can offer a considerable deepening of our understanding of the soul. Anthroposophy's unique method of research opens up a new dimension of soul experiences that depth psychology has not even touched upon. This new dimension has opened the door to the innermost realms of the human soul. The purpose of tomorrow's lecture will be to describe these things in detail.

2

THE RIDDLES
OF THE HUMAN SOUL IN
THE LIGHT OF ANTHROPOSOPHY

IN THE PREVIOUS LECTURE, I tried to characterize the most important results of research done within the different schools of depth psychology. We have seen that depth psychology is concerned with studying the soul's unconscious and its relation to human consciousness. We have also seen that its research method is analogous to that used by modern natural science in its study of the relationship of the outer physical world to human consciousness.

Today I will describe the findings of anthroposophical research in the realm of the soul. To begin with, I must mention that depth psychology and Anthroposophy spring from different roots. While I mentioned yesterday that depth psychology arose from the practical needs of psychiatry, Anthroposophy has its roots in the pure need for knowledge, and that means the need for a true and encompassing knowledge of human nature in general. Both recognize that only a part of the psyche can be experienced by our everyday consciousness, whereas most of soul life is shrouded in the darkness of the unconscious. This is why true self-knowledge is so difficult.

We find, however, that the research methods of depth psychology and Anthroposophy differ right from the start. While the former is concerned with immediately exploring the unconscious, the latter remains initially in the realm of consciousness. The following illustrates why this is so. One could perhaps characterize the difference between the conscious and the unconscious aspects of the soul by imagining them as two rooms: one full of light, so that everything in it can be clearly seen, the other one dark, so that nothing in it is visible. (We will ignore the transitional realm between them for the moment.) If one conceives of things this way, it is quite reasonable to assume that your aim will be to bring some light into the darkness of the second room.

Anthroposophy has a different approach. It states that the image of the soul with two different rooms is not completely accurate. We saw yesterday that the concepts we form out of our own inner consciousness have the character of abstract, imageless thoughts, unless they are triggered by our sense impressions. In contrast to this, the concepts that "trickle" out of the unconscious always appear in the form of images or symbols. We achieve our clearest possible thinking in the thoughts we form when working with mathematics or logic, where we are most awake. Anthroposophy points to something that has not yet been taken into account by most philosophy or psychology: the fact that when we work mathematically, for instance, our clear thinking is directed toward the object of our thinking, the content, but not toward the *activity* of thinking itself. This may seem strange at first, but it will become clearer when I make the following comparison.

I can decide to bend my arm. This is a decision of my will. What happens? As soon as I have made this decision, it is conveyed somehow to my muscles, and I bend my arm. I can see this happen and so become conscious of it. But what actually happened between my decision and its execution, I cannot observe and know. Modern physiology speaks of the function of motor nerves in this connection, but this is mere speculation and theory, and does not stem from direct experience. Now when I am confronted with a math or physics problem, as a student is in an exam, I find myself in exactly the same situation as the one described above. What do I do? I set my thinking in motion, and with luck, I find the solution to my problem. It lights up in me somehow. I could then exclaim with Archimedes: "Eureka, I have found it!" But I don't know what actually happened in my soul to bring about the "lighting up" of the correct thought, just as I have no idea how my arm bent after I decided to bend it. In this case one says that one has "found' the solution—so it must have been present somewhere in my consciousness if I was able to find it. Where this is, however, is hidden from my experience. Thus Anthroposophy suggests that there must be something like a "dark area" in our consciousness, and that this dark area is thinking itself when considered as an activity. Out of this recognition arises the necessity to explore and shed light on this dark area, the act of thinking itself, before trying to take on the sphere of the unconscious.

The Anthroposophical Method of Research

Anthroposophy takes a fundamentally different approach to discovering the secret of the soul from that of depth psychology. Instead of forming theories and hypotheses, it attempts to arrive at direct experiences. Since we cannot directly experience the activity of our own thinking, we can try to retrain our thought life in such a way that our field of inner perception is enhanced and broadened, so that things previously unseen become visible. Such a retraining of inner perception can be achieved by voluntarily beginning a path of inner education. This inner schooling consists of exercises in concentrated thinking and certain meditations. They are described in Rudolf Steiner's basic works *How To Know Higher Worlds* and *An Outline of Esoteric Science*, as well as many of his other writings. Here I can only hint at the principle of these exercises. Anyone interested in details may find them in the above-mentioned books.

In the same way that one can strengthen one's arms and legs by repeating certain exercises regularly over a period of time, one can increase the scope and intensity of one's thought life by diligently following the thought exercises regularly and patiently. I have to admit that here we are talking not about weeks, but rather about months and years. Such an exercise may be concerned with a deduction from a mathematical theorem, or a philosophical thought that at one time led you to a particular insight. It is essential not only to remember the concept but to follow the reasoning that led to it, from the beginning up to the point where one can once more experience the initial flash of understanding. If such exercises are repeated regularly over a long period of time, the strength of one's thinking is enhanced to such an extent that one can experience not only the object of thinking, but also the activity of thinking itself. One can observe oneself thinking, so to speak.

To experience this is a veritable breakthrough in soul life, a profound change. The experience has several different aspects. Here I will outline only three.

When, by training the mind, one is able to observe one's own thinking in the way described here, the human soul in this moment is not dependent on the physical body. It is independent of the brain and the nervous system. We are dealing here with a pure soul activity. Anthroposophy therefore recognizes the soul as a separate entity with its own reality apart from the physical body.

When we acquire the ability to observe our own thinking, it is truly possible to discover one's own "I." To say "I" to oneself is surely the expression of an inner recognition of one's individual soul. Symbolically this could be expressed with the image of the snake biting its own tail, or of a complete circle. In our ordinary consciousness we often say "I," but after we make the crucial discovery mentioned here we realize that so far we have never penetrated to our real "I." The symbolic circle has never been fully closed. In our normal consciousness we are in a sense always "on the way" to self-discovery; we never quite reach the goal. Therefore, when we say "I" to ourselves, we don't envision a clearly defined concept, such as an outer object we can name. Our "I" always remains dark for us, more like a vague feeling. The circle of self-recognition is only closed when we arrive at the point where we can observe our own thinking activity.

What thinks in us is obviously our "I"; it is we ourselves. Therefore, when we can observe ourselves thinking, we also discover our "I" in its full reality. Anthroposophy thus comes to the remarkable conclusion that this "dark area" within us that seems to surround our thinking is indeed nothing else but our core, our "I," to which all the activities of normal consciousness are related. Strangely, even though all our thinking and striving is related to an inner core, the core itself remains more or less hidden from our consciousness throughout our life. We only see it in the full light of consciousness once we are able to observe our own thinking inwardly after having gone through the process of inner schooling. Thus, when a student of Anthroposophy apprehends her own "I" for the first time, it is as if she wakes up in the midst of her normal consciousness. She awakens to a new reality, a higher consciousness. As I will explain, Anthroposophy calls this *imaginative consciousness*.

A third fact appears when imaginative consciousness is attained: it becomes possible to solve the mystery of everyday consciousness. This mystery presents itself, for instance, in the following problem: Yesterday, my sketch showed how our normal consciousness borders on the surrounding world where we receive our sense impressions. But we do not only *receive* sense impressions. We also extend our own thoughts and concepts toward these impressions. We connect our concepts to our sense impressions. Now we can ask how this is significant. What connection is there between our sense impressions and our concepts?

Philosophers have asked this fundamental question throughout human history, from ancient Greece to the present day. It cannot be answered as long as we stay within the limits of our everyday consciousness and its experiences. This does not mean that the most diverse answers have not been given. However, all these answers only constitute theories and hypotheses; they do not stem from genuine experience. I want to name here only two of the most famous theories, which were hotly debated, especially during the Middle Ages. The proponents of the one theory called themselves *realists*. They held that thoughts not only exist within the human mind, but are part of the outer reality of the world as well. For the realists, outer reality consisted not only of physical matter but also of "thought substance." And just as human beings see colors with our eyes and hear tones with our ears, we can apply our thinking like a "spiritual eye" and thereby "perceive" the thoughts contained in the world. When, in our soul, we then connect our thoughts with our sense perceptions, we only reunite what we have experienced with our different organs of perception.

Opposed to the realists were the *nominalists*. They held that thoughts themselves have nothing to do with the world around us. They believed that the human mind and soul produces thoughts out of itself, and that these exist only in the mind. Concepts are only names (*nomina*) and descriptions we give to the different phenomena in the world. We name things in order to group and order them, which makes them easier to understand. As we know, this nominalist attitude has prevailed, becoming the foundation for judgment in modern natural science.

Imaginative Consciousness

How things really are can only be experienced from the lofty standpoint of imaginative consciousness. At first it may seem as if the only content of this consciousness were the "I"-core that now becomes visible to the inner eye. This, however, is not the case; it is only one aspect of the experience. At the moment when the anthroposophical scientist awakens to his higher consciousness, he discovers that it has a far greater range than ordinary consciousness. In other words, he is able— one cannot express it otherwise—to immerse himself immediately into the inner workings of nature; not, of course, in a physical sense, but in a spiritual one. An anthroposophical scientist thus recognizes that the realists of the Middle Ages were right in a certain sense. Everything we encounter in nature—minerals, plants, and animals—consists not only of material substance but also of thought substance. It all contains objective cosmic thoughts. The cosmic thoughts that are hidden, so to speak, in all natural phenomena become objects of spiritual recognition because the thinker has strengthened his receptive capacity through the above-mentioned exercises. He has caused a new organ of perception to arise within himself, just as a plant brings forth a blossom after a certain period of growth. Anthroposophy calls this higher consciousness *imagination*, because it is an experience of images, a supersensible "seeing." Now it becomes clear that the objective thoughts contained in nature are somewhat different from what the medieval realists imagined. They are not mere abstract thoughts, but living, creating, form-giving, and transforming forces that give everything alive— animals, plants, and even minerals—their specific configuration. When, for instance, you look at an oak tree with its thousands of leaves, each with the same characteristic form and color, or when you consider a herd of sheep in which each animal has the typical form, you may well ask, what forces are at work here that guide the flow of the sap, the chemical composition in this tree, in such a way that all the leaves have the same shape and color? Or, in the other instance, that all the sheep in the herd have the characteristic form and typical behavior of sheep? These are indeed supersensible forces—spiritual, thoughtlike prototypes, archetypes of the natural forms that have the capacity to be filled with material substance. These are the forces that become visible to imaginative consciousness, thereby revealing to anthroposophical research that the human soul has a far wider range than ordinary day-time consciousness recognizes. In a very real way, the soul reaches into the inner realm of nature.

Of course, we know nothing of all this in our ordinary waking consciousness, and for good reason. Were we to have the immediate experience of these facts every day, we would not be able to distinguish our own soul from the surrounding world. We would be so interwoven with nature that we could not recognize ourselves as an "I." That we can develop our individual "I" is due to our ability, in the course of our development, to suppress the experience of these interconnections, to keep them unconscious so that we know nothing of them. The suppression of these spiritual facts can also be described in another way; it is the same process, only expressed differently. When we develop our ordinary consciousness, we restrict the range of our experiences to such an extent that it no longer reaches into the realm of nature, but only to its boundary. When we then come in touch with this boundary, we recognize it as different from ourselves, and we experience ourselves as an "I." The same situation can also be explained in yet another way: our soul, in the course of developing ordinary consciousness, unites itself utterly with the physical body, identifies with it completely. Consequently, it can only recognize what the sense organs can grasp. The physical sense organs function in such a way that they let us perceive nature as from the outside. They cannot penetrate into her inner realm.

Now we can see that what sense impressions tell us is only half the story. The soul also answers with its thoughts. What happens during this activity? Again, what happens here can only be observed from the standpoint of imaginative consciousness. The soul, when confronted with a particular sense impression, extends a supersensible organ—like a searchlight, perhaps—into its own inner being and looks for the thoughts that belong to this sense impression. These thoughts are present in nature as well as in our soul, because the soul, as we have seen, projects into the natural realm, even though we are not conscious of it. Having found the proper thoughts, the soul lifts them up into consciousness, and for this it uses the brain and nervous system as it uses the sense organs to perceive outer nature.

This amazing process is still a bit more complicated, however. The living, creating, form-giving forces that are present in nature as well as in the human soul cannot immediately enter our waking consciousness. What enters our consciousness is only a copy, a mirror image, of the living reality. And the mirror that produces this image is our brain. We bring the living cosmic thoughts into such a relationship with our brain that it can produce a copy of them that we then perceive with our normal consciousness. So Anthroposophy posits that thinking itself— if we consider it to be an activity that seeks to grasp the living thoughts weaving in the world as well as in our soul—is a soul activity totally independent of the brain. The brain is only needed to produce the mirror image of living reality so that our everyday consciousness can see it. The process of recognition is indeed that complicated when seen from the standpoint of anthroposophical research.

Within all this lies the mystery of everyday consciousness. As I mentioned before, our everyday consciousness is structured as it is to give us the ability to set ourselves apart from the surrounding natural realm so that we can experience ourselves as an "I." In this sense Anthroposophy is in full agreement with the claims of Adler and Jung that those forces that create our everyday consciousness are the same as those that make us into a being that calls itself "I." We can even take a further step and agree with what Adler has emphasized so strongly: that the "I"-consciousness always goes hand in hand with a strong egoism. This is certainly the case. Anthroposophy, however, identifies a different cause for this than Adler's psychology, which teaches that egoism arises as a compensation for a certain inherent feeling of inferiority.

For Anthroposophists, the root of egoism appears to lie in the following two circumstances. First, as we grow into adulthood, we identify more and more with our physical body, feeling cut off from the world around us. This makes us want to assert our ego strongly. The second reason is that in our everyday consciousness we never quite find the answer to the question: "Who am I?" This makes us egoistic and "self-seeking," in the true sense of the word. This self-seeking only comes to rest and is satisfied when the inner experience of the "I am" is truly felt. For then the restless striving has come to an end. This can only happen if consciousness is raised to the higher level of imagination.

Experience shows that when higher consciousness is attained, some of our seemingly natural tendencies reverse themselves. Part of the new consciousness is the realization that the forces that have so far formed our everyday consciousness have a constricting, narrowing effect, which estranges human beings from the universe. I could also say that they are forces of antipathy, of hatred, if you will. As soon as the new, higher consciousness is attained, inner development takes a new direction. The forces of antipathy, hatred, and contraction have reached their goal. They can now turn into forces of sympathy, love, and expansion. Imaginative consciousness can expand since it has found the "I" to be independent of the physical body.

Yet another phenomenon shows itself for the seeker of higher knowledge at this stage: When human beings have attained full waking consciousness at adulthood, they do not always remain awake. They enter into other forms of consciousness at regular intervals. One of these is the dream state. What actually happens when we fall asleep at night and enter into the dream state? For imaginative consciousness, it appears that the soul that was given over entirely to the body while awake leaves the body to a certain degree. The degree is exactly the same as in someone who has attained imaginative consciousness. Thus a certain expansion of consciousness takes place in the dreamer, and it is the same expansion that higher consciousness affords the spiritual scientist. However, in the person who has not undergone the necessary schooling, the consciousness dims as it expands. Let me illustrate this again with a sketch (figure 2).

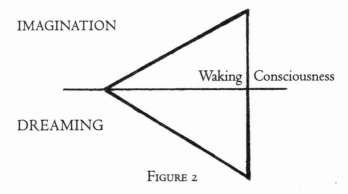

IMAGINATION

Waking | Consciousness

DREAMING

FIGURE 2

Let us suppose that the middle line represents the level of clarity of our waking consciousness. The clarity in the dream is somewhat dimmer. As consciousness is dimmed, so is the experience of the "I," our core.

When we dream, we are actually just as removed from our physical body as the spiritual researcher is in imaginative consciousness, and our consciousness is expanded just as much. We can turn this around and say: The spiritual researcher is in the same world as the dreamer. But the spiritual researcher is in this world with a clarity of consciousness that is as far above normal consciousness as that of the dreamer is below it. At the same time, the "I"-consciousness is as much brighter in the researcher as it is dimmer in the dreamer. Because of this, the spiritual researcher is in a position to explain, with the help of supersensible observation, the essence of the dream state. What indeed is this?

When we dream, our soul is literally spread out, to a very large extent, beyond the physical body. The soul is interwoven with the sphere of the living, objective thoughts that interpenetrate the whole world. To this sphere also belongs the living, form-giving archetype that underlies our own physical body, just as an archetype underlies every living animal or plant. Steiner called these living, form-creating thought-beings "etheric formative forces" (*ätherische Bildekräfte*) to emphasize their nonmaterial yet actively plastic character. Indeed the human body is supported by such an organization of etheric formative forces. These not only provide the body with its characteristic form before and after birth but also protect it during its whole lifetime from

the forces of decay and disintegration by constantly maintaining its
vital functions such as breathing, circulation, digestion, and metabolism. Sometimes an anomaly arises within the activity of these forces.
This manifests itself, depending on the extent of the anomaly, in a lack
of well-being or in illness. In the dream state, one is directly aware of
the activities of the etheric formative forces. The dreamer is sensitive to
them especially during times of illness. But they show themselves in
symbolic pictures, not in their real form. Thus Anthroposophy cannot
agree with the assumption of depth psychology that all dream experiences stem directly from the soul. Some are simply images caused by
physiological functions in either the healthy or the sick physical body.
Of course there are also other kinds of dreams, and I will talk about
them too. But you can see from the description here that the spiritual
researcher, having attained imaginative consciousness, is able to penetrate not only into the inner workings of nature, but also into the zone
that lies between waking and sleeping—the dream state.

Inspired Consciousness

The path of spiritual-scientific research is not completed with the
attainment of imaginative consciousness. That is only the first stage.
There are two further stages that I will describe here, albeit only in a
sketchy fashion.

To the thought exercises that lead to the first stage there can be
added exercises of the feelings, of the heart. These exercises will significantly enhance the forces of caring, of devotion, and of openness
toward the outer world. When such schooling of the feeling life is
added after the attainment of imaginative consciousness and the
desired goal is reached, seekers are able to free themselves from the
physical body to an even higher degree than was the case in the first
stage. Consequently, they awaken into a still deeper level of their inner
being, the Self, and attain an even brighter, clearer consciousness than
before—they reach more deeply into the "I." This is again only one
side of the coin. The other side is that consciousness expands again to
such an extent that it enables one to experience directly *what lies behind the*

world thoughts, the archetypes, what brings them into being. What is this experience? To the modern person it sounds unbelievable and fantastic, yet it is a real experience: *One sees differentiated spiritual beings who appear in a hierarchical order.* We can also call them *divine beings,* for they are the ones the ancients called their gods, and of whom Christian esoteric tradition speaks as the hierarchy of angels, archangels, *archai,* Powers, Thrones, and so on. The anthroposophical researcher comes into direct contact with these beings, enters into a spiritual conversation with them, if you will. The experience on this level is not only a beholding but like an intense listening. And what one hears is what has been called "the music of the spheres," a cosmic music. It is the way in which these divine beings speak to the soul of the listener. This hearing is also perceived like a spiritual "inbreathing." Thus Anthroposophy calls this experience *inspiration.*

I will only mention one aspect of this rich experience. It is revealed to the seeker at this stage that he or she is not the only one who comes into contact with these spiritual hierarchies, but that every single human being does. This happens at regular intervals throughout our life every time we fall into a deep, dreamless sleep. When we lose our daytime consciousness as we fall asleep, our soul separates even more from the body than it does in the dream state. At the same time that our consciousness expands, it is dimmed to an even greater degree, so much so that we could almost call it unconsciousness. It is not complete unconsciousness, but a very dim state of awareness. Our "I"-consciousness is at that moment completely extinguished. We now find ourselves in the same surroundings that spiritual researchers find themselves in when they have attained inspirational consciousness. Or I could say it the other way around: The spiritual researcher, when in the state of inspirational consciousness, is in the same world as the sleeper, only the researcher's consciousness is as much brighter than his or her daytime consciousness as the sleeper's is dimmer.

Ordinarily we consider the sleeping state as being unconscious in contrast to our waking consciousness, and between these two we have the dream state. Inspired consciousness is so significantly brighter that to one who has attained it, ordinary consciousness appears as a sleep—

spiritual sleep, unawareness of the spirit world. Such a person sees imaginative consciousness as a dream state in the higher sense. Now Rudolf Steiner was not the first to acquire inspired consciousness; there is a long line of initiates preceding him. They gave a name to the state of inspired consciousness: the "state of enlightenment." I only have to remind you of Buddha's experience under the bodhi tree.

Anthroposophical researchers can observe what actually happens in sleep because they are in the same state as the sleeper, only they experience it in full consciousness. A great deal could be said about this; however, I will select only one phenomenon here. I have already mentioned that everyone, while sleeping, is in the presence of certain exalted spiritual beings without being aware of it. When one awakens from sleep one knows nothing of these encounters. But we do carry something into waking life that is like an "afterglow" of what has been experienced in sleep, and that is the ability to have religious feelings and thoughts. It is a remarkable fact that most people, even though they know nothing of such sleep encounters, have a certain deep feeling that something supersensible, superhuman, creative, divine must lie hidden beyond ordinary life. And they have a deep longing that is expressed in the word *religio*—the longing to reconnect somehow with the divine spiritual that is felt to be behind the physical world. This longing is indeed satisfied every night in sleep, but the price we pay for it is the loss of our waking consciousness. We sink deeply into unconsciousness, and when we wake in the morning we bring with us religious feelings to a greater or lesser degree. This is a great gift that we receive from the sleep experience. If it were possible to keep someone from sleeping for a long period of time, among other undesirable consequences, that person's ability to have religious feelings would completely die. She would become a convinced atheist. We owe the fact that we can have religious thoughts to our going to sleep every night. In sleep lie the roots of religious feeling, even though it may sound strange to many of you. In ancient times people were well aware of the sacredness of sleep. In more recent times, the poet Novalis has expressed such thoughts in his *Hymns to the Night*.

There is something else that reveals itself to anthroposophical research: when we awaken from sleep, we not only bring back this general aftereffect of our sleep experiences, we also bring back more concrete, specific effects. Depending on the destiny of the soul's life on earth, it meets with spiritual beings that have a special relationship with it. When the soul returns to waking consciousness, passing through the dream world and the realm of etheric formative forces, these spiritual beings clothe themselves in those symbolic pictures that, as we have already indicated, trickle through from the unconscious into consciousness. Those are the "archetypes of the collective unconscious" that Jung discovered and that constitute, according to Jung, the essential content of the world's great religions.

Again Anthroposophy can wholeheartedly agree with Jung about this discovery. Those archetypes do indeed exist, but in our day and age, when the impressions of the outer world caused by automobiles, airplanes, radio, television, and so on are so overwhelming and loud that they outshine and crowd out the more subtle impressions of the unconscious, we hardly ever become aware of the archetypes anymore. They seem to show up only in pathological conditions, often in a distorted form. In older times, when daily life was simpler, quieter, and more regulated, the archetypes had a stronger influence on people's consciousness. This was also the case because they lived closer to the dream state. Here Anthroposophy can take another step and agree with Jung that these experiences of the archetypes are of a collective nature, and are available to everyone. Every man and woman will have these experiences, regardless of whether he or she is Mr. Jones or Mrs. Miller. They are differentiated only according to different cultural or racial conditions or to the time period in which they manifest.

Here again Anthroposophy is able to enlarge and even to clarify the findings of depth psychology. Jung can merely assert that the archetypes exist. They come from the collective unconscious, present themselves in symbols, and are experienced unconsciously, and their true reality cannot be wrested from the unconscious. Thus for Jung, the source of the archetypes remains in the dark, and all he can do is advance hypotheses about their nature. In his earlier writings he considered them to be the result of thousands of years of human experience that have entered the hereditary stream; later he conceived the archetypes to be constitutional dispositions of recognition, experience, and behavior that are inherently rooted in the human being.

Accordingly, he ascribes to them mere psychological significance, and regards their content as images, symbols, of superhuman beings. And he considers the individual's relationships with these beings as mere projections of the psyche into the metaphysical-transcendental realm. By contrast, Anthroposophy can refer to actual experience, because in the state of higher consciousness the so-called unconscious is illuminated for the researcher. We discover that such archetypes as God the Father, the Earth Mother, the Trinity, the God-Man, the Devil, and so on, have their origin in certain realities of the spiritual world and its relationship to human beings. Anthroposophy is able to trace the origin of each of the archetypes in a concrete way. Within the framework of this lecture I cannot go into details; for these I refer you to Steiner's writings and lectures. In my next lecture, I will only discuss one of the archetypes in detail.

Intuitive Consciousness

We still have not arrived at the end of the spiritual-scientific path of research. It is possible to reach a third stage on this path by adding to the above-mentioned exercises of thoughts and feelings a third one: a training of the will. This consists above all else in giving one's will a "moral education" in the highest sense of the word. Again, you can find the relevant exercises in Steiner's basic works. When these have been carried out sufficiently to attain the intended goal, one gains the ability to have even more experiences in one's soul-spiritual being, independently of the physical body, than those one had in imaginative and inspired consciousness. Such a person then truly awakens in his innermost core. This means a rise to the highest degree of enlightened consciousness that one is capable of in the present state of development. Anthroposophy calls this stage *intuitive consciousness*. Again, my description so far covers only one side of what is happening. On the other side, intuitive consciousness has a far wider range than inspired consciousness; it provides the opportunity to experience the higher spiritual beings more directly. It is as if one is immersed totally in their being. While before they revealed themselves in images, in the "music of the spheres," and in the "cosmic Word," they now merge completely with the person who is in this state of consciousness (figure 3).

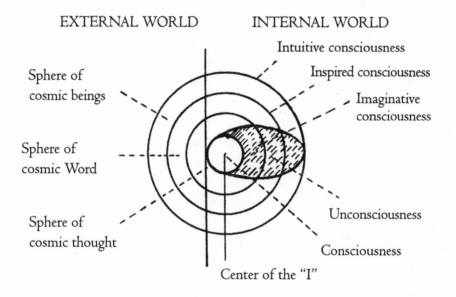

FIGURE 3

At this, the highest stage of supersensible consciousness to which Anthroposophy can lead, another important truth is revealed: in their inner core, human beings are essentially identical with those high spiritual beings that weave and create in the world as described above. If I may use a picture here, a drop of the ocean of spirit that flows all around the world lives in every person's inner being. The seeker can now see that, unlike the plants, animals, and stones, humanity is not only the creation of the divine beings but is their heir, their offspring. Just as a child of human parents is human, so can human beings call themselves the divine child of these higher beings. These beings are in the cosmic sense our parents, our ancestors.

Yet something more is revealed at this stage of higher consciousness. In the course of human existence, it happens again and again that we come into direct contact with spiritual beings, just like the initiate who has undergone arduous training. This happens to every person when the separation of the soul from the body goes further than in the dream state and even in sleep: that is, when death occurs. Since ancient times death has been called "the brother of sleep." In death the soul separates so completely from the body that the latter disintegrates and "returns to dust." But it is not only the body that disintegrates; the "I" experience as we have it in our everyday waking consciousness does as well. It is extinguished not only temporarily, as in sleep, but permanently and completely. This means that the personality we know and identify with during our earthly life vanishes in death. It does not endure beyond our death. But something does remain and endure, and that is the "I" that we cannot find all our life long, unless we are initiated into the higher stages of consciousness that I have described here. This "I" lives on and is finally distilled into the innermost core of our being. This core then lives with the spirit beings in direct communication—as if with its older brothers and sisters, so to speak.

Now I can say this again the other way around: The spiritual researcher is in the same condition in intuitive consciousness as people who have died. Only the spiritual researcher experiences this in full consciousness, while still alive and in the body (figure 4).

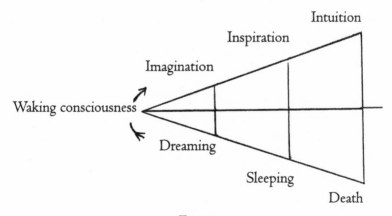

FIGURE 4

Thus spiritual science is in the position to solve the riddle of death—and the solution to this riddle is immortality. Not immortality of the ordinary personality, of course, but immortality of the inner, spiritual human core. This can be revealed during earthly life only in intuitive consciousness. The immortality of the inner human core becomes experience in the intuitive state of consciousness. For this reason Anthroposophy is also able to describe concretely what life after death is like. It is shown to the spiritual scientist that the human core, after having spent a certain length of time in the spiritual world, does not remain there forever but returns to earth again and enters a new life. In other words, spiritual science arrives at the fact of reincarnation, and at the same time the meaning of reincarnation is revealed: Every human being possesses such a wealth of talents and potential that a single life on earth would never be sufficient to develop them all. On the other hand, the possibilities that life on this earth offers us in the course of a lifetime in the challenges of the material earth, the hindrances and difficulties that help us to develop strength and fortitude, cannot be fully exhausted in a single life. Therefore a soul has to descend to earth not eternally, but many times and under many different conditions—just as many times as it takes to acquire everything that can be learned and experienced here. When a soul has developed all this it will go on to different forms of existence. I cannot speak of those now; it would overstep the limits of this lecture.

What is said with all the foregoing? It is possible to know not only the nature of death but also the secret of human birth. Just as we learn that the secret of death consists in the fact of the soul's excarnation from the body, so we learn that the mystery of human birth is solved when we see that the soul incarnates into a new body that has been prepared for it with a precise combination of inherited traits and talents. With this knowledge we have once more gained an understanding of the dignity of human birth. True human dignity lies in the fact that the human race does not merely perpetuate the species, as is the case with the animals. The sheaths are prepared again and again for human individualities to develop their full potential here on earth. The deeper meaning of human birth is that in the case of human beings, the evolution of the species is given a higher purpose; it serves the development of individualities from one incarnation to the other.

The Dignity of Human Birth

Now I have come to the point where Anthroposophy is obliged to do more than augment and rectify certain views of depth psychology, as in the cases I have pointed out earlier in this lecture. When it comes to the opinion of Freud, who maintains that the sex drive, the drive to propagate, is the all-encompassing driving force in the human psyche, we have to declare that we find ourselves in strong opposition to such a theory.

When we look back from our present condition into earlier times when daytime consciousness was not yet developed in the same way as ours is today, we find that humankind was still much more closely connected to the sphere of dreams, of sleep, and to those conditions of consciousness that lie beyond birth and death. The myths, religions, and ritual practices of those times give impressive witness to this fact. A great deal of importance was given to everything that had to do with the succession of generations, with marriage, and with the creation of offspring. All this was expressed in a wealth of rituals, cults, and ceremonies, beginning with the puberty rituals to which young men and women were subjected, and the numerous and varied marriage ceremonies practiced then, some of which have survived to this day.

When psychoanalysis claims that the archetypal, basic human drive is the sexual drive, one can only say that this is a grotesque misunderstanding.

The reason for the many rituals and customs surrounding the generation of offspring was this: In those days, people still had an understanding of the mystery of human birth that went far beyond its merely physical aspects. We encounter the knowledge of reincarnation in ancient India, as well as in other old cultures. In all ancient cultures we find at least an inkling, a feeling, for the preexistence of human souls before birth and for the fact that birth is essentially a process of incarnation. All those customs and ceremonies were meant to prepare the younger generation for marriage and childbearing in such a way that they would have an understanding of the deeper connections of life and birth and bring to these experiences the right attitude. This can be absolutely confirmed from what is known about the old puberty and marriage rituals.

Over the course of time, humankind began to develop more and more the clear daytime consciousness that we possess today. With that there arose a danger that we would completely lose our knowledge of the mystery of human birth. This would cause our attitude toward the dignity of the birth process to change and we would look at it merely as a physical function. To avert this danger, an event took place that (with all its other important consequences) would once again enable humankind to have a true understanding of the mystery of birth, and would retain our human dignity. I am talking here about the Christ event. We are told about the birth of Christ with the words that the Angel Gabriel speaks to Mary: "Hail Mary, full of grace, you are blessed among women; you will bear a son, and you shall call him Jesus." Mary answered: "Behold, I am the Lord's handmaiden, and it shall be with me according to thy words." In the figure of Mary we are shown a woman, a mother, who for all times can be a model for the right attitude toward human birth. We are then told that Mary will conceive her son from the Holy Spirit. Hereby the *innermost secret of every human birth* is revealed. For every human mother receives her child from the Holy Spirit in the sense that the child is born out of the spiritual world from where human individualities descend to begin a new life. Only in the Bible story the secret is told in special reference to the Christ, who is characterized as the archetypal representative of humanity. He is called the "Son of God." But in him is revealed what is, as I have already mentioned, the inner secret of every human birth. One may assert that the warm, loving veneration that was offered to the Virgin Mary in the Middle Ages has done its share to preserve human dignity for the whole culture of that time.

By the fifteenth and sixteenth centuries human consciousness had progressed so far in its evolution that we were almost completely cut off from an awareness of the spiritual worlds. Waking day-consciousness had taken over. The danger became even greater that we would forget the secret of human birth altogether.

And now we see something remarkable happen that can awaken us to the mystery of birth. This time it does not happen in the form of a historical event but in a remarkable painting. I am talking about the *Sistine Madonna* by Raphael. When you look at this painting, forgetting all that you may know about its content intellectually, and just try to see what the figures in the painting are telling you, you see two figures, one male, one female, kneeling on the ground. Above them is the Virgin Mother, as if floating down from heaven to earth. She is carrying the child in her arms, and the child looks as if it had just now parted from all the little angel heads in the background and flown into the arms of its mother so that she can carry it down to earth. It is clear that the child in this picture is descending from heaven. One can take the mother as a symbol of the human soul and the child as the young "I" on its way to incarnation. Over the centuries this painting has made a profound impression on many who have gazed at it. In this way it has perhaps helped us once more, at least on the feeling level, to have an inkling of the secret of our birth.

It was not until the middle of the nineteenth century that Darwin's theory of evolution arose and was embraced with great enthusiasm by the majority of people. With this theory, the human being is degraded to the status of "most developed animal," and with that comes the assumption that the human is nothing more than a being within a species, the same as the animal. Within this mode of thinking the secret, the dignity of human birth is completely forgotten. This opened the way for Freudian psychoanalysis, which is nothing but psychological Darwinism or Darwinized psychology. Psychoanalysis declares the sexual urge, which is necessary for the propagation of the species, to be the basic, most important drive in the human soul. If this view should become the predominant one in our culture, human birth would eventually be seen as no different from the animal's. Our whole existence would become animallike, and culture would fall into barbarism. There are many alarming signs in our century that this could indeed happen.

For this reason it became necessary for our time that the mystery of human birth should be revealed once more, but now in a form appropriate to the trend of our epoch, which demands scientific explanations. Here, in my estimation, lies one of the most important contributions of Anthroposophy, for it has been able to unveil the secret of human birth through a truly scientific research method. The anthroposophical path of research is admittedly different from the usual approach, but this is necessary because of the character of the matter under investigation.

By arriving at the experience of the immortality of the human essential core, the "I," we see it passing through repeated lifetimes, and human birth is once again recognized as a process of incarnation. Of course, it is also true that the human species is propagated by the birth of new human beings, and the sex drive is certainly active in our lower nature. But our essential being does not express itself in the sex drive. That natural drive is elevated to serve a higher purpose: the evolution of the individuality. If this knowledge is taken up into our feelings and emotions, we will arrive at a moral and practical attitude toward the birth process that is in accordance with human dignity.

I have tried here to show how the riddles of the human soul find their answers in depth psychology and in Anthroposophy. If Anthroposophy, as we have seen, goes far beyond what depth psychology in its different versions has to offer, we are in no way of the opinion that our research into these riddles is in any way complete. We confess with Heraclitus, whom I quoted at the beginning of these lectures: "No one can fathom the depth of the human soul, even if he or she walked to all the corners of the earth." We are convinced that complete knowledge about the soul will never be attained. The future will bring more and deeper insights into its workings, insights of which we may not even dream today.

Anthroposophy does not pretend to have found everything there is to know about this subject. But its discovery of those facts that help us recognize the dimensions and dignity of our soul has offered an important service for our time. Without this renewed way of looking at the human soul, the danger indeed exists that humankind could sink into the abyss of a subhuman existence.

3

DEPTH PSYCHOLOGY AND
ANTHROPOSOPHY

IN THE FIRST TWO LECTURES, we encountered the answers that depth psychology and Anthroposophy each have been able to give to the riddle presented by the human soul. To conclude our comparisons, tonight we will look in greater detail at the differences between the two modes of research. I hope it has become sufficiently clear from my last two lectures that Anthroposophy finds its answers through the recognition of an objectively real divine-spiritual world that appears in three stages: cosmic thoughts, the cosmic Word, and the world of manifest spiritual beings. There is no mention of these at all in depth psychology.

I also explained that the different results of these two research methods arises out of the initial attitude with which each approaches the subject. Depth psychology remains entirely within the realm of ordinary consciousness, drawing conclusions, and at the same time suggesting theoretical hypotheses about the unconscious. Anthroposophy, having developed a path of schooling that leads to an expansion of consciousness, is able to recognize not only the true nature of the so-called unconscious by making it conscious, but also to describe how the human soul in its three aspects relates to the divine and spiritual worlds.

One can also characterize the difference between the two approaches thus: Anthroposophical research works within the spiritual element, recognizing three distinct parts of the soul: the physical, the soul, and the spiritual elements. Depth psychology remains entirely in the soul element.

Let me remind you that in anthroposophical terminology the *spiritual element* constitutes the "core" of the human being, but is hidden from our ordinary consciousness and is awakened only when one attains the higher levels of consciousness: imagination, inspiration, and intuition. The *soul element* is experienced dimly in the dream state, and in its full brightness in our normal, waking state.

Soul and Spirit in Depth Psychology and Anthroposophy

The fact that depth psychology is concerned with the soul element alone, ignoring the spiritual, has been critically recognized by the creator of "logotherapy," Viktor Frankl. Depth psychology could defend itself against such criticism by pointing out that its foremost concern has *always* been the psyche; this is certainly justified. However, the problem is that depth psychology is especially concerned with exploring the unconscious. For Anthroposophy, the so-called unconscious is nothing else but the veiled, undiscovered spiritual element. When seen in this light one has to admit that depth psychology does indeed have to do with the spiritual in the human being.

This is why I want to compare these two important disciplines in a very precise manner. Whereas Anthroposophy aims to lead human beings to the development of the higher self and thereby to true self-knowledge, depth psychology can only grasp the higher self through its projections into the realm of the psyche. But in this way it cannot accomplish what in reality should be its ultimate goal. This inadequacy prompted Victor Frankl to develop his "logotherapy."[1]

Of course, the spiritual element is also evident in depth-psychological theories, because in reality the human being is always active in its totality. However, in the images of the soul given by psychoanalysis and individual psychology, the spiritual merely glints through, quite muted and almost unrecognizable. You have to look for it in Freud's theory where he talks about moral impulses and value judgments; in Adler's theory you find it in social impulses and common ideals. These certainly constitute very important factors in the development of the soul, but there does not seem to be a sufficient explanation for their origin and effectiveness. Thus in his later years Freud found it necessary to assume, in addition to the sex drive, a second basic drive in the psyche, the "death wish," which he supposed to be at the root of conscience. A proponent of individual psychology, E. Wexberg, had to confess in 1928: "The opposing forces of growing individualism and the personality cult on the one hand, and the necessity of developing a feeling of communality on the other hand, are causing those insurmountable problems that so tragically show themselves again and again in the life of individuals as well as in the life of nations."

In Jung's psychology of the complexes, the spiritual is decidedly more evident. It is represented by the collective unconscious and the world of archetypes. Even so, it does not appear here in its true form and reality, but clothed in the soul element in the form of projections. In Jung's assumption that the processes and experiences that call forth the archetypes cannot ever be wrested from the unconscious, we find proof that, in his depth psychology, we cannot speak of a human spiritual awakening.[2]

Admittedly, Jung has taken a very important first step in the direction of a spiritual awakening. He speaks of the necessity of reuniting the two elements of the soul that are split asunder into its conscious and unconscious parts. And he considers the reawakening of the central core of the human being, which he called the "Self" (situated between the conscious and the unconscious), to be the highest goal of human development.

Furthermore, what Jung calls the Self, in contrast to the everyday ego, can be considered identical with what Rudolf Steiner has called the immortal "I," the "higher ego," which goes through a sequence of repeated earthly lives. And finally, Jung speaks of the "individuation process" in which one becomes truly oneself. This is identical with Steiner's concept of the process of individualization, which is the highest goal one can achieve. But in spite of these similarities, Jung does not fully recognize the character of the Self, since he has nothing to say about reincarnation.

The World of Images in Imaginative Consciousness

Judging from Jung's descriptions of the world of archetypes—which he himself encountered when he was in a state of enhanced consciousness—one could equate this experience with the one that Steiner calls *imaginative consciousness.* This is the first of the stages described in anthroposophical literature. Indeed the concept of imagination is very familiar to Jung. He and his pupils are fond of psychologically interpreting and unraveling the imaginative and symbolic pictures we find in myths, fairy tales, visions, rituals, alchemical manipulations, and so on. But they do not dare to go further along the path of discovery of the archetypes, assuming that it would be dangerous, or even impossible. According to Jung, penetrating into the world of archetypes is fraught with ever-increasing dangers, dangers that would jeopardize a person's mental health. This world of images proves to be overwhelmingly powerful. Whoever tries to give herself up to it feels as if her ego is being squashed, so to speak. Or one might suffer from delusions of grandeur if one identifies too much with the images. These dangers are well known to Anthroposophy; one becomes acquainted with them on the path to higher knowledge. I did not mention them in my last lecture because I only wanted to give a schematic overview of the stages of anthroposophical initiation. If Anthroposophy encourages further steps toward enlightenment in spite of these dangers, it is because of the special preparations that pupils undertake. These give students the strength to withstand these overwhelming experiences and protect them from harm. I spoke in my last lecture about certain thought exercises that lead to the ability to immerse oneself in the natural world in a new way. The cosmic thoughts are revealed; the living, formative forces that give shape to all natural things.

Through the experience of imaginative consciousness, not only do Anthroposophists acquire a relationship to their own soul that is different from that of depth psychology, but a view of the natural world opens up to them that differs from the one held by contemporary natural science. In the previous lecture, we saw that depth psychology completely shares the viewpoint of natural science in regard to the natural world, inasmuch as it looks at nature as consisting entirely of matter. From this basis all kinds of theories and hypotheses are constructed that keep changing according to the latest scientific findings. Anthroposophy has gone beyond this, discovering the creative, formative spirit "behind" natural phenomena.

The spirit that is grasped in this way protects the anthroposophical researcher from the danger of being overwhelmed by the powerful experiences of this stage of consciousness. This may also be expressed as follows: We have seen that imaginative consciousness is attained by the above-mentioned thought exercises. They strengthen the intensity and energy of thinking to such a degree that the "I"—which, as we have seen, is active in the thinking process quite independently of the physical brain—can hold its own against the onslaught of living pictures. As the spiritual scientist slowly grows accustomed to the new experience, he or she does not identify with the pictures in an illusory way, but is able to observe them freely and use them in his or her own creative way. Steiner has called this world "the world of free imaginations." They are free in contrast to the "compulsory" forms of imagination that we experience in our dreams.

In the stages of higher consciousness we are able to interpret these dream pictures correctly. How are they "compulsory"? I said yesterday that the soul detaches itself from the body in the dream state to the same degree that it detaches itself in imaginative consciousness. Now I have to modify this statement somewhat. "The body" in this case consists of the functions of the brain and the nervous system that we need for our everyday consciousness. As I said yesterday, dream consciousness is dimmed to the same degree that imaginative consciousness becomes brighter. How do we explain this difference? It happens because, as the soul retreats from the functions of the brain and nervous system, it binds itself more intimately to the processes of breathing, blood circulation, and metabolism. These are at work in the body with the help of the living, creating, formative forces I mentioned in yesterday's lecture. In the dream state, the soul is thus bound up with different physical functions than in the waking state. This quite often causes the dream pictures to be governed not only by physiological processes but also to be strongly compulsive. It is often impossible for the dreamer to disentangle himself from the powerful pictures. The same holds for the mythological pictures that have appeared since ancient times to people in their dreams. This was especially true before the time of the Greeks, when independent thinking evolved. These dream images arose with great, elemental power and could not be erased. Because their origin was bound up with the physical body and its functions they also had, aside from other meanings, physiological significance.

Something similar happens when—in depth-psychological or self-analysis, without spiritual-scientific schooling—the world of dream pictures is brought up into ordinary consciousness, where it is interpreted in a literary or artistic fashion. The so-called "free associations" are not really free, but are caused by half-conscious dream impressions. This way of dealing with dream pictures poses the danger of getting caught in their suggestive power. Jung himself made a distinction between "passive" and "active" imagination, and claimed that active imagination allowed him an entirely free choice of images. He used these images for therapeutic purposes with his patients, and he came very close to imaginative consciousness in Steiner's sense. Even so, the approach is different. Depth psychology is aimed at therapy, Anthroposophy at higher knowledge. For Jung it was important to enter as much as possible into the realm of the unconscious that lies precisely between full waking consciousness and dream consciousness. Imagination in the sense of Anthroposophy happens entirely in the sphere of clear, enhanced consciousness.

In this difference we find the reason Jungian psychology has remained at the aforementioned level while Anthroposophy can lead to higher stages of spiritual awakening. When one leaves behind the dream with its compulsive imaginations, one can go on into the realm of sleep, where ordinary consciousness is completely dimmed. Here the unconscious must seem entirely impenetrable. Sleep also has two aspects: on the one hand, the soul is still further withdrawn from the body than in the dream; on the other hand, it dives even more deeply into the bodily processes, but in the opposite direction and for a different purpose than in the waking state. Sleep results in regeneration and rejuvenation, while waking results in fatigue and weariness. Jung definitely had an inkling of this unique, intimate fusion of body and soul that results in the deep unconsciousness of the sleep state. He once said, "If the light of knowledge could be brought to the unconscious, the true nature of matter and psyche would be revealed."

When we attain the state of inspiration in the anthroposophical sense, our awareness goes even further in the opposite direction from the sleep state. Instead of losing consciousness we become more awake. I have to point to one other significant aspect of the anthroposophical path: the ascent from imaginative to inspired consciousness is not a simple progression where the next stage is added on when one does more exercises. One must first be able to erase the world of images (as occurs naturally when we pass from dream into sleep). Pupils must erase the world of images into which they have just entered by their own volition. The "I" has to be strong enough to do this. Now one encounters a vacuum; one stands before an abyss of spiritual emptiness. This vacuum then produces the "spiritual suction" that brings in the "World-Word" (*Welten-Wort*, Logos) that is experienced in inspired consciousness. The preparatory exercises prove their worth especially in this phase. Without the strengthened "I," one would not have the power to erase the world of images and achieve the necessary spiritual vacuum.

The crossing of the threshold between imagination and inspiration is certainly the most important and profound experience for the spiritual scientist. It enables him to come into conscious, active contact with higher spirit beings. By crossing this threshold, the Anthroposophist obtains the equivalent to what in ancient times was called "initiation." Then it was achieved in a temple with the help of a hierophant. Now it can be achieved in a way commensurate with modern consciousness. At this point, I have to mention something else that is fundamentally important for our comparison of depth psychology and Anthroposophy.

The Archetype of the God-Man and the Metahistorical Secret of History

Yesterday I mentioned that to the person who has reached the stage of inspiration, it is revealed that during deep sleep every person comes into contact with certain spirit beings. We are not conscious of this, but as we awaken we pass through the dream sphere, and then the impressions we had during deep sleep sometimes clothe themselves in those images that Jung has called the archetypes of the collective unconscious. Today I will take a closer look at one of these archetypes. This is the archetype of the God-Man who is represented in Christianity as Jesus Christ. For Jung, he is the archetype of all archetypes, since he is the symbol for the highest aim of humankind: the fulfillment of the individuation process. With this achievement the human "I" becomes the bearer of the Self that has always been considered to be the collective unconscious, embracing all humanity. The collective unconscious has been felt to be superhuman, transpersonal, and divine. In older times, when the development toward individual consciousness had not yet begun, the symbol for the collective unconscious was Adam, the first man. With the emergence of individual consciousness, the symbol has changed and appears now in the figure of what St. Paul calls the "New Adam." Now the highest goal for humankind can be characterized in the words of St. Paul, which I quoted in my first lecture: "I live, yet not I, but Christ in me."

While on the path of investigation, the spiritual scientist encounters the Christ as a real divine being. This encounter takes place precisely at the moment when the threshold from imaginative to inspired consciousness is crossed. Indeed the seeker recognizes this being as the one who is making it possible to cross this threshold at all. Thus the encounter with the Christ becomes the essential experience for the spiritual scientist on his or her path. The Christ being becomes the "initiator" who imparts the secrets of the spiritual world and at the same time the deeper secrets of his own being. At this moment, the whole panorama of the events in Palestine as they have been recorded in the Gospels also passes in review before one: Christ's incarnation in the person of Jesus of Nazareth, his passion, and his resurrection. Steiner describes this moment in his autobiography: "My inner development culminated in the moment when I stood before the Mystery of Golgotha in profound inner devotion." This means that only since the event of the Mystery of Golgotha has it become possible for human beings to follow the path described here, where the "I" awakens to ever deeper awareness and thereby experiences the spirit worlds as well as its own being in a conscious way.

In ancient times, certain individuals were also initiated into the knowledge of higher worlds with the possibility of interacting with divine beings, but this could only happen through the "temple sleep." The pupil was induced to fall into a deep, deathlike sleep, was ritually entombed, and then awakened again. He then possessed higher knowledge. The whole community of the mystery temple was involved in this, helping the new initiate along the way and shielding him from the dangers that were described above. As a consequence, the secret knowledge was not his own, private affair, but belonged to the mystery community. This was the reason that betrayal of the secret knowledge was punishable by death.

It was known in ancient mystery schools that one day an important event would take place: the god with whom the initiates were able to communicate in secret would incarnate in the flesh. That is why the image of the mother with the divine child at her breast or in her lap is found in many variations throughout the ancient world, in the Indian, Egyptian, Greek, and Celtic cultures. But it had only prophetic significance.

Now the events described in the Gospels can certainly be looked at as symbolic pictures of inner experiences that the personality of Jesus had to undergo: the baptism in the Jordan, passion, death, burial, and resurrection into the full glory of the spirit. These are reminiscent of the experiences the initiates had in the old mystery temples.

However, they do not only have inner, symbolic meaning. They were real events of cosmic significance: the incarnation of a God in human flesh. The birth, life, death, and resurrection are real events, fully visible and played out on the stage of history. This is the profound significance of the events in Palestine; they are doubly meaningful. They were inner, mystical experiences for the person Jesus of Nazareth, but they were also historical events—not only in the banal sense that the man Jesus lived and had a spiritual awakening that enabled him to do certain amazing deeds for which he was then punished by the death on the cross. No, they are much more: they represent a "metahistorical" cosmic fact. Through the "Mystery of Golgotha," as Steiner has called the whole sequence of events, the basic situation of human beings in regard to themselves and to the spiritual world has been altered.

Jung, in his essay about the transformative symbolism in the Christian Mass, asserts the archetypal character of the Christ being and emphasizes that the human being must find the Christ within, bring him to birth, and thereby become a "Christophorus," a "Christ-bearer." He describes this as merely an inner process that is portrayed by Christianity as a unique historical event and is symbolized in the ritual of the mass. The question "what actually happened in Palestine?" does not enter in—understandably, as we might say in his defense. This question goes beyond psychology, and he wants to remain within the psychological in his reflections. At the end of the essay he emphasizes: "With the statement that I consider such a metaphysical event to be a psychological process, I don't by any means say that it is 'merely physical,' as my critics love to say." Nevertheless, Jung portrays the rituals of the Christian mass as having significance only for the inner life of the soul. And, he adds, they have been taught and practiced in one form or another ever since humankind existed, because they are rooted in the human being and are part of human soul life. The profound difference between the pre-Christian and post-Christian situations is not recognized. Jung does point out that mysticism and gnosis both took the incarnation of Christ mostly to be a metaphor for the inner, mystical development of the soul, and that they almost ignored the historical reality. Thereby they were in danger of "psychic inflation" for their ability to "bring the Christ to birth within themselves." The church, on the

other hand, recognizing this danger, has always upheld the importance of the real, historically unique character of the Christ event.
Jung leaves it at that.

For Anthroposophy, as I have said before, the significance of the
Christ event lies precisely in its double aspect. It is indeed a mystical
fact, because it can be recreated over and over again as an inner process. It has appeared in pre-Christian and post-Christian initiation in
manifold metamorphoses. The former had the character of prophecy; the latter signified the *imitatio Christi*. (In the esoteric Christianity
of the Middle Ages the path of initiation consisted essentially of the
inner experiencing of the "seven stages of the Cross," as described in
the Gospel of St. John. This Gospel makes the initiatic character of
Christ's passion eminently clear.) However, the Christ event is at the
same time also a historical event, in the sense that it has changed forever the inner constitution of humanity, so that the very methods of
initiation had to be transformed. Anthroposophy, inasmuch as it is
able to attain to purely spiritual experience—or, to put it differently,
to arrive at the experience of an objectively real spirit world—can
lead us further than the subjective experiences of the soul. As we have
seen in the previous lectures, not only does it penetrate into the realm
of nature, where the workings of the creative, formative forces are to
be seen "behind" natural phenomena. It has also discovered the
"metahistorical" secret behind human history that gives history its
true meaning. This secret works behind the scenes in the evolution of
human consciousness. For instance, in pre-Christian times human
beings had to lose their "I"-consciousness entirely in order to obtain
higher knowledge. In post-Christian times, we can transform it into a
higher, spiritual "I"-consciousness. It also means that Christ, if one
truly wants to see him as an archetype unique among all archetypes,
could not be found in the innermost soul in pre-Christian times.
This is only possible as a consequence of the Mystery of Golgotha.
He cannot, in contrast to all other archetypes, be brought into physical existence out of spiritual experience, but had to be found first in
the physical sense world as historical fact. Only on the path of spiritual awakening will he reveal himself in his archetypal significance.

During my last lecture, I drew a sketch (figure 5) to illustrate the different levels of consciousness where the ordinary waking consciousness is shown as the fulcrum, so to speak, between those levels that are below and those that are proportionally above it. That sketch also shows the levels of consciousness the human being has attained in the course of history. If we turn this sketch ninety degrees (figure 6), we can see how the evolution of human consciousness is connected to the metahistorical secret of history that has to do with the Christ event.

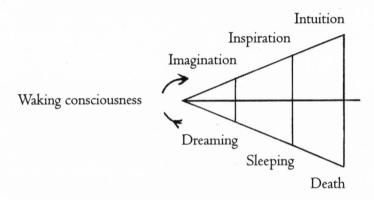

FIGURE 5

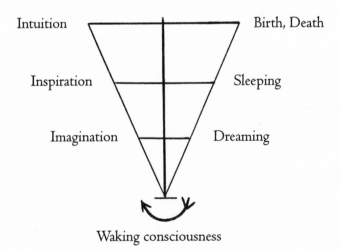

FIGURE 6

Here we can see how humankind in the beginning had a consciousness that was very dim in regard to the outer world but had the capability of seeing into that world where the soul lives between death and a new birth. The next step is the one where human beings could perceive what went on in sleep, and then the one where they were aware of dreamlike mythological pictures. Finally, we descended into the current state of consciousness—in which we are clearly at home in the outer world but are completely unaware of our spiritual nature. We have a certain "I"-consciousness, but we identify with our physical body to such a degree that our "I" has a strongly egoistic character, as we have seen in the other lectures. This descent is characterized in Christian terms as the "Fall" that human beings experienced at the beginning of our earthly existence and have suffered from ever since. Through the event of Golgotha this "sinful I" has been redeemed. Thus human beings have the ability to develop themselves, to purify, to expand, and to raise themselves, step by step, to higher awareness. Then human beings will be reconnected with the spirit world, but now in full, waking consciousness. In this way the incarnation of the Christ has indeed made it possible to complete the individuation process.

The Individual and Humankind

Understood in the above sense, Anthroposophy stands on specifically Christian ground. That is why it could arrive, by means of the unique path of spiritual training, at the highest stage of knowledge that is possible in our time: initiation. This corresponds to the completion of the human individuation process in Jung's terminology. At this highest stage of knowledge it was also possible to recognize the fact of human reincarnation. This answers the age-old riddle of the relationship of the individual human Self to the collective consciousness of the species.

Jung's psychology has not been able to give a satisfactory answer to this riddle. There are instances where Jung asserts the absolutely individual character of the Self. There are other situations, however, where he makes the Self the representative of the collective unconscious of the species. This ambivalence is again the consequence of Jung's inability to go *beyond the soul realm* in his scientific endeavors. Thus the recognition of the "metahistorical secret," as I called it a few moments ago, was not possible for him.

Spiritual science has been able to affirm that the inner core of the human being, the "I," is indeed an individual, unique from all other individuals. However, since the "I," in its repeated incarnations, takes part in all cultural epochs and acquires all the knowledge necessary for further development, it is in this sense a citizen of the whole world, not just of one epoch. In this sense the human is a universal being. It would be wrong to call this universality collective, species-bound. Rather it should be called metahistorical, because it takes part in the whole of humankind's development through all stages of history.

Reconciliation of Knowledge and Faith

What I have been able to describe for you so far about the anthroposophical path of knowledge will help us to see that it is the only modern path capable of reaching what Jungian psychology seeks, what it has stated to be its highest, ultimate goal: the reconciliation of religion and science, of faith and knowledge. Certainly the conflict between these two spheres has become more and more apparent in the last few centuries. The reason can be sought in the fact that the treasures that are hidden in the world of the unconscious have been increasingly suppressed in our culture and in our consciousness. We also have to admit that this state of affairs has led to a "cultural illness." Jung and his pupils have tried to bring new impulses of healing to this cultural illness by emphasizing the value and importance of the religious content of the archetypes of the collective unconscious. They show their patients a way to reconnect with the world of weaving pictures that well forth from the unconscious, encouraging them to shift their attention to a point between consciousness and the unconscious. The fact that Jung and his students have been able to give new validity to religious ideas and concepts has brought it about that recently, quite friendly contacts have been made between "Jungians" and representatives of both Christian churches, the Protestant as well as the Catholic. This is quite natural, since psychotherapy and pastoral care have a great deal in common. For instance, the well-known German organization Arzt und Seelsorger ("Physician and Minister") has for many years been holding well-attended conferences that deal with the concerns of both psychotherapy and pastoral care.

These circumstances should not prevent us from recognizing that because of the gap between knowledge and faith, religious life today is still in a precarious situation, and cannot ultimately be helped by Jungian psychology. This is because Jung, while rediscovering the unconscious, stopped at the first stage of spiritual knowledge, the one Steiner called imagination. He was not able to bring the essence, namely, the "I," into consciousness. He declared this to be impossible. Or, to put it differently, Jung was, and above all wanted to be, a psychologist, and concerned himself only with the psyche. When he speaks of the unconscious, he means a soul phenomenon only. He does not know, nor does he want to know, that the so-called unconscious in humanity is spiritual, and that it constitutes the sphere in which human beings are connected to the real spiritual world. Thus he merely focuses on the psychological aspect of religious experience; he is not concerned with its metaphysical aspect, and thereby gives credence to the opinion that religious experiences have mainly a personal, psychological significance.

In my view, the essence of religious experience is that it enables human beings to establish a true relationship to a real, transpersonal, divine world. This has been understood since the beginning of human existence. That is why religious life will never be satisfied with a mere psychological explanation of its content, even though much of value might be unearthed by psychology. Admittedly, religious experience differs from spiritual science inasmuch as it has to do with feelings and faith, not with knowledge. In this respect it is actually closer to depth psychology, which is also not interested in spiritual cognition. This similarity has no doubt been the reason that there are many instances of active cooperation between representatives of depth psychology and traditional churches.

One can ask two questions here: Can the psychological explanation of a religious experience have a future in our day and age? After all, our time stands under the sign of science, and of the increasing demand for conscious awareness. In this cooperation between religious groups and psychologists, the reconciliation between science and religion is achieved by a compromise; religious experiences are reduced to mere psychological significance. There is no real reconciliation of science and religion. This has been recognized by a number of individuals, especially in the Catholic Church, who are vehemently opposed to the friends of depth psychology.

Something very different has been achieved by Anthroposophy, which is better suited to meet the true demands of religious life in our time. Anthroposophy has opened a way to full illumination of the so-called unconscious, and has thereby discovered that in their inner core, human beings are in reality connected to the spiritual world, and it has opened the way to experience this world. It has succeeded in showing *how* humanity is connected to the spiritual world—and has created a conceptual basis for this knowledge, thereby giving new significance to religion. At the same time, spiritual science has integrated its understanding of nature and humanity with its knowledge of the spirit world, thereby creating a whole, harmonious worldview. I tried to give you a picture of this worldview in the preceding characterization of the Christ event. In this way, science and religion are truly reconciled, and neither of them gives up its essence. Anthroposophy is neither a newly founded religion, since it is wholly founded on knowledge, nor does it, as many of its critics claim, destroy true religious feeling by being too scientific. At the higher levels of consciousness, as I have described them for you, understanding takes on the character of deep religious feeling. For it is not necessary, in order to have a religious experience, that the object of the experience be shrouded in darkness. Such feeling can unfold in all its intensity even more when one is able to see its object in the clear light of conscious recognition. In fact our day and age demand such clear vision for the reawakening of true devotion. In this way Anthroposophy can become the source for a renewed religious experience, and already has for many.

Admittedly, this twofold character of Anthroposophy is still a stumbling block for many of our contemporaries. For some it is too religious, for some too scientific. Yet the decisive task for our epoch—and, I may add, especially for the German and Central European spiritual life of our epoch—is undoubtedly this: to bring to birth a renewal of religious life out of the spirit of science, and thereby bring about a reconciliation of religion and science. The great German philosopher Schelling recognized this 150 years ago. In his essay "The Nature of German Science," he wrote: "The German nation strives with all its being toward religion, but, according to its particular character, also toward a religion that is connected to knowledge and grounded in science. Thus Bacon's famous dictum that superficial philosophy leads away from God, while truly and deeply understood philosophy leads back to him, has been proven true in a remarkable way. Rebirth of religion through science, this is truly the task of the German spirit, the definite goal of all its endeavors."

Since Anthroposophy has created the basis for a reconciliation of religion and science, it is able to heal the cause of modern humanity's inner strife: the conflict between knowledge and belief that is at the root of so much mental crisis and illness nowadays. We must admit, however, that in those cases where an inner crisis has already led to an acute mental illness, it is not possible to use Anthroposophy directly as a healing agent. Of course the same is true of depth-psychological theories by themselves. But just as therapeutic methods have been developed out of depth-psychological theories, there are ways to use Anthroposophy as a foundation for therapy.[3] To describe these therapies lies outside the scope of these lectures, just as would a description of depth-psychological therapies.

In closing, I should say that modern people, thrown as they are into contemporary civilization and exposed daily to the contrasting views of knowledge and faith, of natural science and religion, are constantly obliged to struggle for a balance between these polarities. This is true even if they have entered the anthroposophical path of knowledge. Our soul life often still swings too far in either one or the other direction, creating a certain one-sidedness. This makes us subject to criticism by either the adherents of traditional churches or by intellectuals involved in modern scientific thinking. But in these lectures we were not so much concerned with the difficulties and dangers that can arise on the anthroposophical path (as much as on any other path of knowledge), but with the achievements that can be expected if one follows the path faithfully. Initially, these achievements have certainly been made by the founder of Anthroposophy, Rudolf Steiner.

NOTES

Citations from the works of Jung and Steiner use published English translations when available. In notes to Steiner's works, "GA" indicates references to
the *Gesamtausgabe*, the collected edition of Steiner's works published by the
Rudolf Steiner–Nachlassverwaltung, Dornach, Switzerland.

JUNG AND STEINER

Chapter One

1. See among others R. Goldschmit-Jentner, *Die Begegnung mit dem Genius*
   (Frankfurt am Main, 1954).
2. See J. Hemleben, *Rudolf Steiner: An Illustrated Biography* (London: Sophia
   Press, 2001).
3. L. Frey-Rohn, *Von Freud zu Jung: Eine vergleichende Studie zur Psychologie des
   Unbewussten, Studien aus dem C.G. Jung-Institut*, Zurich XIX (Zurich, 1969).
4. See G. Wehr, *Jung: A Biography*, trans. David M. Weeks (Boston: Shamb-
   hala, 1988).
5. F. Husemann, *Das Bild des Menschen als Grundlage der Heilkunst*, vol. I (Stuttgart,
   1951).
6. A. Arenson, *Leitfaden durch 30 Vortragszyklen Rudolf Steiners* (Stuttgart, 1930).
7. Rudolf Steiner, *Der Goetheanumgedanke inmitten der Kulturkrisis der Gegenwart,
   1921–1925*, GA 36 (Dornach, 1961).
8. C.G. Jung, "A Review of the Complex Theory," *The Structure and Dynamics
   of the Psyche, Collected Works*, vol. 8, trans. R.F.C. Hull (Princeton, N.J.:
   Princeton University Press, 1969), p. 102.
9. Rudolf Steiner, *A Way of Self-Knowledge*, trans. Christopher Bamford
   (Anthroposophic Press, 1999), p. 18.
10. There is an extensive body of critical writing from theologians as well as
    scientists. See L. Werbeck, *Eine Gegnerschaft als Kulturverfallserscheinung*, vol.
    2. (Stuttgart, 1924). For an overview of critical secondary literature, see
    K. von Stieglitz, *Die Christosophie Rudolf Steiners* (Witten, 1955), pp. 336–
    340. About Jung, see H.J. Herwig, *Therapie der Menschheit: Zur Psychoanalyse
    Freuds und Jungs* (Munich, 1969).
11. J. Gebser, *Abendländische Wandlung*, in *Rahmen der Workausgabe* (Schaffhausen,
    1975). For more on Gebser, see his *Ever-Present Origin* (Athens, Ohio:
    Ohio University Press, 1986).
12. A. Gehlen, *Anthropologische Forschung* (Reinbek, 1961).

13. C.F. von Weizsäcker, *Die Tragweite der Wissenschaft*, vol. I (Stuttgart, 1964).

14. See appendix 5 below: "The *Unus Mundus* and the Cosmic Christ."

15. J.A. Cuttat, *Hemisphären des Geistes* (Stuttgart, 1964).

16. Rudolf Steiner, lecture of October 20, 1920.

17. Rudolf Steiner, "Anthroposophy: A Striving for a Spiritual Understanding of Nature Permeated by Christ," Vienna, June 11, 1922 (ms.).

18. Rudolf Steiner, *The Christ Impulse and the Development of Ego Consciousness*, ed. Lisa D. Monges and Gilbert Church (Anthroposophic Press, 1976), p. 146.

19. W. Bitter, ed., *Psychotherapie und Religiöse Erfahrung* (Stuttgart, 1965).

20. U. Mann, *Theogonische Tage: Die Entwicklungsphasen des Gottesbewusstseins in der altorientalischen und biblischen Religion* (Stuttgart, 1970); and *Tragik und Psyche: Grundzüge einer Metaphysik der Tiefenpsychologie* (Stuttgart, 1981).

Chapter Two

1. F. Poeppig, in the journal *Die Kommenden* (Freiburg), June 10, 1963.

2. C.G. Jung, *Memories, Dreams, Reflections*, ed. Aniela Jaffé, trans. Richard and Clara Winston (New York: Vintage, 1965), p. 3.

3. Ibid., pp. 4–5.

4. *Nachrichten aus der Rudolf Steiner Nachlassverwaltung*, no. 13. For the following see the biography by G. Wehr, *Rudolf Steiner* (Munich, 1987), which attempts to consider all biographical as well as historical and spiritual factors in Steiner's life.

5. F. Poeppig, *Rudolf Steiner der grosse Unbekannte: Leben und Werk* (Vienna, 1960), p. 17.

6. This age is not given by Steiner himself; it can be found in Poeppig's commentary. As the author has been told by H.E. Lauer, it would make more sense to place this event a little later, at the time of the change of teeth.

7. Rudolf Steiner, "Self-Education: The Self-Development of Man in the Light of Anthroposophy," Berlin, March 14, 1912 (ms.).

8. Ibid.

9. Rudolf Steiner, *Autobiography: Chapters in the Course of My Life: 1861–1907*, trans. Rita Stebbing (Anthroposophic Press, 1999), p. 16.

10. Ibid., pp. 18–19.

11. Ibid., p. 22.

12. Ibid., p. 23.

13. Ibid., p. 24.

14. Ibid., p. 26.

15. Jung, *Memories, Dreams, Reflections*, p. 9.

16. Ibid., p. 7.
17. Ibid., p. 9.
18. Ibid., p. 15.
19. Ibid., p. 68.
20. R. Meyer, *The Wisdom of Fairy Tales*, trans. Polly Lawson (Anthroposophic Press, 1988).
21. Rudolf Steiner, *The Fall of the Spirits of Darkness*, trans. Anna Meuss (Bristol, U.K.: Rudolf Steiner Press, 1993), p. 49.
22. Jung, *Memories, Dreams, Reflections*, p. 188.
23. Ibid., p. 19.
24. Ibid., p. 28.
25. Ibid., pp. 41–42.
26. Ibid., pp. 33–34.
27. Ibid., p. 63.
28. Steiner, *Autobiography*, p. 59.
29. Ibid., pp. 161–62.
30. Jung, *Memories, Dreams, Reflections*, p. 72.
31. Ibid., p. 109.
32. Steiner, *Autobiography*, p. 49.
33. Ibid., p. 32.
34. Jung, *Memories, Dreams, Reflections*, p. 99.
35. Steiner, *Autobiography*, p. 46.
36. Rudolf Steiner, *Briefe*, vol. I, GA 38 (Dornach, Switzerland, 1985), pp. 35ff.
37. Rudolf Steiner, *Nachrichten der Rudolf Steiner-Nachlassverwaltung*, GA 13 (Dornach, Switzerland, 1965), pp. 1ff.
38. Ibid.
39. Rudolf Steiner, *Theosophy of the Rosicrucian*, trans. M. Cotterell and D.S. Osmond (London: Rudolf Steiner Press, 1966), p. 7. The Rosicrucian manifestos can be found as appendices in Ralph White, ed., *The Rosicrucian Enlightenment Revisited* (Lindisfarne, 1998).
40. Rudolf Steiner, *Goethes Geistesart*, GA 22 (Dornach, 1956).
41. Steiner, *Autobiography*, p. 239.
42. Jung, *Memories, Dreams, Reflections*, p. 184.
43. Ibid., pp. 196, 199.

Chapter Three

1. Rudolf Steiner, *Freud, Jung, and Spiritual Psychology*, trans. May Laird-Brown et al. (Anthroposophic Press, 2001), pp. 31–58.

2. C.G. Jung, *Two Essays on Analytical Psychology, Collected Works,* vol. 7, trans. R.F.C. Hull (Princeton, N.J.: Princeton University Press, 1966), p. 3.

3. Rudolf Steiner, *Geisteswissenschaftliche Behandlung sozialer und pädagogischer Fragen,* GA 192, May 1, 1919, p. 61ff.

4. Jung, *Two Essays on Analytical Psychology,* p. 4.

5. See Rudolf Steiner's public lectures *Aus dem Mitteleuropäischen Geistesleben,* GA 65 (Dornach, 1962), and *Aus Schicksaltragender Zeit,* GA 64 (Dornach, 1959).

6. Some of these lectures appear in English in Steiner, *Freud, Jung, and Spiritual Psychology.*

7. Ibid., p. 31.

8. Ibid., pp. 42, 52.

9. Ibid., p. 32.

10. In the beginning Jung did show sympathy for Freud's sexual symbolism. Jung said before the first International Congress for Psychiatry and Neurology in September 1907 in Amsterdam: "I find that in [his sexual theory] one could follow [Freud] most easily, because mythology here has done some very instructive preparation in that it expresses the most fantastical thinking of whole nations." Jung points to relevant publications and to the allegorical-symbolical language of poetry and continues: "Freud's symbolism is therefore nothing unheard of, only the psychiatrist is not used to it in his practice." C.G. Jung, *Freud and Psychoanalysis, Collected Works,* vol. 4, trans. R.F.C. Hull (Princeton, N.J.: Princeton University Press, 1967), p. 23.

11. Steiner, *Freud, Jung, and Spiritual Psychology,* pp. 41–43.

12. C.G. Jung, *Psychological Types, Collected Works,* vol. 6, trans. R.F.C. Hull (Princeton, N.J.: Princeton University Press, 1974), p. xiii.

13. Steiner, *Freud, Jung, and Spiritual Psychology,* p. 43.

14. Ibid., pp. 48, 53.

15. Ibid., p. 58.

16. Ibid., p. 61.

Chapter Four

1. Jung, *Analytical Psychology,* pp. 74–75.

2. Rudolf Steiner, *From Symptom to Reality in Modern History,* trans. A.H. Parker (London: Rudolf Steiner Press, 1976), p. 93.

3. Rudolf Steiner, *Behind the Scenes of External Happenings* (London: Rudolf Steiner Publishing, 1947), p. 8.

4. Ibid.

5. Steiner, *The Fall of the Spirits of Darkness*, p. 138.

6. C.G. Jung, "Wotan," *Civilization in Transition, Collected Works*, vol. 10, trans. R.F.C. Hull (Princeton, N.J.: Princeton University Press, 1975), pp. 179-193.

7. Steiner, *The Fall of the Spirits of Darkness*, p. 144.

8. Ibid., p. 196.

9. Ibid., p. 199.

10. On the year 1917, see R. Riemeck, *Mitteleuropa: Bielanz eines Jahrhunderts* (Freiburg, 1965).

Chapter Five

1. Rudolf Steiner, *A Psychology of Body, Soul, and Spirit: Anthroposophy, Psychosophy, and Pneumatosophy*, trans. Marjorie Spock (Anthroposophic Press, 1999), p. 5.

2. See E. Bock, *Rhythm of the Christian Year* (Edinburgh: Floris, 2000).

3. W. Bitter, *Analytische Psychotherapie und Religion* in *Transzendenz als Erfahrung* (Weilheim, 1966).

4. Rudolf Steiner, *Theosophy: An Introduction to the Spiritual Processes in Human Life and in the Cosmos*, trans. Catherine E. Creeger (Anthroposophic Press, 1994), pp. 22–23.

5. Rudolf Steiner, *Philosophy, Cosmology, and Religion*, trans. Lisa D. Monges and Doris M. Bugbey (Anthroposophic Press, 1984), p. 4.

6. Cf. Rudolf Steiner, *Philosophy and Anthroposophy* (Spring Valley, N.Y.: Mercury Press, 1990).

7. Steiner, *Theosophy*, p. 24, 29–30.

8. Rudolf Steiner, *Anthroposophical Leading Thoughts*, trans. George and Mary Adams (London: Rudolf Steiner Press, 1973), p. 20, no. 17.

9. Steiner, *Theosophy*, p. 134. Emphasis in the original.

10. Ibid., p. 149.

11. Ibid., p. 132.

12. Ibid., pp. 134–35.

13. Rudolf Steiner, *How to Know Higher Worlds: A Modern Path of Initiation*, trans. Christopher Bamford (Anthroposophic Press, 1994).

14. Steiner, *Theosophy*, p. 58.

15. K. von Stieglitz, *Die Christosophie Rudolf Steiners* (Witten, 1955).

16. Jolande Jacobi, *The Psychology of C.G. Jung: An Introduction*, trans. Ralph Manheim (New Haven, Conn.: Yale University Press, 1973); Frieda Fordham, *An Introduction to Jung's Psychology* (New York: Viking, 1996); and H.F. Ellenberger, *The Discovery of the Unconscious* (New York: Basic Books, 1981).

17. Jung, *Psychological Types*, p. 421.

18. C.G. Jung, *The Archetypes and the Collective Unconscious, Collected Works*, vol. 9.I, trans. R.F.C. Hull (Princeton, N.J.: Princeton University Press, 1990), p. 5.

19. Jung, *Psychological Types*, p. 460.

20. Jung, *Two Essays on Analytical Psychology*, p. 173.

21. Jung, *Psychological Types*, p. 448.

22. H. Poppelbaum, *The Battle for a New Consciousness* (Spring Valley, N.Y.: Mercury Press, 1993).

23. Rudolf Steiner, *From Buddha to Christ*, trans. D.S. Osmond (New York: Anthroposophic Press, 1978), pp. 91–92.

24. Jung, *Two Essays on Analytical Psychology*, p. 119. Steiner's concept of "soul" should not, however, be identified with Jung's "psyche." Cf. Erich Neumann, *Krise und Erneuerung* (Zurich, 1961), pp. 65ff.

Chapter Six

1. Rudolf Steiner, *The Spiritual Guidance of the Individual and Humanity*, trans. Samuel Desch (Anthroposophic Press, 1992), p. 3.

2. Rudolf Steiner, *Esoteric Development* (Anthroposophic Press, 1982), p. 27.

3. Rudolf Steiner, *Wonders of the World, Ordeals of the Soul, Revelations of the Spirit*, trans. Dorothy Lenn and Owen Barfield (London: Rudolf Steiner Press, 1963), pp. 30–34.

4. Ibid., p. 38.

5. Marie Steiner, in the foreword to Rudolf Steiner, *Das Initiaten-Bewusstsein: Die wahren und die falschen Wege der geistigen Forschung*, GA 243 (Dornach, 1960), p. 10.

6. Rudolf Steiner, lecture of August 14, 1924, in *Karmic Relationships*, vol. 8, trans. D.S. Osmond (London: Rudolf Steiner Press, 1975) pp. 16–30.

7. Erich Neumann, *The Great Mother*, trans. Ralph Manheim (Princeton, N.J.: Princeton University Press, 1972); M. Esther Harding, *Woman's Mysteries, Ancient and Modern* (Princeton, N.J.: Princeton University Press, 1971).

8. Rudolf Steiner, *Wonders of the World*, p. 42.

9. Ibid.

10. Rudolf Steiner, *From Jesus to Christ*, ed. Charles Davy (London: Rudolf Steiner Press, 1973), p. 17.

11. Ibid., p. 20.

12. C.G. Jung, *Answer to Job*, trans. R.F.C. Hull, second ed. (Princeton, N.J.: Princeton University Press, 1969), p. 79.

13. G. Zacharias, *Psyche und Mysterium* (Zurich, 1954), p. 44.

14. C.G. Jung, *Aion: Researches into the Phenomenology of the Self: Collected Works*, vol. 9.ii, trans. R.F.C. Hull (Princeton, N.J.: Princeton University Press, 1968), pp. 181–83.

15. See Rudolf Steiner, *Founding a Science of the Spirit*, ed. Matthew Barton (London: Rudolf Steiner Press, 1999); *Theosophy of the Rosicrucian*; *The Gospel of St. John*, trans. Maud B. Monges (Anthroposophic Press, 1962).

16 Rudolf Steiner, letter of August 16, 1902, GA 39.

17. Rudolf Steiner, *Spiritual Guidance of the Individual and Humanity*, trans. Samuel Desch (Anthroposophic Press, 1992), pp. 3–4.

18. Ibid., pp. 8–9.

19. C.G. Jung, "Analytical Psychology and Education: Three Lectures," *The Development of Personality, Collected Works*, vol. 17, trans. R.F.C. Hull (Princeton, N.J.: Princeton University Press, 1954), p. 115.

20. Rudolf Steiner, *The Foundations of Human Experience*, trans. Robert F. Lathe and Nancy Parsons Whittaker (Anthroposophic Press, 1996), p. 49.

21. Rudolf Steiner, *Spiritual Guidance*, p. 10.

22. Ibid., p. 17.

23. Ibid., p. 19.

24. Ibid., pp. 29–30.

25. Ibid., p. 21.

26. Cf. G. Wehr, *Spirituelle Interpretation der Bibel als Aufgabe: Ein Beitrag zun Gespräche zwischen Theologie und Anthroposophie* (Basel, 1968); also *Die Realität des Spirituellen* (Stuttgart, 1970); *Wege zu religiöser Erfahrung: Analytische Psychologie im Dienste der Bibelauslegung* (Darmstadt, 1974); *Stichwort Damakuserlebnis, Psyche und Glaube* 3 (Stuttgart, 1982).

27. C.G. Jung, "Brother Klaus," *Psychology and Religion: West and East, Collected Works*, vol. 11, trans. R.F.C. Hull (Princeton, N.J.: Princeton University Press, 1969), p. 320.

28. Jung, *Answer to Job*, ibid.

Chapter Seven

1. Rudolf Steiner, lecture of January 24, 1918, GA 67.

2. Rudolf Steiner, *Mystics after Modernism*, trans. Karl E. Zimmer (Anthroposophic Press, 2000), p. 199.

3. Rudolf Steiner, *Christianity as Mystical Fact*, trans. Andrew Welburn (Anthroposophic Press, 1997), pp. 179, 183.

4. Rudolf Steiner, *Karmic Relationships*, vol. 4, trans. George Adams et al. (London: Rudolf Steiner Press, 1983), pp. 79–80. For a detailed description of Steiner's inner development, see Wehr, *Rudolf Steiner*.

5. C.G. Jung, "Freud and Jung: Contrasts," *Freud and Psychoanalysis, Collected Works*, vol. 4, trans. R.F.C. Hull (Princeton, N.J.: Princeton University Press 1961).

6. C.G. Jung, "The Real and the Surreal," *The Structure and Dynamics of the Psyche, Collected Works*, vol. 8, trans. R.F.C. Hull (Princeton, N.J.: Princeton University Press 1969), p. 382.

7. Rudolf Steiner, *Intuitive Thinking as a Spiritual Path: A Philosophy of Freedom*, trans. Michael Lipson (Anthroposophic Press, 1995), pp. 38, 43, 143. Other translations of this work have been published under the titles *The Philosophy of Freedom* and *The Philosophy of Spiritual Activity*.

8. C.G. Jung, "The Spirit of Psychology," *Eranos Year Book*, 1946.

9. J. Hupfer, "Der Begriff des Geistes bei C.G. Jung under bei Rudolf Steiner," in *Abhandlungen zur Philosophie und Psychologie* I (Dornach, 1951).

10. A. Morawitz-Cadio, *Spirituelle Psychologie: Zur Psychologie Jungs als Notwendigkeit der Gegenwart* (Vienna, 1958).

11. Jung, *Psychological Types*, p. 59.

12. Rudolf Steiner, *The Tension between East and West*, trans. B.A. Rowley (Anthroposophic Press, 1983), pp. 33–34.

13. Rudolf Steiner, *The Archangel Michael: His Mission and Ours* (Anthroposophic Press, 1994), p. 161.

14. Rudolf Steiner, lecture of May 1, 1919, GA 192.

15. Rudolf Steiner, *Old and New Methods of Initiation*, trans. Johanna Collis (London: Rudolf Steiner Press, 1991), p. 150. Steiner's efforts at such spiritualization of thinking can be found already in his pre-anthroposophical early works, such as *Intuitive Thinking as a Spiritual Path*, especially chapter three, "Thinking in the Service of Understanding the World." They continue into his later works. In the 1919 Dornach lectures *The Mission of the Archangel Michael* (GA 194) we find the statement: "We have created ideas, thought forms that lack the power to penetrate into life." It is not sufficient to merely study man's surroundings in a scientific manner. We need a spiritual knowledge "that is so strong that at the same time it can become a new science." Most people, however, speak of something abstract, otherworldly, when they speak of spirit.

16. Karl Kerényi, C.G. Jung et al., *Essays on a Science of Mythology*, trans. R.F.C. Hull (Princeton, N.J.: Princeton University Press, 1969).

17. Rudolf Steiner, lecture, December 14, 1919. Steiner often pointed to the one-sidedness inherent in defining things without questioning how this process is justified. "Human intellect can serve very well in daily life, but the moment you enter into supersensible regions it is doubtful that it can be a means of recognition, even though one can still consider it a

useful tool." Similar statements appear in the descriptions of the spiritual-scientific path, where Steiner emphasizes that deductive reasoning cannot lead to a recognition of higher worlds. Furthermore "when one wants to understand the things that belong to reality, one cannot *define*. One must *characterize*, because it is necessary to look at the facts and the beings from all different viewpoints. Definitions are always one-sided." Rudolf Steiner, *Occult Science and Occult Development: Christ at the Time of Golgotha and Christ in the Twentieth Century*, trans. D.S. Osmond (London: Rudolf Steiner Press, 1966).

18. Rudolf Steiner, lecture of May 1, 1919, GA 192.

19. Steiner, *The Fall of the Spirits of Darkness*, p. 129.

20. Ibid., p. 139.

21. C.F. von Weizsäcker's detailed statements are quite revealing; see "Über einige Begriffe aus der Naturwissenschaft Goethes in ihrem Verhältnis zur modernen Naturwissenschaft," in *Die Tragwiete der Wissenschaft*, vol. I (Stuttgart, 1966), pp. 222–43. See also Wolfgang Schad, *Goetheanismus und Anthroposophie* (Stuttgart, 1982).

22. Rudolf Steiner, lecture of February 21, 1918, in *Das Ewige in den Meschenseele*, GA 67.

23. Steiner, *Autobiography*, p. 71.

24. Rudolf Steiner, lecture of February 7, 1918, GA 67.

25. Ibid.

26. Rudolf Steiner, *Methodische Grundlagen der Anthroposophie, 1884–1902*, GA 30 (Dornach, 1961), p. 203.

27. Johann Wolfgang von Goethe, "Perceptive Power of Judgment" in Goethe, *Scientific Studies*, ed. Douglas Miller (Princeton, N.J.: Princeton University Press, 1995)

28. Rudolf Steiner, lecture of February 21, 1918.

29. Jung, *Psychological Types*, p. 68.

30. H.E. Lauer, *Erkenntnis und Offenbarung in der Anthroposophie* (Basel, 1958). Steiner himself discussed the problem extensively.

Chapter Eight

1. L. Frey-Rohn, "Die Anfänge der Tiefenpsychologie von Mesmer bis Freud," 1780–1900, in *Studien zur Analytischen Psychologie C.G. Jungs* (Zurich, 1955).

2. Rudolf Steiner, *A Theory of Knowledge Based on Goethe's World Conception* (Anthroposophic Press, 1968).

3. Rudolf Steiner, *Anthroposophical Leading Thoughts*, pp. 13, 21, 22.

4. Rudolf Steiner, lecture of June 25, 1918, GA 181.

5. Rudolf Steiner, foreword to *Philosophy and Anthroposophy*, GA 35. Not translated. The essay itself is published by Mercury Press (Spring Valley, N.Y., 1988).

6. Rudolf Steiner, *Philosophie und Anthroposophie, 1904–23*, GA 35 (Dornach, 1984), p. 156.

7. Rudolf Steiner, lecture, March 12, 1918, GA 181.

8. I. Progoff, *Das Erwecken der Persönlichkeit* (Zurich, 1967).

9. Jung, *Aion*, p. 3. Emphasis in original.

10. Jung, *The Structure and Dynamics of the Psyche*, p. 325.

11. R. Treichler, *Der schizophrene Prozess* (Stuttgart, 1967), p. 135.

12. Rudolf Steiner, *Spiritualism, Mme. Blavatsky, and Theosophy*, trans. Christopher Bamford and Mado Spiegler (Anthroposophic Press, 2002), p. 202.

13. Rudolf Steiner, *The Stages of Higher Knowledge* (Anthroposophic Press, 1981), p. 6.

14. Rudolf Steiner, lecture of April 20, 1918, GA 67.

15. Steiner, *Stages of Higher Knowledge*, pp. 9–10.

16. Rudolf Steiner, *Anthroposophy and the Inner Life*, trans. V. Compton-Burnett (London: Rudolf Steiner Press, 1992), p. 77.

17. Letter of March 31, 1960, in Miguel Serrano, *C.G. Jung and Hermann Hesse: A Record of Two Friendships*, trans. Frank MacShane (New York: Schocken, 1968), p. 74.

18. See Aniela Jaffé, *The Myth of Meaning in Jung's Work* (New York: Putnam, 1971).

19. See Rudolf Steiner, *An Outline of Esoteric Science*, trans. Catherine E. Creeger (Anthroposophic Press, 1997), chapter 4.

20. Rudolf Steiner, *The Riddles of Philosophy* (Anthroposophic Press, 1973), p. 15.

21. Emil Bock, *Moses: From the Mysteries of Egypt to the Judges of Israel*, trans. Maria St. Goar (Rochester, VT: Inner Traditions, 1986), p. 13.

22. Rudolf Steiner, *According to Luke*, trans. Catherine E. Creeger (Anthroposophic Press, 2001), p. 201.

23. Rudolf Steiner, lecture of October 3, 1919.

24. Rudolf Steiner, lecture of August 8, 1918, GA 181.

25. Erich Neumann, *Origins and History of Consciousness*, trans. R.F.C. Hull (Princeton, N.J.: Princeton University Press, 1995). See also M.-L. von Franz, "Der kosmische Mensch als Sielbild des Individuationsprozesses und der Menschheitsentwickelung," in W. Bitter, *Evolution* (Stuttgart, 1970).

26. Rudolf Steiner, *Christianity as Mystical Fact*, trans. Andrew Welburn (Anthroposophic Press, 1997), p. 97.

27. U. von Mangoldt, *Buddha lächelt, Maria weint* (Munich, 1958).
28. Jung, letter to Gerhard Zacharias, August 24, 1953.
29. Rudolf Steiner, *Spiritual Guidance of the Individual and Humanity*, p. 19.
30. Jung, *The Archetypes and the Collective Unconscious*, p. 23.
31. Cf. Rudolf Steiner, *The Reappearance of the Christ in the Etheric* (Anthroposophic Press, 1983).

Chapter Nine

1. Rudolf Steiner, *Materialism and the Task of Anthroposophy*, trans. Maria St. Goar (Anthroposophic Press, 1987), p. 260.
2. Gebser, *Abendländische Wandlung*, pp. 56ff.
3. Rudolf Steiner, *A Theory of Knowledge Implicit in Goethe's World Conception*, trans. Olin D. Wannamaker (Anthroposophic Press, 1988), p. 3.
4. Rudolf Steiner, *Human and Cosmic Thought*, ed. Charles Davy (London: Rudolf Steiner Press, 1961), p. 39.
5. Steiner, *Theosophy*, pp. 29, 30.
6. Cf. A. Morawitz-Cadio, "Versuche zur Unterscheidung von Seele und Geist," in *Natur und Kultur* 53–54 (Munich, 1961). See also Lauer Appendix.
7. Cf. *Heilende Erziehung* (Stuttgart, 1962).
8. See W. Bitter, *Der Verlust der Seele* (Freiburg, 1969).
9. Steiner, *Anthroposophy and the Inner Life*, p. 13.
10. Rudolf Steiner, *Ideas for a New Europe: Crisis and Opportunity for the West*, trans. Johanna Collis (Sussex, England: Rudolf Steiner Press, 1992), p. 3.
11. Jung, *Two Essays on Analytic Psychology*, p. 124.
12. Jung, *The Structure and Dynamics of the Psyche*, p. 204.
13. Rudolf Steiner, *The Riddles of Philosophy* (Anthroposophic Press, 1973), p. 60. See also Steiner's *Mystics after Modernism*.
14. Rudolf Steiner, *The Archangel Michael: His Mission and Ours*, ed. Christopher Bamford (Anthroposophic Press, 1994), p. 141.
15. Jung, *Civilization in Transition*, p. 320.
16. Jung, *The Archetypes and the Collective Unconscious*, p. 207.
17. L. Frey-Rohn, *Von Freud zu Jung* (Zurich, 1969).
18. C.G. Jung, *Psychology and Alchemy, Collected Works*, vol. 12, trans. R.F.C. Hull (Princeton, N.J.: Princeton University Press 1968), p. 17.
19. C.G. Jung, *Mysterium Coniunctionis, Collected Works*, vol. 14, trans. R.F.C. Hull, second ed. (Princeton, N.J.: Princeton University Press, 1970), p. 551.
20. Jung, *The Structure and Dynamics of the Psyche*, p. 215.

21. Rudolf Steiner, *How to Know Higher Worlds*, trans. Christopher Bamford (Anthroposophic Press, 1994), pp. 16–18.

22. Rudolf Steiner, *Philosophie und Anthroposophie*, p. 261.

23. Jung, *Psychology and Religion*, p. 544.

24. Steiner, *An Outline of Esoteric Science*, pp. 18–19.

25. Jung, ibid., p. 543.

26. Jung, *The Archetypes and the Collective Unconscious*, p. 212.

27. Ibid. pp. 211, 213, 214.

28. Aniela Jaffé, *From the Life and Work of C.G. Jung* (San Francisco: Harper & Row, 1971).

29. M.L. von Franz, in G. Zacharias, ed., *Dialog über den Menschen* (Stuttgart, 1968); see also von Franz, *Number and Time: Reflections Leading toward a Unification of Depth Psychology and Physics* (Chicago: Northwestern University Press, 1974).

30. Jung, *The Structure and Dynamics of the Psyche*, p. 215.

31. Steiner, *Archangel Michael*, p. 188.

32. Jung, *Memories, Dreams, Reflections*, p. 359.

33. Frey-Rohn, *Von Freud zu Jung*.

34. Jung, *Mysterium Coniunctionis*, ibid.

Chapter Ten

1. C.G. Jung, "Psychological Commentary," trans. R.F.C. Hull, in W.Y. Evans-Wentz, ed., *The Tibetan Book of the Dead*, second ed. (Oxford: Oxford University Press, 1949), pp. xli–xlii.

2. Ibid., p. lii.

3. Steiner, *How to Know Higher Worlds*, p. 13.

4. C.G. Jung, *The Relations between the Ego and the Unconscious. Collected Works*, vol. 7, trans. R.F.C. Hull (Princeton, N.J.: Princeton University Press, 1966), p. 173.

5. Rudolf Steiner, letter of August 16, 1902, GA 39.

6. Steiner, *Anthroposophical Leading Thoughts*, p. 13.

7. Jung, *Memories, Dreams, Reflections*, p. 192.

8. Steiner, *Ideas for a New Europe*, p. 28.

9. Steiner, *Autobiography*, p. 267.

10. Karlfried Graf Dürckheim, *Überweltliches Welt: Der Sinn der Mündigkeit* (Weilheim, 1968), p. 76.

11. Jacobi, *Der Weg zur Individuation*, p. 74.

12. Rudolf Steiner, *Four Mystery Dramas* (London: Rudolf Steiner Press, 1997).

13. Rudolf Steiner, *Secrets of the Threshold*, trans. Ruth Pusch (Anthroposophic Press, 1987), p. 58.

14. Steiner, *A Way of Self-Knowledge*, pp. 7-9.

15. Steiner, *Anthroposophy and the Inner Life*, p. 30.

16. Jung, *Memories, Dreams, Reflections*, p. 181.

17. M.-L. von Franz, "Die aktive Imagination in der Psychologie C.G. Jungs," in W. Bitter, ed., *Meditation in Religion und Psychotherapie* (Stuttgart, 1958), pp. 136–48. See also A.N. Ammann, *Aktive Imagination: Darstellung einer Methode* (Olten-Freiburg, 1978).

18. Steiner, *Anthroposophy and the Inner Life*, pp. 16–17.

19. Steiner, *A Way of Self-Knowledge*, pp. 26–29.

20. Ibid., p. 157.

21. Jung, *Psychology and Alchemy*, p. 41.

22. Jung, *The Relations between the Ego and the Unconscious*, p. 240.

23. Steiner, *A Way of Self-Knowledge*, pp. 28–29.

24. Rudolf Steiner, lecture of March 12, 1918, GA 181.

25 Rudolf Steiner, *The Karma of Vocation*, trans. Olin D. Wannamaker (Anthroposophic Press, 1984), pp. 93–95.

26. Jaffé, glossary to *Memories, Dreams, Reflections*, p. 391.

27. Steiner, *Intuitive Thinking as a Spiritual Path*, pp. 226–28.

Chapter Eleven

1. Cf. Heinrich Dumoulin, *Zen Enlightenment: Origins and Meaning* (New York: Weatherhill, 1979).

2. W. Vissert's Hooft, *Kein andere Name: Synkretismus oder Christliche Universalismus?* (Basel, 1965).

3. Beckh, "Rudolf Steiner und das Morgenland," in *Vom Lebenswerk Rudolf Steiners*, ed. F. Rittelmeyer (Munich, 1921).

4. Rudolf Steiner, *Luzifer-Gnosis: Gesammelte Aufsätze 1903-1908*, GA 34, p. 371.

5. H. Beckh, *Buddha und seiner Lehre* (Stuttgart, 1958).

6. Beckh, "Rudolf Steiner und das Morgenland," p. 279.

7. Ibid., pp. 283ff.

8. Rudolf Steiner, *Metamorphoses of the Soul: Paths of Experience*, vol. I (London: Rudolf Steiner Press, 1983), pp. 131–32.

9. Emil Bock, *St. Paul: Life, Epistles, and Teaching*, trans. Maria St. Goar (Edinburgh: Floris, 1993), p. 9.

10. Rudolf Steiner, *The Bhagavad Gita and the Epistles of Paul*, trans. Lisa D. Monges and Doris M. Bugbey (Anthroposophic Press, 1971), p. 61.

11. Rudolf Steiner, *Metamorphoses of the Soul*, vol. 2, trans. C. Davy and C. von Arnin (London: Rudolf Steiner Press, 1983), pp. 113–14.

12. On the theological understanding of the idea of evolution with reference to Franz von Baader, see E. Benz, *Perspektiven Teilhard de Chardins* (Munich, 1966).

13. Steiner, *Metamorphoses of the Soul*, vol. I, p. 133.

14. Steiner, *Theosophy*, p. 89.

15. Rudolf Steiner, *From Buddha to Christ* (Anthroposophic Press, 1978), pp. 57, 66.

16. Ibid., p. 68.

17. Ibid., p. 72.

18. Rudolf Steiner, *The Spiritual Hierarchies and the Physical World: Reality and Illusion*, trans. R.M. Querido (Anthroposophic Press, 1996), p. 29.

19. Jung, *Psychology and Religion*, p. 493.

20. C.G. Jung, "Commentary on *The Secret of the Golden Flower*," *Alchemical Studies, Collected Works*, vol. 13, trans. R.F.C. Hull (Princeton, N.J.: Princeton University Press, 1968), p. 4.

21. Ibid.

22. Jung, *Psychology and Religion*, pp. 532, 534.

23. Ibid., pp. 559-76.

24. Ibid., p. 534.

25. Ibid., p. 537.

26. Jung, *Memories, Dreams, Reflections*, p. 275.

27. Jung, *Psychology and Religion*, p. 577.

28. Jung, *Memories, Dreams, Reflections*, ibid.

29. Ibid., p. 283.

30. Rudolf Steiner, *The Tension between East and West*, trans. B.A. Rowley (Anthroposophic Press, 1983), p. 81.

Chapter Twelve

1. W. Bauer, "Rechtgläubigkeit und Ketzerei im Ältestan Christentum," in *Beiträge zur historischen Theologie*, vol. 10 (Tübingen, 1964).

2. Steiner, *Christianity as Mystical Fact*, p. 148.

3. See G.R.S. Mead, *Fragments of a Faith Forgotten*, reprint (Kila, MT: Kessinger, 1997).

4. Rudolf Steiner, *The Gospel of St. Mark*, trans. Conrad Mainzer (Anthroposophic Press, 1980), p. 142.

5. Steiner, *Anthroposophical Leading Thoughts*, p. 180.

6. Rudolf Steiner, *Mystery of the Universe*, trans. George and Mary Adams et al. (Rudolf Steiner Press, 2001), p. 213.

7. M. Verino, "Gnosis und Magie," in A. Böhm, ed., *Häresien der Zeit* (Freiburg, 1963).

8. M. Buber, *Werke*, vol. 3, *Schriften zur Bibel* (Munich-Heidelberg, 1964).

9. See G. Wehr, *Martin Buber in Selbstzeugnissen und Bilddokumenten* (Reinbek, 1968), pp. 128ff.

10. Schilpp-Friedmann, ed., *Martin Buber: Philosophen des 20 Jahrhunderts* (Stuttgart, 1963), p. 614.

11. M. Buber, *The Eclipse of God: Studies in the Relation between Religion and Philosophy* (Humanity Books, 1998).

12. Jung, *Memories, Dreams, Reflections*, p. 201.

13. Jung, *Civilization in Transition*, pp. 82–83.

14. G. Quispel, *Gnosis als Weltreligion* (Zurich, 1951), p. 46.

15. H.J. Herwig, *Therapie der Menschheit: Studien zur Psychoanalyse Freuds und Jungs* (Munich, 1969), p. 85.

16. H. Schlier, in *Handbuch theologischer Grundbegriffe*, vol. 2 (Munich, 1970), p. 196.

17. G. Koepgen, *Gnosis des Christentums* (Salzburg, 1939).

18. See Victor White, *God and the Unconscious*.

19. G. Wehr, *Die Realität des Spirituellen* (Stuttgart, 1970).

20. Steiner, *Anthroposophical Leading Thoughts*, p. 175.

Appendices

I.

1. See R. Treilicher, *Vom Wesen der Hysterie* (Stuttgart, 1964); and "Der schizophrene Prozess als Zeitkrankheit und als Hygienisches Problem," in *Weleda-Nachrichten* 29 (1952) and *Der schizophrene Prozess* (Stuttgart, 1967).

2.

1. Jung, *Two Essays on Analytical Psychology*, pp. 30, 238.

2. Jung, *The Archetypes and the Collective Unconscious*, p. 284.

3. Jung, *Aion*, p. 8.

4. Steiner, *An Outline of Esoteric Science*, pp. 356–58.

5. Steiner, *A Way of Self-Knowledge*, p. 135.

6. Ibid., p. 137.

7. Ibid., p. 84.

8. Steiner, *An Outline of Esoteric Science*, p. 361.

9. Steiner, *Secrets of the Threshold*, p. 129.

10. Steiner, *The East in the Light of the West*, pp. 9–40.

11. Rudolf Steiner, *From Limestone to Lucifer*, trans. A.R. Meuss (London: Rudolf Steiner Press, 1999), p. 203.

12. Jung, *Aion*, pp. 30–31.

13. Steiner, *A Way of Self-Knowledge*, p. 68.

3.

1. J. Gervel, *Imago Dei: Genesis 1:26f. im Spätjudentum, in der Gnosis, und in den paulinischen Briefen* (Göttingen, 1960). H. Martin Schenke, *Der Gott "Mensch" in der Gnosis: ein religionsgeschichtlicher Beitrag zur Diskussion über die paulinische Anschau und von der Kirche als Leib Christi* (Göttingen, 1962).

2. G. Wehr, *Jakob Böhme in Selbstzeugnisse und Bilddokumenten* (Reinbek, 1971), pp. 96–105.

3. E. Benz, *Adam: Der Mythus von Urmenschen* (Munich-Planegg, 1955).

4. G. Wehr, *Der Urmensch und der Mensch der Zukunft: Das Androgyn-Problem im Licht der Forschungsergebnisse Rudolf Steiners*, second ed. (Freiburg, 1979); also G. Wehr, *Heiliger Hochzeit* (Munich, 1986), pp. 103ff.

5. Rudolf Steiner, *Cosmic Memory: Atlantis and Lemuria*, trans. Karl E. Zimmer (Blauvelt, N.Y.: Rudolf Steiner Publications, 1959), p. 91.

4.

1. Rudolf Steiner, *Reverse Ritual*, trans. Eva Knausenberger (Anthroposophic Press, 2001), pp. 43–55.

2. H.E. Lauer, *Erkenntnis und Offenbarung* (Basel, 1958).

3. Steiner, *Philosophie und Anthroposophie*, pp. 225ff.

4. Ibid., p. 261.

5. Cf. G. Wehr, *Spirituelle Interpretation der Bibel als Aufgabe* (Basel, 1968).

6. Steiner, *Philosophie und Anthroposophie*, p. 263.

7. C.G. Jung, *Psychology and Religion* (New Haven, CT: Yale University Press, 1938), p. 57.

5.

1. M.-L. von Franz, "Symbole des Unus Mundus," in *Dialog über den Menschen* (Stuttgart, 1968); also von Franz, *Number and Time: Reflections Leading toward a Unification of Depth Psychology and Physics* (Chicago: Northwestern University Press, 1974). See also Jung, *Mysterium Coniunctionis*.

2. Steiner, *The East in the Light of the West*, p. 80.

3. Ibid., p. 88.

4. Most of Steiner's important lectures on this subject are collected in *The Reappearance of Christ in the Etheric*.

5. H. Hasso von Veltheim-Ostrau, *Der Atem Indiens: Tagebücher aus Asiem* (Hamburg, 1955), p. 263.

6 Ibid., p. 268.

7. Jung, letter of August 24, 1953. Quoted in Bitter, *Der Verlust der Seele*, p. 213.

8. Ibid., p. 214.

THE RIDDLES OF THE SOUL

3.

1. Frankl puts great emphasis on the *spiritual in the human being*, but he never speaks about the *spiritual in the world*. The failure to recognize the latter severely limits the possibilities for logotherapy, since the psychological disturbances that logotherapy tries to deal with are often rooted in the fact that a connection between the "spiritual in the human being" and the "world spirit" cannot be found. This is a consequence of the materialistic worldview of our time.

2. Alice Morawitz-Cadio, a pupil of Jung, writes in her *Psychologie Spirituelle* (1958): "It is Jung's monumental achievement to have opened up for us once more the sight of the spiritual in the human psyche, and to have developed empirical understanding of the spirit within the soul. This is an immensely important turning point for our time." Her "spiritual psychology" attempts to develop Jung's ideas further with the help of some anthroposophical insights. She admits that "the tendencies toward spiritual interpretation contained in Jung's theories have not been sufficiently clarified to be useful for the practitioners in the field. In fact this aspect of Jungian psychology is not understood by Jung's disciples, and is often even suppressed.... My spiritual psychology is not fully identical with Jung's psychology, at least not in its general scientific form." Morawitz-Cadio's book is a significant attempt to build bridges between Jung's depth psychology and Steiner's Anthroposophy.

3. See Husemann, *Das Bild des Menschen als Grundlage der Heilkunde*.